# When Your Child
# Has an Eating Disorder

# When Your Child
# Has an Eating Disorder

*A Step-by-Step Workbook for
Parents and Other Caregivers*

**Abigail H. Natenshon**

Jossey-Bass Publishers
San Francisco

Jossey-Bass books and products are available through most bookstores. To contact Jossey-Bass directly call our Customer Care Department within the U.S. at (800) 956-7739, outside the U.S. at (317) 572-3986 or fax (317) 572-4002.

Jossey-Bass also publishes its books in a variety of electronic formats. Some content that appears in print may not be available in electronic books.

ISBN 0-7879-4578-1

FIRST EDITION
*PB Printing*          10 9 8 7 6 5

# Contents

*To my sweet and accomplished daughter,*
*Elizabeth Rachel, who, with the help of*
*Anat Baniel and the late Moshe Feldenkrais,*
*has found the bridge between the impossible*
*and the possible and has deftly crossed it.*

# Acknowledgments

Writing this book has been a process that like everything worthwhile in life has unfolded painstakingly through hard work, learning, and commitment. My research for this book has been carried out primarily through the hearts and minds of my patients and their families, feeling and breathing "texts" who have given of themselves through countless hours of intimate sharing. By allowing me to enter their lives, they have enriched my own. Invaluable wisdom arises out of the reality of the interactive moment, especially when one's patients and their families are quick to learn and easy to love.

I feel extremely fortunate to share my life with my loving husband, Lou, who has nourished me through this project as he has throughout our marriage, sharing with a full heart still another of life's peak experiences. I am infinitely grateful as well to my children, Adam and Elizabeth, who have taught me everything I need to know about parenting, whose interest and encouragement throughout this writing process have sustained us through all too many nights when dinner was less than a home-cooked and relaxed event; and special, heartfelt thanks to you, Ad, for your invaluable insights and astute editorial assistance.

I also offer my thanks to the people who inspired me to get started: my cousin Leslie Horvitz and my friends Lyn and Ralph Haber, Carol Adorjian, Mel Marks, and Judy Lavin, all of whom are accomplished and talented authors, who waded through my initial writing efforts to find a kernel of substance. And I thank my dear friend and mentor Karen Sager, also an accomplished author, for her infinite wisdom and moral support when I needed it the most. Thanks as well to Craig Johnson, Tim Walsh, Walter Kaye, Howard Natenshon, Garry Sigman, Peter Hurst, and Michael Oberman for their interest, forthcoming assistance, and valuable contributions. I would also like to thank the gracious members of my family, Rosemary Caine Natenshon; Jennifer Irving Kochman; Marjorie Weinert Ford;

my mother, Zelda Horvitz; and my sisters, Barbara Irving Eisenbud and Nina Weisberg, for their invaluable input and encouragement.

I am fortunate to have been associated through the years with the finest and most talented nutritionist I know, Lynn Freedman, my partner and my friend. I extend my thanks to Vivian Meehan, the president of ANAD (National Association for Anorexia Nervosa and Associated Disorders), to Patricia Santucci, and to Mary Ann Kirk for reading the manuscript and sharing their extensive expertise. I am particularly grateful to Dr. Santucci for her assistance with the discussion of medications in Chapter Four and to Dr. Kirk, a talented specialist in this field and a friend whose wisdom and most forthcoming insights have been deeply appreciated. Many thanks to Ivan Eisler, Daniel le Grange, and James Lock, who have been gracious in reading and commenting on the work, and to Bruce Wexler, who carried me through this project with equanimity and skill.

My deepest gratitude goes to my editor at Jossey-Bass Publishers, Leslie Berriman, who always seemed to have the right words to tweak my thinking to an awakening of new awareness and new directions, and always through kindness and encouragement. A great problem solver and skilled listener, Leslie has had the capacity to hear what had not yet been spoken and to envision results not yet attained. Thanks also to Jossey-Bass production editor Lasell Whipple and copyeditor Elspeth MacHattie, who have seen this project through to fruition with tremendous respect, sensitivity, and professionalism.

And very very special thanks to a parent who chooses to remain nameless, a friend, a mentor to an eating disorder recovery, and an extraordinary human being who has been highly committed to her family, to the work of recovery, and to making this book the best it could possibly be.

Finally, I could hardly forget to extend special love and gratitude to Harpo and Mila, my poodle and tabby cat, respectively, who never left my side or my keyboard throughout the many, many hours of writing, night and day. Sitting in on therapy sessions as well, these two have been involved from this project's inception—Mila atop the monitor with her paws dangling over the screen and Harpo curled up at my feet. You guys have been great companions.

Abigail H. Natenshon
*Highland Park, Illinois*
*July, 1999*

Acknowledgments

# Introduction

Over the years, countless numbers of parents have asked me to suggest a "good book" that could guide them in their efforts to prevent or confront eating disorders in their children. Unable to find one that effectively and positively addresses these issues for parents, I decided to write the book they were seeking. This workbook is not only about eating disorders; it is about your child, about you, about your relationship with each other, about parenting, and about advocacy. It is about one of the most misunderstood of all recoveries from one of the most widespread psychiatric disorders. It is about making changes and solving problems. What do food and eating have to do with the quality of your child's existence and his or her ability to solve problems? Everything—as you will soon discover.

## EATING DISORDERS: THE TIP OF AN EMOTIONAL ICEBERG

Your child's eating habits provide a window into his or her emotional health and capacity to deal with life. Dysfunctional eating patterns may be indicators of emotional imbalances, distortions in thinking, or developmental tasks not yet achieved that could derail your child's effective maturation into adulthood. Understanding the complexities of the disease and your child's reasons for subscribing to it will provide you with an ever-deepening knowledge of your child and his or her needs.

Whether you are hoping to prevent your child from becoming eating disordered, feeling your child may be suffering from an eating disorder now, or sensing your child's current treatment is not as effective as it should be, you, like your child, are affected by the disease. You may not be used to thinking of eating disorders as diseases, because the term disease means different things to different people. Those who consider a disease an incurable condition that happens *to* them, that renders them helpless and without control, may find it pessimistic or alarming to call an eating disorder a disease. Perhaps a more practical and fruitful way to define disease is as a biochemically determined condition that negatively affects every aspect of a person's life and that, in the instance of eating disorders, is *eminently curable.* This is the definition I use in my work and in this book, and I use the terms disease and disorder interchangeably throughout the text.

## YOUR RESPONSES AS YOU READ

As you read this book, keep in mind that your natural response may be to see yourself or your child in many of the situations described. "That's *me.* That's *her!*" But it's important to resist that response and keep an open mind, neither immediately rejecting nor too quickly buying into the conclusion that your child has an eating disorder. If, as you continue to read the material and do the exercises, you do become aware that what your child is struggling with is likely to be an eating disorder, don't despair. Despite the frightening stories you may have heard or read about in the media, it is my personal experience, as a psychotherapist who has worked extensively with these cases for the past twenty-five years, that the vast majority of eating disordered patients *do* get better, totally and lastingly better, and go on to live fulfilled, productive, and gratified lives. In fact, reading this book could put you in a position to *prevent* what might otherwise be the onset of an eating disorder in your child, before it has a chance to take hold.

## PERSONAL CHALLENGES

In the process of working through this problem with your child, you may find yourself facing challenges greater than you bargained for. In addition to confronting your child, you will need to confront two other very important people— yourself and your partner. Because your own attitudes toward eating, weight, food, and problem solving significantly influence your child, you may need to consider making some personal changes of your own.

## A PLACE TO BEGIN

You will find this book to be relevant to you before, during, and after your child has been diagnosed with an eating disorder. It will continue to be a resource for you weeks, months, or even years after the treatment process has begun. *When Your Child Has an Eating Disorder* is not designed to be a substitute for eating disorder treatment but rather an inspiration to find the best possible treatment. Through its material you will become an expert in your own right in eating disorders and their treatment, a mentor to your child's recovery progress, and an invaluable participant in your child's treatment team. This book will help you formulate your questions even as it provides the answers you require. If nothing else, it will give you a place to begin, a running start and the continuing momentum to carry you along in your efforts to support your child's recovery. It may also be valuable to your child, helping him or her to explain to you what this disease is about, as well as how to approach, respond to, and conquer it. This book will, above all, give you some degree of control in an ordeal that might otherwise feel out of control and confusing.

## A BLESSING IN DISGUISE

Though the effects of disease may be far-reaching and adverse, the benefits of overcoming it may be equally far-reaching and profound. Time and again, recovered patients and their families have declared: "How else could I have learned so much about what I need to know to get along in the world," ". . . to come to know myself so completely," ". . . to live comfortably within my family and my own skin," ". . . to choose an appropriate life partner?" Eating disorder recovery is an investment in your child's future and in your own future with your child. An eating disorder that begins as an ordeal may also become an unparalleled opportunity for growth and maturation. In the end, recovered individuals cease to be victims of food, of circumstance, and of others. They become empowered, self-contained, and self-actualized human beings. Eating disorder recovery allows both parent and child to take back control of their lives and destinies.

## PARENTS AS PART OF THE SOLUTION

This book is based on my experience that if parents are not part of the solution, they become part of the problem. Mine is a highly controversial stance. Many professionals and parents alike maintain that children, especially during this kind of crisis, need *independence* from parents, not interference, in order to develop into healthy, recovered adults. Many parents, out of respect for their child and with the very best intentions, back away from involvement with their disordered child just when they need most to *join* with him or her. Time and again I hear parents complain of their "hands being tied" because they fear "provoking" their child or dampening their child's "freedom." However, the onset of an eating disorder is a clear and definitive statement that the time is not appropriate for parents to disappear from their child's emotional landscape, whatever the life stage in which the disorder makes its appearance.

## PARENTS' ROLES IN RECOVERY

As a parent, you would likely go to great lengths to shield your child from pain. The recovery process requires unrelenting courage on your part to assist your child to stand firm and *face* emotional pain in an effort to work through it. You will need courage too, first to approach a resistant or defiant child and then to back off in response to your child's growing resourcefulness. Though it is your child's job to look after his or her own disease and recovery, it is *yours* to provide him or her with the permission and opportunity to do so. Your role will vary from situation to situation and from one stage of recovery to another, but you will always be a player in your child's recovery just as you are in your child's life as a whole. Here are some typical roles for parents of children with eating disorders, and the tasks associated with those roles.

| *Parental Role* | *Parental Task* |
| --- | --- |
| Observer | Identifying the problem |
| Educator | Educating your child about the disease |
| Facilitator | Encouraging your child to accept treatment |
| Researcher | Finding the appropriate treatment |
| Partner in recovery | Participating in the treatment team |
| Interpreter of the treatment process | Supporting the work of the therapist |
| Mentor | Keeping the treatment successful |
| Guardian of the relationship | Making changes as your child does |

The next section will assist you in using this book to your best advantage as you learn how to fulfill these roles and tasks.

# How to Use This Book

The workbook format is an ideal vehicle for taking in information practically and at a lively pace; it facilitates learning through doing. However, this workbook is more than an interactive teaching device. It is rich with ideas that have never before been offered in a publication for parents. It puts you behind the scenes, into the minds and hearts of your eating disordered child, the person treating your child, other parents, and most significantly, yourself.

You may begin your reading anywhere. Each chapter is capable of standing alone. Some parts will be more relevant to you than others, so feel free to skip sections or exercises that do not speak immediately to your needs and those of your child. However, you will probably find that the more you participate in the resources presented here, the more profound your insights will be and the more benefits you will derive.

The organization of the book reflects the chronological course of disease and treatment. Divided into three parts, each deals with one stage of the process you will need to undertake to promote your child's recovery. Part One, "The Truth About Eating Disorders," addresses your initial responsibility to educate yourself about eating disorders, recognize them, and understand their function for your child. Part Two, "Taking Action," leads you through proactive discussions with your child about how to proceed, choosing from among various treatment options, and seeking professional help. Part Three, "Recovery," presents ideas that will help you assist your child during the recovery process.

Advocating for you as you advocate for your child, this book will guide you in your search for the best professionals and will help you discover which elements of your child's treatment might require fine-tuning to bring about the best results. You will find a richness of experience in the personal case scenarios and an assurance that you aren't alone in addressing these problems. This book is your guide to creating wellness in your child and in your family.

## USING EXERCISES AND OTHER TOOLS

*Exercises,* lettered sequentially throughout each chapter (Exercise A, Exercise B, and so on), are intended to inspire a deeper understanding of yourself and your child. More specifically, some clarify the ideas, theories, and suggestions offered in the text. Some help you determine how the material relates specifically to your child, enhancing your sensitivity to him or her and honing your listening and response skills. Other exercises help you make assessments, set goals, and anticipate and rehearse interventions so you are better prepared to handle actual situations. Others help you evaluate the quality of the professional services your child receives, your child's progress in recovery, or your own responses to the process.

*Activities* suggest more open-ended tasks, stimulating in-depth self-assessment and self-awareness. By offering you the opportunity to think and write beyond the scope of this book, the activities will give useful direction to your insights about yourself and the process you are going (and growing) through as you help your child. The activities are meant to arouse and stimulate your curiosity about yourself and your self-awareness, much as the process of psychotherapy would do. Consider recording your responses to the activities in a personal journal. This personal journal can ground you during the tough times, providing a helpful point of reference and reassurance about how far you have come. Sometimes, putting words to otherwise vague or ambiguous thoughts can give clarity to feelings, problems, and goals. Directing your focus inward, the journaling process itself can be a great comfort.

As you consider problems posed by this book and the personal issues it raises, you may find that you could benefit from sorting through some of these issues with the help of a psychotherapist. As in the psychotherapy process, the questions posed by this book do not necessarily require answers. They are meant to inspire internal searching and, like planted seeds, may come to fruition at later times. Specific answers are less significant than the *process by which you arrive at them.* This means you need not agree with all the concepts put forth in this book for them to be useful to you. Even if some ideas prove to be no more than a stimulus that helps you initiate the problem-solving process for you and your child, they will be of infinite value.

Other tools you will find useful are the *troubleshooting tips* and the *taking stock* sections, which introduce or recapitulate important ideas and skills.

## BEING CREATIVE

Use this book independently or in the company of your total family, your partner, or your child (or in any combination of these ways). Bring it to therapy, if you like, as a stimulus to uncovering and dealing with significant personal issues. You may want to invite your child or partner to complete some of the same exercises you have worked on, in order to detect disparities in perspectives. Each exercise can be a jumping-off point for discussions between you and your child, your family, or your child's therapist. Each exercise provides a means to better listen to and resonate with your child. Each provides excellent fodder for thought and personal growth. Interactive in nature, the exercises offer a new language for you and your child, a language about solutions, healing, optimism, and alternatives that encourages the sharing of information and increased closeness.

You may want to consider reading through the entire workbook initially, doing only those exercises and activities that apply to your current situation. You may then find it helpful to respond to the remaining exercises and activities as they become applicable to your child's evolving recovery. The exercises and activities are tools for you to use over and over again to keep yourself informed about your child's progress as he or she heals, and about your family's response to the process as it unfolds.

## REMEMBERING THE GOAL

The complexity of the disease and the breakdown of the process step by step and stage by stage may sometimes seem confusing, intimidating, or discouraging. It may be helpful to keep in mind that *when recovery goes smoothly, it can go simply and sometimes quickly.* My having broken down the process into several parts is a technique meant to create a structure within which you and your child can work with an eating disorder. You have the potential to make a great impact on your child's life and on his or her eating disorder recovery. This book will enable you to make your actions count and to be the best parent you can be.

# When Your Child
# Has an Eating Disorder

# The Truth About Eating Disorders

Part One of this workbook is intended to help you understand what eating disorders are and how to recognize them in your child. The two chapters in this part identify common misconceptions about eating disorders and give you a framework for positive action, enabling you to become an effective advocate for your child's health and well-being.

*What You Can Do*

1. Trust your instincts. If you feel there is something amiss with your child, follow up on it.

2. Learn all you can about eating disorders, their impact, and their idiosyncracies.

3. Learn to recognize hidden signs of disease.

4. Understand that eating disorders are not just about food.

5. Recognize and put aside your own misconceptions about eating disorders.

6. Understand that your child, having turned to a disorder for emotional comfort, is in emotional pain, though she may not recognize it.

7. Understand what the eating disorder indicates about your child's needs and coping capacities.

8. Recognize any resistance you may have to acknowledging illness or confronting your child and prepare yourself to surmount these obstacles.

9. Understand that you are not responsible for your child's illness.

10. When encouraging your child to accept help, remember that if one approach doesn't work, there is always another way.

# Learning All You Can

*The beginning of wisdom is to call things by their right names.*

Chinese proverb

Eating disorders present a very real threat to the quality of our children's lives and to the relationships that hold our families together. At once public yet intensely private phenomena, these diseases have become rampant in our society, afflicting children at increasingly younger ages. Eating disorders are all but impossible to recognize in their early stages; in their later stages their dysfunctions approximate normal and accepted attitudes and behaviors of our time—after all, who isn't concerned about looking better, eating better, and staying in shape? Because of the stigma surrounding these diseases, people are often reluctant to consider them, to recognize their existence and their meaning. Misinformation lies at the very root of the epidemic, as eating disorders remain shrouded in myths and misconceptions.

In my experience with hundreds of eating disordered individuals and their families, conquering these diseases is firmly within reach of the vast majority of individuals who attempt recovery and occurs in almost every case where families extend themselves to become knowledgeable and involved in constructive ways. Your commitment to your child's eating disorder recovery now is like taking out an insurance policy for your child's health and well-being during her adult years, as the skills required for eating disorder recovery are general life skills.[1] Moreover, a clear understanding of what eating disorders are—and what they are not—will give you and your child a distinct advantage in your efforts to prevent or to begin to heal this disease.

## DISPELLING MYTHS, CLARIFYING MISCONCEPTIONS

Before you can effectively help your child address issues concerning food, weight, diet, and eating disorders, you must free yourself of any misconceptions you may have about these issues. Here are two sets of common attitudes and beliefs that could interfere with your efforts to support your child's recovery.

*Common Myths About Food, Weight, and Diet*

Myth 1.   Dieting is the most effective way to lose weight.

Myth 2.   The more exercise you do, the healthier you are; you can never be too fit.

Myth 3.   Sweets and snacks are bad for you.

Myth 4.   Nobody eats breakfast.

Myth 5.   Everybody is preoccupied with becoming and staying thin.

Myth 6.   A meal is anything you put in your mouth around mealtime.

Myth 7.   Fat-free eating is always healthy eating.

Myth 8.   Meat and dairy products are fatty foods that should be avoided.

Myth 9.   It is normal for teenagers to abuse substances, if only recreationally.

Myth 10.  Food is fattening.

If reading these myths has been eye-opening for you, you come by your misconceptions honestly. We live in a fat phobic, thin-is-in society, bombarded by messages about food and weight that are confusing and erroneous.

*Common Myths About Eating Disorders—And What the Facts Are*

Myth 1.   *An eating disorder is mainly about eating too much or too little.* Eating disorders have less to do with food and more to do with how an individual thinks, feels, and copes with life stresses.

Myth 2.   *Eating disorders are contagious. People become ill through exposure to others' disordered behaviors.* Exposure may encourage *experimentation,* but an eating disorder will not take hold unless there is a chemical predisposition and a ripe emotional environment.

Myth 3.   *Exposure to information through the media or reading can cause disease.* Again, only individuals who are emotionally predisposed and biochemically susceptible to disease will succumb, just as eating strawberries may cause an allergic reaction but only in the individual who is allergic to strawberries. Media exposure may trigger disordered *behaviors* in some children who are not susceptible to the disease itself. Disordered behaviors not connected to disease are easily extinguished.

Myth 4. *A person never fully recovers from an eating disorder, in the same way that a recovered alcoholic will always remain an alcoholic.* Depending on the strength and motivation of the patient and family, recovery from eating disorders tends to be complete and everlasting in a substantial percentage of patients (as described in Chapter Six). Another large percentage recovers adequately but may require additional therapy on occasion to prevent a relapse. Only about one-fifth of eating disordered patients do not achieve any degree of recovery.

Myth 5. *Once an anorexic achieves a normal weight, she is recovered.* Changes in weight and eating behavior alone or changes in emotional function alone do not constitute recovery. Both types of change must occur simultaneously for recovery to take place. In point of fact, however, if an anorexic patient has been capable of restoring her weight, such behavioral changes indicate an internal emotional environment healthy enough to support the *process* of recovery, and the odds are good that the patient is either recovered or close to it.

Myth 6. *Anorexics are always noticeably thin.* Particularly at the beginning of the disease and in the lattermost stages of recovery, anorexics may exhibit no visible effects from disease; in fact, disease characteristics sometimes resemble the patient's quest for good health and a demonstration of self-control.

Myth 7. *Anorexics eat little or nothing at all, having lost their appetites.* Anorexics do eat. What distinguish them from others are the motivations and purposes behind their eating rituals and responses to food. If they eat little, it is not because they don't long for food. What motivates them is their fear of becoming fat and their belief that giving in to their hunger is equivalent to losing control.

Myth 8. *You can't be a highly functional person if you have an eating disorder.* Most individuals with eating disorders remain highly functional though the quality of certain role functions may be compromised.

Myth 9. *Eating disorders affect only adolescent girls.* Eating disorders are not limited by gender, age, nationality, social class, or culture.

Myth 10. *Persons with bulimia eat a lot and are not primarily concerned with being thin.* Bulimia is motivated by the urge to be thin and generally begins through dieting efforts. The bulimic purge is also motivated by the need to *undo* or *expel* shameful or uncomfortable feelings by flushing them away.

Myth 11. *A binge always involves eating large quantities of high-caloric food in a short period of time.* This is not necessarily the case. One recovering bulimic found herself in a Seven–Eleven store mindlessly purchasing a low-fat muffin on the heels of a serious argument with her boyfriend. Next thing she knew, she was hiding behind the building, stuffing the unchewed muffin down her throat. She consumed only one muffin and its caloric content was minimal, but this episode qualifies as a binge due to its motivation, the aftereffects on her psyche, and her amnesic, trancelike state. Some bulimics consider five grapes a sizable enough binge to warrant purging. Bingeing should not be confused with purposeless eating.

Myth 12. *Laxative and diuretic use results in weight loss.* Laxatives and diuretics expel fluids from the body. This is interpreted by the scale as weight loss, but it is not. Moreover, the bloating that results arouses the patient's desire to use additional laxatives or diuretics.

Myth 13. *A person who eats meals does not have an eating disorder.* Some anorexics may eat three meals a day plus snacks but be so restrictive and exclusive in their food *choices* that they still manage to deprive their bodies of necessary nutrients.

Myth 14. *Physicians can be counted on to discover and diagnose an eating disorder.* The symptoms of eating disorders do not readily show themselves in the typical physical examination.

Myth 15. *Parents are the cause of their child's eating disorder.* Parents are not the cause of their child's disorder. They may *contribute* in some ways to the onset of disease, but they cannot be considered responsible for a disease that results from an integration of neurochemical and sociocultural factors, unless of course they have abused their child.

Myth 16. *If a person can stop bingeing, her purging will cease.* Purging is not necessarily the result of overeating or of bingeing. It is an ingrained habit, an effort to undo uncomfortable feelings and shameful behaviors or a response to a feeling of being too full, too fat, or unworthy.

Myth 17.   *Undereating and overeating are functions too diverse to be part of the same eating disorder syndrome.* Undereating and overeating are flip sides of the same coin; they are both manifestations of feeling out of control.

Myth 18.   *The severity of the symptoms is the best indicator of how hard it will be to recover from an eating disorder.* It is not the severity or the frequency of symptoms that determines the prognosis of a child with an eating disorder but the health and resiliency of her underlying personality along with early disease detection and family support.

Recognizing these myths as the misconceptions they are will help you begin to understand the nature of eating disorders and to identify any personal beliefs that may not be helpful to your child.

**Activity** **Journaling Your Experience**   Consider keeping a journal of your experiences with your child's disorder from this point on through recovery. Writing about your emotions and interactions can be helpful both in identifying and probing your ideas and feelings now and in focusing your efforts later. Chronicling your experience will allow you to look back periodically and see how far you and your child have come, and it will keep you on track toward your objectives.

## EATING DISORDERS: WHAT THEY ARE

Eating disorders are diseases of

- The body, affecting nutrition and physical health.
- The mind, affecting cognition (thinking) and attitudes.
- The psyche, affecting feelings and emotions.
- The ability to be sociable, affecting relationships and personal interactions.
- The soul, affecting one's quality of life and capacity to enjoy inner peace.

They may exist side by side with other disorders, such as disorders of

- Mood (depression, bipolar disorder, and other affective disorders)
- Anxiety (obsessive-compulsive behaviors, panic attacks, phobias, and post-traumatic stress disorders typically resulting from sexual, physical, or emotional abuse)

- Adjustment (psychosocial stressors such as a romantic breakup, a separation from family, a move, a natural disaster, a death in the family, starting college)
- Sexuality (avoidance of sex and compulsive sexual behavior)
- Personality (narcissistic, hysterical, borderline, avoidant, dependent, obsessive-compulsive, and paranoid)
- Substance abuse (drug, alcohol, nicotine, caffeine, laxative, diet pill, and diuretic addiction)

Bulimic women are three to five times more likely to abuse alcohol and drugs than are women in the general population. Substance abuse or dependence, particularly involving alcohol or stimulants, occurs in about one-third of individuals with bulimia nervosa.[2] There is close to a 50 percent crossover between eating disorder relapse and previous chemical dependency.[3] When alcohol or drug addiction coexists with an eating disorder, that addiction needs to be addressed prior to or simultaneously with the eating disorder.

Eating disorders are rarely found apart from symptoms of depression, anxiety, low self-esteem, obsessiveness, or some combination of these. Effective eating disorder treatment will simultaneously address all categories of underlying emotional issues and problems. The reverse is not true, however. Though other types of psychotherapy address emotional issues, they do little to address or affect dysfunctional eating habits.

## Some Definitions

Parents need to know how different eating disorders are defined so they know how to recognize them in their children.

Many people assume that anorexics eat too little or starve, and that bulimics eat too much and purge. In fact, anorexics, though they restrict their food drives, rarely have a complete suppression of appetite, and in an effort to become "more perfect" anorexics, approximately 50 percent of them purge when the hunger drive overcomes the drive for thinness. Bulimics, in their effort to lose weight or become anorexic, have been known to fast, sometimes up to five days. Ultimately foiled in these efforts they gorge themselves then resort to purging to compensate for their "indiscretions." For this reason, bulimia nervosa has been called *failed anorexia.*

Because these two syndromes share a primary drive to restrict food intake, a fear of weight gain, and distorted cognitions relating weight and shape to self-concept, anorexia and bulimia must be seen and treated as different aspects of the same syndrome, not as two separate diseases. The task for food restricters is to learn to eat and live normally; the task for binge-purgers is the same, though compounded, because they must also strive to gain control over deeply ingrained and habitual purging behaviors.

Symptoms of disease vary from person to person and may not precisely match clinical definitions. By the time symptoms are easy to recognize and classify, you can be assured that the disease has been evolving for some time.

**Anorexia Nervosa**    When a person chooses to restrict food, sometimes to the point of starvation, the potentially life-threatening disorder is known as *anorexia nervosa*, often referred to simply as *anorexia*. This classification is characterized by the patient's refusal to maintain body weight at or above a minimally normal weight for age and height, fear of becoming fat, distorted body image, and absence of menses. Individuals with anorexia may eventually develop a true lack of appetite, though the essence of the disease lies not in the loss of appetite but in the individuals' efforts to *control* appetites—of all kinds. Fearing food and their own destructive urges when they allow themselves to indulge, anorexics deny their bodies, even when experiencing the pain of hunger.

*Restricting type* refers to anorexics who do not eat enough to maintain body weight. *Binge-eating type* and *purging type* refer to those who regularly engage in binge-eating or purging behaviors such as self-induced vomiting and misuse of laxatives, diuretics, or enemas.[4]

**Bulimia Nervosa**    Though anorexia has been in evidence for three hundred years, it was not until the late 1960s that Marlene Boskind Lodahl (now White) coined the term *bulimerexia* to describe women who binged and vomited. Lodahl understood bulimerexia to be similar but unrelated to anorexia nervosa. When later researchers discovered that bulimic behaviors were a variant of self-starvation, they elected to rename the syndrome *bulimia nervosa*.

*Bulimia nervosa,* often termed simply *bulimia,* is the repeated cycle of out-of-control bingeing accompanied by purging (purging type) or by fasting or excessive exercise (nonpurging type) to compensate for the intake of calories. Compensatory bulimic behaviors used in the effort to prevent weight gain include vomiting or abusing laxatives, diet pills, diuretics, enemas, or ipecac syrup, a liquid intended for use in first aid to induce medically necessary vomiting. Ritalin too is now being abused as an appetite suppressant. Though bulimia begins as a device to regulate diet and control weight, it ultimately becomes a means to regulate mood, with the individual finding solace in the act of purging.

(This book uses the terms anorexia and bulimia not loosely but to mean specifically anorexia nervosa and bulimia nervosa.)

**Eating Disorders Not Otherwise Specified**     *Eating disorders not otherwise specified* (EDNOS) is a diagnostic category used to describe disorders of eating that do not meet the criteria for any specific disorder. It is estimated that roughly one-third of those who present for treatment of an eating disorder fall into this category.[5] This diagnosis might be used to describe chronic dieters who purge only foods they label fattening, anorexics with menses, anorexics who maintain a normal weight, individuals who spit out food before swallowing, those who experience involuntary vomiting (a condition known as *rumination*), and so forth. It is my opinion that EDNOS are largely responsible for the wholesale underdiagnosis of eating disorders in the United States today.

**Binge-Eating Disorder or Compulsive Overeating**     Binge-eating disorder (BED), or compulsive overeating, is characterized by eating when one is not hungry or by continual eating without regard to physiological cues, sometimes resulting in frequent episodes of binge eating, with the individual reporting an inability to stop or to control the behavior. Binge eaters typically eat to the point of feeling extreme discomfort or even pain. *Deprivation-sensitive* binge eating arises out of excessive dieting or food restriction; *addictive* or *dissociative* binge eating is the practice of self-medicating or self-soothing with behaviors that typically evoke feelings of emotional tranquility or numbness.[6] One in five young women today reports this experience with food.[7] Forty percent of binge-eating disorders occur in men and boys.[8]

Typically experiencing an obsessive preoccupation with body image, individuals with BED do not seek to avoid weight gain through purging or other drastic measures. They tend to exhibit less extensive levels of psychopathology and show strong motivation to desist from these behaviors, which can be tenacious and recurring. Because some of the symptoms of BED differ from those of other eating disorders, this disease is mistakenly viewed as being less serious and not as deserving of intensive treatment. A highly functional and thin BED patient of mine has complained that no one gives credence to the extent of her psychological suffering, depression, and self-loathing after a binge. They say, "You're thin! What are you complaining about?"

If victims of BED cease dysfunctional behaviors without attending to underlying emotional or relational issues simultaneously, their efforts invariably result in failure. Because many of the underlying issues of the binge eater tend to be similar to those of anorexics and bulimics, the same treatment techniques apply. It is important to understand that not all people with binge-eating disorder are overweight, that not all overeaters are binge eaters, and that being overweight, even to the point of obesity, does not qualify a person as a binge eater.

**A Word About Obesity**     There are a variety of causes for obesity. Obesity can be the result of food *grazing*, of eating too much highly caloric food, of genetic predisposition, or of early childhood eating patterns. When obesity is not the result of an effort to resolve emotional problems through the act of eating, it may not indicate the presence of an eating disorder; nevertheless, in some instances it might be considered a chronic medical condition, like hypertension or diabetes.

**Why Food?**

Food represents an island of sanctity, something that children can control without interference. A parent may dictate whether a child can use the car, at what time she must come in for curfew, and when she must stop receiving phone calls for the night, but no one can make her eat or stop vomiting—*no one.* Children with eating disorders are often good kids who want to do everything right and who are loath to cause problems for those they love. Food abuse provides a way for them to take control inoffensively, turning inward what might otherwise have become disruptive acting-out behaviors.

In addition, we live in a culture that glorifies thinness. Our society's instructions to women contradict the physiological dictates of nature. Unlike previous generations, for whom voluptuous icons such as Sophia Loren or Marilyn Monroe were the feminine ideal, we live in an age in which women are expected to grow thinner as they grow older. Just when their bodies begin to crave and produce increased fat in order to sustain the rising levels of estrogen that prepare them to fulfill their natural womanly function of carrying on the species, they are asked to grow smaller. This is not so for men, who account for only about 10 to 15 percent of the eating disordered population.

The history of food restriction goes back beyond our society's cultural quest for thinness. Richard Bell, in his book *Holy Anorexia,* describes medieval Italian saints who, through self-starvation in the service of purity and the search for perfect holiness, met all the criteria of anorexia nervosa as we know it today.[9] Though the culture of the times has changed from admiring thinness as a sign of self-denial and asceticism to equating thinness with beauty, the human instinct for control and self-mastery has remained constant. Anorexia is a means through which the individual exhibits rigid control over her out-of-control feelings, purging herself of yearnings and sensual pleasures.

## How Food Works

Every food has its own distinct chemical makeup. Every body has its own unique chemical requirements and needs. Certain types of foods are brain altering, releasing endorphins (pleasure-producing chemicals) that for some people provide a biochemical fix, anesthetizing emotional pain. Certain individuals may develop specific cravings (for carbohydrates, for example) from a depletion of naturally occurring neurotransmitters such as serotonin. In addition, food-related rituals, such as drinking six glasses of iced tea before dinner or eating the exact same foods every day, in the same sequence, and at the same time of day or night, evoke an empowering sense of magic; controlling food creates an illusion of controlling all things.

One mother told me that even after the family had spent months in treatment, she still was not able to fully understand how abusing food made her daughter feel better. It seemed contradictory to her that her daughter could be so eager to lose weight and yet also binge eat, and that her daughter needed to lose weight yet also needed to consume as many as 2,500 calories a day during recovery. Her confusion stemmed from not understanding that *a healthy eating lifestyle is determined by how food is used and for what purposes, not by how much food is consumed.* Whether too heavy or too thin, an overeater or an undereater, having too little or too much control over food, the eating disordered child needs to learn to integrate a sense of balance into her eating lifestyle.

In eating disorder recovery, any prescription for caloric intake should be less about gaining or losing weight and more about refeeding the body, turning on a sluggish and malfunctioning metabolism, and regaining a sense of regulation and authentic, spontaneous self-control with regard to eating as well as *all* of life's functions. It is not a person's weight that determines whether she is healthy or sick; recovery is the process through which an individual learns what she needs in life and how to get it, or in other words, how to care for herself with wisdom and moderation.

**Activity** **Journaling Eating Habits** You may find it helpful to establish an awareness of your own eating habits. Set aside a three-day period to keep tabs on yourself. During that time, take note of the foods you eat, when you eat them, in what quantity, and why. Are you eating when you are hungry or bored? Does food serve emotional functions for you? Are there patterns that begin to emerge? What are these patterns? How might your food patterns be influencing your child's eating? Remember that idiosyncratic eating does not necessarily indicate the presence of an eating disorder. Exhibit 1.1 illustrates the format you might use for your food journal.

## Beyond Food

With eating disorders, what you see is not necessarily what you get. Your task is to see beyond and through the smoke screens of deception and misconceptions about eating disorders; in approaching your child, your task is to see *beyond food.* What should you be looking *for?* For example, might you be observing something other than excellence in your high school student who appears to be a paragon of achievement, self-discipline, and physical fitness? Your objective in considering your child's circumstances at this point is not so much to diagnose disease as to understand and fully appreciate *who your child is and what she might be going through.* An eating disorder is like a lens through which your child perceives and interacts with the world. Symptoms have very aptly been called the soul's voice.[10] It is for you to understand how that lens may be distorting her vision and impairing her functioning.

Because no eating disorder is exactly like any other, not all the following explanations may pertain to your child. After reading each section, consider whether it describes your child. Start the process of thinking beyond food. Exhibit 1.2 summarizes the many components of an eating disorder.

**Exhibit 1.1. Sample Food Journal Format.**

| Food Consumed | Time of Day | Feelings Before | Feelings During | Feelings Afterward | Observations |
|---|---|---|---|---|---|
| | | | | | |

**Exhibit 1.2. What Eating Disorders Are About.**

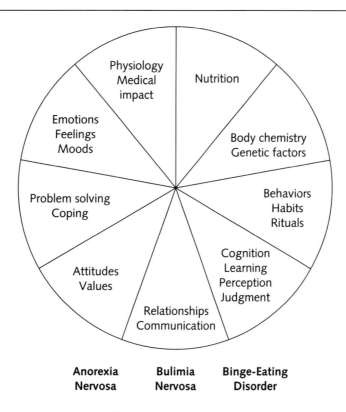

Anorexia          Bulimia          Binge-Eating
Nervosa           Nervosa          Disorder

Eating disorders are not just about food.

**Eating Disorders Are Disorders of Control**     "There have been too many disappointments in life that have been just too painful. I can't endure it anymore, so I simply shut down." Natalie has learned to control her feelings by denying them, and to control her daily stressors by avoiding risk.[11] She controls her hunger by sheer will. She controls herself by denying herself access to food. She controls her anorexia in order to be perfect at it. She controls her parents' lives by staying as sick as she is. Her effort is to alter her world rather than to adjust to its demands. Despite her efforts she does not have enough control of her life to resolve her problems by dealing with them directly. She may ultimately not have enough self-control to keep herself alive.

**Eating Disorders Are Disorders of Thinking**     Individuals with eating disorders think in distorted ways about themselves, the world, and their place in it. They think that gaining 5 pounds invariably leads to gaining 50 or 150 pounds and that freedom with food would lead to a wholesale freedom to self-destruct through excessive behaviors. One young anorexic woman believed that if she recovered, she would become promiscuous and obese, flunk out of school, and run away from home.

Persons with eating disorders spend a majority of the day preoccupied with thoughts of what they have eaten and what they will eat, precluding learning and concentration. They tend to be black-and-white, all-or-nothing thinkers, distorted in their perceptions of reality and of themselves. Finding no middle ground, they think of themselves as fat or thin, good or bad, all A's or a failure.

Their misperceptions about how they look are called *body image distortions.* When they peer into a looking glass, they might as well be standing in front of a fun house mirror. Sonya will not eat anything before a date for fear that her stomach will distend, taking on the size and shape of the food that she has swallowed. Body image distortion can be extreme, as it was for an emaciated patient who was given a therapeutic assignment to use a three-foot by seven-foot strip of paper to cut out a form resembling herself and who asked for additional paper to place side by side with the first to capture the full enormity of her body. Distortions in the perception of reality impair the individual's judgment and ability to solve problems.

**Eating Disorders Are Disorders of Coping**     When Minnie was a child, her mother would send excuses to school explaining why Minnie could not be expected to get her homework in on time, why she couldn't participate in the spring recital, why she had to stay home in bed. Now that Minnie is a young adult facing the pressures of college life, her eating disorder provides whatever excuses she needs to drop out of school and return home: "My eating disorder gives me no other option." Rather than confront difficulties, she chooses to relinquish responsibility for them. Rather than learning to swim, she prefers to eliminate the water.

**Eating Disorders Are Disorders of Identity**     For individuals with a poor sense of self, an eating disorder becomes a substitute self. The disease thrives on the hunger of an internal emptiness, which it both evokes and fosters. One young anorexic woman described her emptiness as "a gaping hole in my chest which lets everybody see right through me. When I am by myself, I feel lost, adrift, terrified . . . without a chance to survive, if not for my eating disorder."

Eloise *is* her eating disorder; after months of hospitalizations and tube-feedings, she was determined to remain ill. She assumed that if she recovered, she would "cease to exist." For her, being without her disease was as unthinkable as being without air to breathe. Similarly, when a recovering anorexic student was told by a dormitory resident assistant of a rumor that there was an "anorexic living in this hall," she was dismayed that he hadn't been able to discern that it was *she* who was being described.

**Eating Disorders Are Disorders of Values and Lifestyle**     Media influences have created and reinforced a schema of values that is replacing society's fading value base of family, community, human connectedness, and faith. One study has shown that 80 percent of ten-year-old girls fear fatness.[12] Forty percent of nine- and ten-year-old girls, many of whom are normal weight or even underweight, are trying to lose weight,[13] some claiming that they would prefer to be dead than fat, others feeling compelled to jog off calories daily. Forty-eight percent of American women express displeasure with their overall appearance.[14] Three weeks after an anorexic young woman gave birth to a child, she received accolades from her friends for losing "all her weight" and fitting into her size two jeans. What is wrong has gone wrong on a grand scale, apparently involving eating disordered and non-eating disordered individuals alike.

Escalating divorce rates, women solidly ensconced in the workforce, and a societal passion for achievement and self-actualization have all contributed to the demise of the communal family dinner. For some children, soccer, gymnastics, and ballet class have taken precedence over food and family, as have parents' own workout schedules. When parents are restricting fat or dieting for health reasons, their children, having no context for such attitudes, learn to see food as the enemy and dieting and exercise as their only defense. Some overly susceptible youngsters—overweight, immobile, underachieving—may develop ill-functioning metabolisms and succumb to the lure of junk food advertising as they sit in front of the TV for protracted numbers of hours. Television and video games are attempts to fill the emptiness in these youngsters' minds and hearts.

**Eating Disorders Are Disorders of Relationships**    Often described by patients as a "secret pal" or "my best friend always there for me," unlike hurtful or rejecting people, eating disorders have staying power. They are disorders of attachment and separateness from others. Often, in an effort to do for other people what the disorder does for her, the eating disordered individual relates to others by attempting to please and protect them. Her refusal to set limits for others increases in direct proportion to increases in her need to restrict herself. Through demands of her own making, she establishes interpersonal connections that produce anguish, ambivalence, and resentment. Darlene, on hearing that her mother had become ill, felt a responsibility to make her mother well and happy, an impossible mission that set Darlene up to feel defeated and out of control. The unrealistic expectations were of her own design, as was the anger that arose out of them. Darlene was as incapable of moderating her caretaking efforts as she was her food intake.

Dolores felt rejected and abandoned by her sister who planned a birthday party for their father and didn't invite her. When asked about her response, she said, "I simply chose not to deal with it. It would have been too painful. So I went to McDonald's instead, and had three Big Macs, two large orders of fries, and a large Coke. Then I made myself sick driving home." Dolores handled her pain by expelling it. Her relationship with food is central in her life, taking precedence over her relationships with others and with herself.

**Eating Disorders Are Disorders of Feelings**    Food abuse puts space and time between an event and the feeling response to it, thus allowing the individual to avoid, postpone, forget, deny, or otherwise anesthetize her feelings. Sara, an anorexic college student, cannot enjoy intimacy with a boyfriend because, without access to her feelings, she knows no way to relate to others beyond physical attraction. For Sara, keeping a safe emotional distance precludes the risk that others will discover her *real* self and hurt her. Always lonely, she is deprived of human connectedness in the same way that she is deprived of food.

Malfunctioning feeling gauges leave an individual incapable of distinguishing internal signals. Hunger may be interpreted as anxiety. Anxiety may be interpreted as hunger. Eating disordered individuals may be unable to distinguish whether another person's advances signify intimacy or aggression.

Knowing no limits or boundaries, these individuals fear that feelings will consume them. One of my emaciated patients is afraid that if she starts to cry, she'll not be able to stop. She is afraid to become happy because then she'll feel disappointed if she can't feel that way always. The excessiveness of her fear of weight gain approaches phobia. She confided to me that her fear of food, weight gain, and stepping on a scale was so intense that she would prefer to be hit by a bus than to deal with any of them. Her deepest fear, however, is of facing herself and her feelings.

**Eating Disorders Are Disorders of Behavior**     Five- and six-year-olds skipping down a sidewalk may be heard chanting the refrain: "Step on a line, you break your mother's spine. Step on a crack, you break your mother's back." To the disordered individual, as to the young child, there is power and a sense of control in rituals, in observable and repetitive behaviors. Without food rituals, eating disordered individuals feel they would have no brakes: if they eat, they would not know when or how to stop; if they eliminate one meal, it would be preferable to eliminate two; if they lose some weight, they would feel compelled to lose more. It is the extreme, unbending, and compulsive nature of unbalanced eating behaviors that is the benchmark of pathology. Disease lurks in the absence of moderation.

 **EXERCISE  A Beyond Food: Recognizing What Eating Disorders Are Really About**   Here are some descriptions of eating disorders as they actually appear in people's lives. To begin learning how to recognize what such behaviors represent, read each description and then write in the type of disorder that it shows, choosing from the following types: disorder of control, thinking, coping, identity, values, lifestyle, relationships, feelings, or behavior. Some descriptions illustrate more than one kind of dysfunction. (See Appendix A for the answers.)

1. A bulimic newlywed is afraid to become pregnant for fear that she will "destroy her children." She is afraid that she won't know if she is giving them too much freedom or too little, showing them too much love or too little, offering them too much food or too little. She is afraid that she will cuddle them when they need food, and feed them when they need cuddling. She is afraid that they will be fat.
   *Disorder of:*

   _____

2. An anorexic youngster is convinced she will gain several pounds if she eats a slice of turkey. She makes certain to do a lot of fidgeting in her effort to work off calories.

*Disorder of:*

_____

3. A young anorexic patient refuses to recover from her disorder because this will please her mother. "This is my disease, not hers."
*Disorder of:*

_____

4. A bulimic college student finds herself dating an alcoholic boy who is abusive to her. Full of shame, she feels defective and deserving of such treatment, responding to the problem with denial and disordered eating behaviors.
*Disorder of:*

_____

5. A bulimic woman feels her thighs expand with each swallow of food.
*Disorder of:*

_____

6. An anorexic college student feels compelled to drop out of college and return home because she fears that her parents will forget about her if she stays away too long.
*Disorder of:*

_____

7. A young girl is frightened by her mother's comment, "Now that you are in recovery, I don't have to worry myself sick about you anymore."
*Disorder of:*

_____

8. When Sally graduates from college, moves into her own apartment, and is about to start a new job, instead of experiencing anxiety, she "numbs out," concentrating on "how skinny I'd like to be, how fat I feel, and how sad it is that I can't see my ribs sticking out anymore."
*Disorder of:*

_____

9. On the night before a race, a bulimic cross-country running star refuses to sleep without her mother at her side.

*Disorder of:*

_____

10. A young woman feels compelled to miss her roommate's evening wedding because the event will interfere with her dinnertime, which has to be at five o'clock precisely.

   *Disorder of:*

   _____

11. A college student takes her own fat-free snacks with her to parties and get-togethers and carries an extra suitcase full of low-fat items when she goes on trips.

   *Disorder of:*

   _____

12. When her boyfriend breaks up with her, an anorexic young woman claims that it wasn't *she* he rejected, it was her eating disorder.

   *Disorder of:*

   _____

13. An anorexic teenager who has been rejected by the college of her choice refuses to attend a family function where people might ask her where she has been accepted.

   *Disorder of:*

   _____

14. Without her thinness, a young woman fears she will have no special qualities to differentiate her from others.

   *Disorder of:*

   _____

The descriptions in Exercise A also illustrate the toll an eating disorder may be taking on your child. Understanding the full impact of the disorder on your child's life will help you make a more educated diagnosis. It will also guide your assessment of treatment needs and your responses to your child. Best of all, learning to understand her as you are now doing will enhance your relationship with her.

**EXERCISE B** **Identifying the Varied Dysfunctions of Eating Disorders** Eating disorders result in various dysfunctions taking a comprehensive toll on a person's existence. To determine whether your child suffers from such dysfunctions, read the following scenarios and the statement that follows each one. If the statement resonates with your observations of your child, circle Y for yes. If it does not, circle N for no.

1. Nancy, an eating disordered college student, cannot get herself to follow the food plan she has worked out with her nutritionist. Confronting even the slightest glitch in carrying out the plan, she feels compelled to give up for the day, determining to follow the plan perfectly the next day.

   Y/N  *My child, in her tireless quest for perfection, has expressed the need to discount and discredit aspects of her life that are flawed.*

2. Despite her plans to study at the library nightly, Nancy rarely follows through on her intentions.

   Y/N  *My child typically cannot abide by what she knows to be best for her.*

3. Resolving to limit her workouts to 45 minutes, Nancy invariably finds herself making internal bargains for "just another 20 minutes," which invariably evolves into 60 to 120 additional minutes.

   Y/N  *My child tends to be excessive in her behaviors.*

4. Feeling that she goes too far with her out-of-control behaviors when she is intoxicated, Nancy finds she is unable to stop drinking at a point before she gets drunk.

   Y/N  *My child indulges in addictive, habitual, and excessive behaviors; such activities may include gum chewing, candy eating, or cola drinking.*

5. Nancy promises herself she will not have sexual relations with her boyfriend, whom she feels is seeing her only for this purpose, but invariably submits to his wishes.

   Y/N  *My child allows herself to be victimized by others.*

6. Nancy determines to call her boyfriend when she wants to see him but instead does nothing but wait passively by the phone till he gets around to calling her.

   Y/N  *My child has difficulty being an active participant in life.*

   Yes answers may indicate that your child is struggling with an eating disorder.

**EXERCISE C** Understanding Food as a Metaphor for Life   To gain more insight into how food relates to issues of control in your child's life, answer the following questions as they relate to your child, writing your thoughts in the space provided.

1. If your child cannot moderate the amount she consumes when she eats potato chips or cookies, the odds are that there are other activities or behaviors she cannot moderate in her life. What might these other activities or behaviors be?

   _____

   _____

2. If your child has admitted to feeling anxious about becoming "too fat" or "gross," what other issues might she be anxious about?

   _____

   _____

3. If your child claims that she "won't allow herself" to feel "fat" or "gross," what else might she not be allowing herself to feel?

   _____

   _____

4. Have you ever noticed your child bingeing on certain behaviors and being overly restrictive of others? Which behaviors do you feel she takes to extremes in her life? What does she do too much? What does she do too little?

   _____

   _____

> **Activity** Relating to Food as a Metaphor in Your Own Life   Think about your own eating behaviors and attitudes. Might they be metaphors for other aspects of your life? Go back to the questions in Exercise C and answer them in relation to yourself. How might your behaviors and attitudes influence your child's? How do your attitudes influence the way you respond to her?

## EATING DISORDERS: WHAT THEY ARE NOT

To understand what eating disorders *are*, it is important to understand what eating disorders *are not*. It is time to explode more of the commonly held myths about this disease, misconceptions that may be impeding your understanding of the disease and your child.

*More Common Myths About Eating Disorders*

Myth 1.  People with idiosyncratic quirks about food are probably eating disordered.
Myth 2.  An eating disorder is a natural and fleeting adolescent life event.
Myth 3.  Eating disorders are generally caused by a concern about weight.
Myth 4.  Eating disorders can be a form of psychosis, especially when people engage in bizarre and compulsive behaviors.
Myth 5.  Eating disorders are addictions from which a person can never fully recover.
Myth 6.  Eating disorders are caused by controlling mothers and passive fathers.
Myth 7.  Eating disorders are caused by passive mothers and controlling fathers.
Myth 8.  There is no way to prevent a susceptible child from developing an eating disorder.

## Not Just About Food

Even for the person who is totally preoccupied with food, food abuse is a metaphor, a symptom of other problems. The individual, feeling unable to take control of her life, tries to take control of food instead. However, this attempt soon backfires, in an ironic twist of reality, and the behavior takes control of *her*. This insidious transfer of power is illustrated in a patient's description of her disease onset: "Vomiting after eating started out first as a luxury and a convenience; it then became an annoying habit; before I knew it, it had become an obsession and the bane of my existence."

The appearance of an eating disorder in the life of a young person might be considered a yellow caution light flashing from deep within the personality, an indicator that something is awry. When I sit down with an eating disordered adolescent to begin treatment, what I see before me is a person who does not know how to feed herself in more ways than one.

## Not About Weight Management

Weight change is one of many possible *indicators* of disease; by itself, it does not determine the presence of disease. Weight gain, loss, or maintenance has significance *only* in how and with what intention it occurs. Weight loss brought about by extreme measures probably indicates the presence of pathology. Eating disorders are anchored in forces deeper and more pernicious than the numbers on a scale. If an anorexic young adult feels that she would be "happy for life" if she could lose ten pounds and she achieves that loss, she then begins to look toward more weight loss to produce more happiness. But she is mistaken in her belief that it is a certain number of pounds that stands between her and happiness.

## Not About Being Crazy

Far from being a sign of craziness, this disease can be seen as a stab at wellness, a search for adaptive solutions to unresolved problems. To the disordered individual, her eating disorder is a survival tool, a stabilizer in an otherwise chaotic world. Although eliciting concern from significant others, the decision not to eat is typically the first time in the individual's life when she has asserted her own will. Her intentions are noble even if her behaviors are questionable. Eating disordered solutions are pseudo-solutions, as they fall short of resolving the individual's problems at their source. This failure creates the need to perpetuate disease, to keep trying for a resolution.

Adolescence and eating disorders coexist quite naturally. The tumultuous adolescent life stage, defined by transition and fraught with change and uncertainty, is a time of confusion and insecurity. Adolescence has been called, lovingly, a state of "temporary insanity." As such it is a time that readily lends itself to behaviors that attempt to establish a sense of stability and control even if at a high emotional and physical price. The task for the recovering patient is to find healthier ways to accomplish this same end.

## Not About Addiction

Propelled by compulsive behaviors and by the feelings and sensations that these behaviors evoke, eating disorders act like addictions. Their driving strength can be seen in these examples:

- An emaciated, anorexic young man described heart pain from the severity of his illness; he was reluctant to go to sleep at night for fear that he would not reawaken. Even in his weakened state, however, and despite his fears, he felt compelled to jog around the block after consuming a piece of Melba Toast.

- An anorexic man hurt in a car accident needed to spend time on a respirator. He could not wait to get off the machine for fear of becoming fat from the accompanying intravenous feedings.
- A bulimic woman who spent well over $100 a day on binge foods was forced to forfeit her home after she went broke. This was not sufficient to stop her bingeing behavior.

Though eating disorders act like addictions, they are *not* addictions. Take note of these distinct differences:

- "Once sick, always sick" characterizes other addictions but does not apply to eating disorders, which are for the most part and in varying degrees curable.
- With addictions, the recovering patient learns abstinence; with food and exercise disorders, the substances that diminish the patient's life (food and exercise) also sustain, nourish, and support it. Being essential to survival, food must remain an unmitigated presence in the person's daily life, ruling out abstinence and self-denial as solutions.
- Eating disorders require regulation and moderation of food and exercise, not withdrawal from them. One reason this task is formidable is that for the child who has an eating disorder, there is a pusher on every corner.

## CAUSES AND TRIGGERS

Knowing *why* their child has an eating disorder is always of concern to parents, as they typically feel responsible for causing the disorder. (Do you?) Parents feel that

- They should have been able to detect the disease sooner.
- They should have been able to prevent its onset.
- They should have had enough control of values at home to outweigh peer and media pressures.
- Their ineptness at parenting caused their child's predisposition to disease.
- Their own issues with food caused their child's disorder.

More practical and salient questions than *why*, however, are *what* to do and *how* to make things better *now*. After reading about causes and triggers of eating disorders, you will have an opportunity to evaluate your own attitudes and behaviors to see whether any of these factors might be *contributing to,* but not the sole cause of, your child's eating disorder.

## Causes

There is no one singular emotional or physical disturbance that can be held responsible for the onset of an eating disorder. Multiple factors come together over time and through life experience to cause the onset of this disease in individuals who are biochemically susceptible, as described in the following sections. Food and weight preoccupation is the common vehicle through which various problems and conditions are manifested (see Exhibit 1.3).

### Factors That Dispose Individuals to Eating Disorders

*Genetic or Organic Factors*

- Genetic vulnerability may be the key to understanding why only a minority of individuals develop eating disorders despite the universal pressures of societal values and diet awareness. Emerging evidence suggests that both anorexia and bulimia are familial and that clustering of the disorder in families may arise partly from genetic transmission of risk.[15] It has also been shown that a single dopamine receptor gene may lie behind an addiction to alcohol, drugs, or food. Some people carry a rarer form of this pleasure gene, with fewer dopamine receptors.[16] People with fewer dopamine receptors "may begin to use substances to satisfy the inherent deficit."[17] Just as alcohol and cocaine boost the level of dopamine in the brain, so do carbohydrates.

- The most relevant heritable factors in the development of eating disorders are personality traits, such as harm avoidance and emotional restraint in anorexia nervosa and emotional lability and behavioral undercontrol in bulimia nervosa.[18] Temperament influences a person's capacity to regulate affect, predisposing a tendency toward eating disorders.

- There is speculation that physical aspects of the brain and central nervous system in eating disordered individuals may differ in some respects from those of the general population, either at the outset or after the disease has become entrenched. The anorexic's feeling of being fat may be mediated in the brain stem, overriding logic emitted from the cortex.

## Exhibit 1.3. Various Causes Come Together to Create Disease.

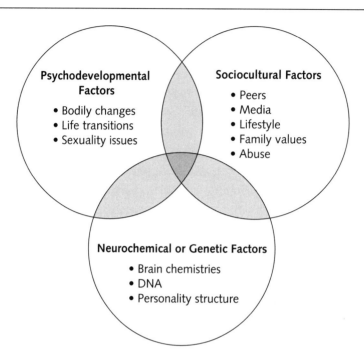

**Psychodevelopmental Factors**
- Bodily changes
- Life transitions
- Sexuality issues

**Sociocultural Factors**
- Peers
- Media
- Lifestyle
- Family values
- Abuse

**Neurochemical or Genetic Factors**
- Brain chemistries
- DNA
- Personality structure

Disparate elements come together to influence the onset of disease. Biochemical imbalances can create a susceptibility to sociocultural influences that give rise to dysfunctional behaviors; dysfunctional behaviors in combination with environmental influences can bring on or exacerbate biochemical imbalances.

*Neurochemical Factors*

- Biochemical imbalances may account for, or contribute to, personality traits such as obsessiveness (compulsive calorie counting, repetitive weighing, a constant preoccupation with food and weight), frequent depressive moods, and perfectionism. There is evidence that neurochemical forces, such as a fragile or deregulated serotonin system, may make certain patients more prone to eating disorders as well as to relapse, an important consideration in addressing the recovery-resistant patient who might otherwise be considered impudent, stubborn, or not *choosing* to get well.

*Psychodevelopmental Factors*

- The interaction of personality traits and adolescent experimentation with dieting might result in "releasing" the risk for an eating disorder in vulnerable individuals.[19]
- Bodily changes with the onset of puberty may be a causal factor.
- Individuation and separation issues such as fear of leaving home and life transitions such as a move, the divorce of parents, a death in the family, or the start of high school or college may set off an eating disorder.
- Issues of sexuality may be precipitating factors.
- Low self-esteem may cause individuals to rely on a veneer of perfection to camouflage what they consider to be their defective or empty internal selves; an eating disorder may be part of this veneer.
- More than 59 percent of bulimic inpatients have experienced physical or sexual abuse such as incest, rape, or childhood molestation.[20] The disease is the patient's effort to regain control and cleanse the body and soul of contamination.

*Sociocultural Factors*

- Pressures from the media and peers can inspire the onset of disease.
- Attitudes determined by lifestyle factors, such as nonassertive responses in codependent households, and activities such as excessive exercise or rigorous dance or athletic practice may be contributing factors.
- Family norms, attitudes, and values may equate happiness with thinness or discourage the uncensored expression of feelings. Unexpressed feelings may ultimately manifest themselves in eating disorders.

**How Parents May Contribute to Disease Development**     Repeat to yourself: "Parents are not to blame." This is a fact that warrants posting on your refrigerator door. *You did not cause your child's eating disorder, you cannot control it, and you cannot cure it.* Eating disorders come into being through a combination of biological and sociocultural factors set off by some sort of stressful precipitant, or trigger. All these factors must be in place for an eating disorder to develop. Sociocultural factors have nowhere to set down roots if the genetic soil is not fertile, and vice versa. The influence of parents and of family environment is but one of multiple factors contributing to disease onset.

Some current theories pinpoint domineering fathers and passive mothers, or vice versa. My experience suggests that these theories are irrelevant. The development of an eating disorder as a coping mechanism comes more decidedly from how a child learns to solve problems and relate to others in her family and less from the personality quirks of either parent.[21] The reality is that somewhere, somehow, your eating disordered child has not learned to feel safe in the world and, more important, in her own skin. She has not learned to take care of herself adequately.

Though you did not *cause* an eating disorder in your child, you may have *contributed* to disease onset; it is important to take a close look at how you may have inadvertently influenced or set off an existing predisposition. Then, by positively influencing your child's environment *today,* you can rectify any difficulties or misunderstandings that your child may have encountered to date.

 **EXERCISE D** **Identifying Parental Contributions to Disease**   A parent may contribute to the onset of an eating disorder in his or her child through the following behaviors. Ask yourself whether or not each behavior pertains to you, and circle Y for yes, N for no.

1. Y/N   Not teaching the child to be responsive to and expressive of her feelings.

2. Y/N   Refusing to engage in conflict and to resolve problems openly as models for the child.

3. Y/N   Teaching the child that anger between people is a precursor to rejection and abandonment that always leads to the loss of love, and that conflict destroys relationships.

4. Y/N   Giving the child the message that expressing anger is synonymous with losing control.

5. Y/N   Not permitting the child enough choices or giving her too many choices.

6. Y/N   Controlling more aspects of the child's life than is absolutely necessary.

7. Y/N   Being overly permissive, resulting in a child who senses she has too much power (ability to harm herself or others) and therefore feels unsafe and insecure when left to her own devices.

8. Y/N  Failing to confront the child when she is obstreperous, upset, or depressed; failing to be assertive in investigating possible abuses of any kind in the child's life.

9. Y/N  Condoning and modeling misconceptions about food and eating and modeling improper eating habits such as skipping meals. In an effort to prevent eating problems, a parent may sometimes create and enable eating dysfunction.

10. Y/N  Abusing substances. The high frequency of substance abuse in families of eating disordered individuals may not be due only to genetic predisposition. Children who live side by side with substance abuse also grow up side by side with the communication patterns and values of addiction: unpleasant feelings should not be expressed, conflict should be avoided at all costs, others must submit to the needs of the abusing individual, and so forth.

Although I believe that all of us can look back on certain aspects of our lives and our parenting with regret, how much more productive it is to look forward to making things *better* than to look backward with self-recrimination and self-loathing. I am also of the belief that if a person makes a decision or takes an action based on conscious choice and in good conscience, there is integrity in that decision that must be respected no matter what the consequences.

 **EXERCISE E Facing Up to the Task**   To achieve some insight into your own attitudes and capacity to be of assistance as an effective mentor to your child during her eating disorder recovery, answer the following questions in the space provided.

1. What are the values I have tried to impart to my child?

   _____

   _____

2. What messages have I given my child about the importance of food and weight, achievement and appearance?

   _____

   _____

3. What messages have I given my child by my comments about *other people's* bodies and weight?

_____

_____

4. How do I feel about my relationship with food? Am I critical of my own body?

_____

_____

5. How would I feel if my child were to regain lost weight during recovery?

_____

_____

6. Can I readily argue my viewpoints with my child and demonstrate genuine feelings, including anger, toward my child? If not, why not?

_____

_____

7. Am I afraid of losing my child's love if I defy or displease her? If yes, why?

_____

_____

8. How would I feel if my child were to express her newly recognized anger toward me?

_____

_____

9. How well do I listen to her? Do I hear her underlying feelings?

_____

_____

10. Does my child feel that I am hearing and being responsive to her? If not, why not?

_____

_____

11. Where and how do I set limits with my child? Are they appropriate limits? Have they changed over time in accordance with circumstances?

_____

_____

12. In what areas have I relinquished limits as she has matured?

_____

_____

13. How do I emotionally support my child? Does she feel that I support her?

_____

_____

14. Where do I find my own emotional support?

_____

_____

15. How has my relationship with my child been affected by her illness?

_____

_____

16. How do I respond when I feel powerless (as I do in the face of this disease)?

_____

_____

17. Do I feel that my child's depression or illness is in any way shameful? If yes, why?

_____

_____

18. Do I see my child as an extension of myself in some ways? If yes, in which ways?

_____

_____

19. How willing am I to look deeply into myself and my own attitudes? What might be stopping me?

_____

_____

20. How open am I to making some changes in myself? What might these changes be?

_____

_____

Your answers should tell you whether you have attitudes and biases that stand in the way of your recognizing and being responsive to signs of disease and whether you have vulnerabilities in the area of food and eating that might hinder your efforts to mentor your child. Equally important, your answers should reveal your *strengths* so that you can make them work for you.

## Triggers

The ripening of a predisposition into a full-blown disorder may be triggered by various kinds of circumstances. Triggers may awaken previously camouflaged or dormant out-of-control feelings, stimulating the individual's need to rely on a device such as an eating disorder for the missing sense of control. A trigger can be an event, a feeling, or a set of circumstances. Whichever it is, it ignites the specific factors that together make a person vulnerable to disease. The event may be temporal, such as a person's leaving home, breaking up with a boyfriend, or starting a well-intentioned diet. The set of circumstances may be an accumulation of situations that occur over time. A trigger for one person may be a benign life event for another.

**Taking Stock** **Identifying Triggers**   Here are some examples of triggers for disease and for episodes of dysfunctional behaviors.

- Certain feelings, such as happiness, depression, anger, or powerlessness
- Specific life situations, such as participating on an athletic team, being invited to the prom, suffering the death of a loved one, or reaching puberty
- Contact with key people, such as an anorexic roommate or a critical coach
- Certain foods, such as sugar, a mood-altering substance
- Specific environments, such as the sorority house, the track, or the health club
- Certain times of day
- Certain occasions, such as arriving home after school or work or studying for final exams
- Certain modes of eating, such as nibbling, grazing, or eating while standing up
- Certain bodily or emotional sensations, such as hunger or pain

- Life transitions, such as starting high school or college, dating, getting married, becoming pregnant, or launching a career
- Starting a diet that seems too good to stop
- Being alone
- A trip to the grocery store
- Having one's boyfriend go away to college

**EXERCISE F Learning to Identify Kinds of Triggers** Triggers often reflect good intentions gone awry. To improve your sensitivity to things that trigger your child's disordered behaviors, consider the following descriptions and before each one write in the letter that corresponds to the kind of trigger it illustrates: (a) a good thing that can become harmful when taken to extremes, (b) the power of another person's words to influence behavior, (c) the misinterpretation of advice or suggestion. Some descriptions illustrate more than one kind of trigger. (See Appendix A for the answers.)

_____ 1. A young woman puts on a bathing suit and realizes that this is a good time to start a diet.

_____ 2. A track coach sitting next to a student in the bleachers muses aloud about how thin the winner of a particular race is. The student takes this comment to mean that there is something about the winner's thinness that is responsible for her success.

_____ 3. An ice skating trainer mentions to a thirteen-year-old student that if her buttocks become any larger, she will no longer look good in her skating costumes.

_____ 4. A husband gently suggests to his wife that she shouldn't eat any hors d'oeuvres at a party because she will want to look good in her bikini the following week: "Remember Mexico!"

_____ 5. A sign in a Midwestern university dining hall posts the calorie count next to each entree on the daily menu.

_____ 6. Anorexia on a Midwestern college campus has become known as the *Greek system syndrome,* the mark of the cool and popular sorority girl. The prettiest girls are known as *twigs.*

_____ 7. A prince puts his arm around the waist of his princess and remarks, "Getting a little chubby here, aren't we?"

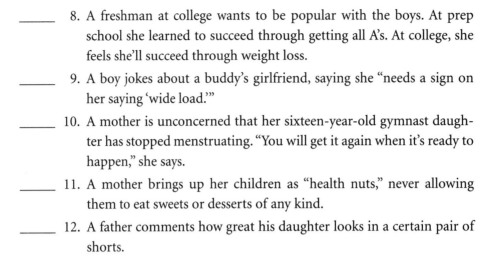

     8. A freshman at college wants to be popular with the boys. At prep school she learned to succeed through getting all A's. At college, she feels she'll succeed through weight loss.

     9. A boy jokes about a buddy's girlfriend, saying she "needs a sign on her saying 'wide load.'"

    10. A mother is unconcerned that her sixteen-year-old gymnast daughter has stopped menstruating. "You will get it again when it's ready to happen," she says.

    11. A mother brings up her children as "health nuts," never allowing them to eat sweets or desserts of any kind.

    12. A father comments how great his daughter looks in a certain pair of shorts.

Once parents free themselves from the myths and misconceptions surrounding eating disorders and begin to look realistically at its causes and behavioral triggers, they become more capable of preventing an eating disorder that might be imminent or of helping their child who already has an eating disorder to recover. The next step is to learn more about the characteristics and symptoms of the disease so you can increase your skill at recognizing it in your child.

# Recognizing Signs of Disease

Does your child have an eating disorder or could he be in the process of developing one? Answering this question can be tricky, as indicators of the disease are generally disguised. Just as photographers see negative spaces and musicians hear rests, you must become sensitive to aspects of disease that may not be immediately apparent to most people. As a parent, you are in an ideal position to entertain a heightened awareness about what might be signs of a disorder in the making and to develop hunches about your observations. You may have heard of the several different kinds of eating attitude assessments, or diagnostic surveys, that could be administered to your child to determine the likelihood of disease.[1,2] However, the results of such tests are difficult for parents to interpret accurately. The most accurate assessment will come from your own sensitive and knowledgeable observations of your child.

**EXERCISE A  Observing Your Child's Attitudes and Behaviors**   Here are some characteristics that in combination with others may be indicators of disease. To begin assessing your child for these various kinds of attitudes and behaviors, consider each characteristic. Does it pertain to your child? Circle Y for yes, N for no.

1.  Y/N   Has undergone excessive or rapid loss of body weight.
2.  Y/N   Has a poor self-image.
3.  Y/N   Feels fat even when thin; describes fat as a *feeling*.
4.  Y/N   Displays quirky eating habits; eats a limited variety of foods or becomes a vegetarian for purposes of food restriction.
5.  Y/N   Denies hunger.
6.  Y/N   Has lost her menses.

7. Y/N   Exercises excessively.

8. Y/N   Frequently weighs himself.

9. Y/N   Has left indicators of laxative, diuretic, or diet pill abuse for you to find.

10. Y/N   Dreams about food and eating.

11. Y/N   Is reluctant to eat in front of others.

12. Y/N   Uses the bathroom frequently during or following meals.

13. Y/N   Compares his body to the bodies of others, such as models and athletes.

14. Y/N   Is moodier and more irritable of late.

15. Y/N   Lacks good coping skills; eats in response to emotional stressors.

16. Y/N   Seeks to avoid risks; looks for safety and predictability as an alternative.

17. Y/N   Fears not measuring up.

18. Y/N   Distrusts himself and others.

19. Y/N   Abhors the feeling of being full, which creates indescribable discomfort, bloating and nausea, along with fear that the discomfort will never go away.

20. Y/N   Hates big family dinners at holiday times; becomes terribly anxious and upset prior to and during the meal.

21. Y/N   Thinks that because he joins you occasionally at restaurants, he must not be disordered.

22. Y/N   Avoids substantive connections with others.

23. Y/N   Believes his life would be better if he were thinner.

24. Y/N   Is obsessed with his clothing size.

If a cluster of these symptoms applies to your child, there is a good chance that he may be struggling with an eating disorder or may soon be developing one.

## LOOKING FOR EXCESSES

It is important to understand that excess and extremism are at the root of eating disorders and also that excesses, whether they concern food, exercise, or any other passion, rarely occur in isolation. My goal here is not to make a crisis out of, or catastrophize, what could be minor problems nor to frighten you into finding eating disorders where they do not exist. It is to help you assess when a diet becomes a disorder and when otherwise healthful exercise becomes a compulsion.

Consider the behavior of this young woman and her mother. Trudy, a college student who sees herself as an athlete, trains hard daily to keep in shape for track, then runs an additional eight miles. Her mother is sure that she can't be disordered because, she says, "Trudy eats." Trudy has not had a menstrual period in years because she lacks the body fat to support production of the hormone estrogen. Running alongside her daughter daily, this parent sees no reason to think that her child is disordered in any way. Yet, if something acts like an eating disorder, feels like an eating disorder, and takes its toll on the quality of a child's existence as does an eating disorder, does it really *matter* what label defines it at the moment? Considering the excesses in her daily exercise, would you anticipate that Trudy is maintaining a functional balance in other areas of her life, including social activities, academics, and recreation? There might well be a benefit in addressing the emotional issues that underlie Trudy's situation even if she does not have a full-blown eating disorder. More to the point, if this were your child, this would be just the kind of situation that should make you look more specifically at exactly what and how your child is eating and how he feels about food, weight, and himself.

In considering Trudy's excesses, her mother flippantly quipped, "But we all have our excesses! You've just got to pick the right ones." True. But some take a greater toll than others. The issue here is not *which* excess you may see in your child but *how* excessive these behaviors are, and *how* that excess serves the child's personality. A behavior is extreme if it puts a person's life off balance emotionally or if it leaves a person functionally vulnerable and at risk, less capable of landing on his feet in times of crisis and, more poignantly, in the process of daily living.

People make positive changes on their own, and it's possible that your child might eventually moderate his extreme behaviors without your help. But you may be taking a gamble by ignoring the situation. These are vulnerable and formative years for your child, setting the stage for all the years to come. The kinds of questions to consider are these: Will the innocent excesses of your well-intentioned child remain as benign as he grows older and more set in his ways? How likely is it that timing, life circumstances, and emotional resiliency will come together favorably so that he can independently develop the strength and capacity to bring his imbalances into balance with the rest of his life functions?

## SEEING BEYOND FOOD; SEEING BEYOND SMOKE SCREENS

Once again, eating disorders are not just about food. Don't be fooled by the smoke screens and barriers your child may be putting up to distract you from his behavior and from issues of food, eating, and weight.

 **EXERCISE B** Seeing Beyond Obstacles to Disease Recognition   You may not recognize an eating disorder simply because you have had no previous experience with this disease. Beyond that, there are many other deterrents to disease recognition. To begin looking beyond these obstacles, read each of the following descriptions and think about whether it pertains to your child. Write your observations and hunches in the space provided.

1. *Evidence of disease is typically not overt.* Eating disorders are highly secretive diseases and often go unnoticed by parents, physicians, therapists, and even the patient himself. Even blood tests fail to reveal eating disorders until the latter-most stages of disease, if at all. Eating disorders go unrecognized in clinical settings in up to 50 percent of cases.[3]

   *This sounds like my child's situation because:*

   _____

   _____

   _____

2. *Symptoms vary dramatically.* No eating disorder looks exactly like another; in fact, no disorder will exactly resemble any definition you will read in a book. There can be extreme variability in symptoms from individual to individual, as well as within the course of a single disease. Anorexics, for example, may restrict food maximally (becoming bony and skeletal), moderately (falling 5 percent to 15 percent below their personal healthy body weight), or minimally (perhaps skipping breakfast and having a salad for lunch, a pattern of calorie rearrangement that may ultimately promote bingeing). Anorexics eat normally, sparingly, ritualistically, or excessively on any given day. Bulimics typically alternate between being highly restrictive and bingeing on food, taking in, at times, from five thousand to ten thousand calories per day. Bulimic individuals may vomit thirty times per day or several times per week. Some

individuals may take thirty to three hundred laxatives per day; others may take one or two or none at all and yet still have an eating disorder. An eating disordered child will probably gravitate toward friends who are very thin, some of whom will be disordered and others of whom will not be, adding to the overall confusion.

*This sounds like my child's situation because:*

_____

_____

_____

3. *Behaviors alone are not reliable and accurate indicators of disease.* Disordered behaviors seen in isolation from other symptoms may actually look healthy to the observer, resembling self-discipline and the capacity to be goal directed. Patients often look good and feel great, invigorated, energized. They tend to be overachievers and perfectionists. Their disease shows up definitively in discreet attitudes and thought patterns.

*This sounds like my child's situation because:*

_____

_____

_____

4. *Disease denial is common.* Disease denial may take the form of resistance to acknowledging disease, nondisclosure of an acknowledged disease, or refusal to consider or heed the health risks of serious disease. It is surprising how many parents are reluctant to acknowledge disease in their children, making excuses for them and their behaviors or considering symptoms to be passing phases, signs of strength, or normal teenage obsessions. Some take comfort in calling the symptoms *food disorders,* a more benign term than eating disorders.

*This sounds like my child's situation because:*

_____

_____

_____

5. *Professionals sometimes err.* Even the most competent physician can be misled by eating disorder myths. In response to a mother's concern that her inpatient

anorexic youngster was refusing to eat protein, sugar, or fats, a doctor heading up a psychology unit in a hospital told her: "We could all take a lesson or two from your daughter. Did you know that Americans eat six times the amount of protein they actually need?"

*This sounds like my child's situation because:*

_____

_____

_____

6. *Weight alone is not an indicator of disease.* Eating disorders are not just about food. To judge the significance of weight gain, loss, or stability, parents have to consider how quickly, through what intentions, and by what means it occurs. Eating disordered individuals can be malnourished even at normal weight.

*This sounds like my child's situation because:*

_____

_____

_____

7. *Feelings are masked.* An eating disorder transforms anxiety, fear, anger, and sadness to anesthetized numbness, stuffing them into inaccessible recesses of the soul. When feelings are not recognized and expressed, the child's needs go untended and the parent's capacity to recognize the child's pain is greatly compromised.

*This sounds like my child's situation because:*

_____

_____

_____

8. *Family dinners are too often the exception, not the rule.* If a child is not sitting down with the family to dine, it is hardly possible for parents to note odd eating behaviors. More important, if parents are not providing an occasion for the child to talk about his day, his thoughts, and his feelings, they will find it difficult to know him fully and to understand what he is going through.

*This sounds like my child's situation because:*

_____

_____

_____

## Subclinical Indicators of Disease in the Making

Subclinical indicators of disease are also known as *soft signs*. Falling short of clinical symptoms, soft signs are found in the feelings, attitudes, life perspectives, and behaviors that underlie disease or predisease states. They tend to be present when symptoms are still evolving, intermittent, or are noticed only as isolated events. Subclinical indicators of disease are to be distinguished from subclinical diseases (EDNOS), which, lacking some essential feature, severity, or duration of bona fide symptoms, fall short of the accepted clinical definitions of eating disorders, as described in Chapter One. Subclinical indicators are hard-to-see forerunners of clinical or subclinical disease, attitudes and behaviors found in individuals who share the eating disordered mind.

Eating disorders are progressive, gradually evolving diseases that develop along a continuum, giving parents a great deal of warning once they learn to read the signs. For example, a child might make a sudden commitment to an extreme form of vegetarianism in which he resists eating beans and other vegetarian proteins; has a proclivity to eating only foods frequently favored by anorexics, such as salads without dressing, frozen yogurt, cottage cheese, cereal, diet drinks, apples, and plain bagels; or has a growing propensity to miss meals because of being otherwise occupied.

A young man might refuse to go to lunch or for drinks after work with his peers at the office. Missing prime opportunities for office socialization and communication, he finds himself alienated at work and ultimately out of a job.

A young woman might marry a man who is as unable to recognize feelings and confront problems as she is. They handle the natural transitions and challenges of their life together by choosing not to deal with them; stressors such as the wedding, job changes, financial concerns, and family relationships are simply not discussed, increasing her depression, affecting her eating patterns, and ultimately jeopardizing their relationship.

A college student who drinks too much and eats too little or too much might decide not even to try to balance his checkbook. Because he does not respect his abilities to regulate himself or his finances, he prefers to be ignorant of any problem he might be called upon to handle if he knew of it. He sees it as safer and more reliable to simply leave an excessive surplus of funds in the account, more than he would actually need or could ever spend.

Subclinical conditions and the soft signs that frequently characterize them harbor highly significant information about the individual's underlying emotional environment, vulnerability to disease, and physiological stressors. *It is in the subclinical and early stage disorder that we find the key to early intervention, to effective and timely recovery, and most important, to disease prevention.* In developing an eye for soft signs of disease, you learn to look for and to see what is not plainly visible. When you perceive possible problems, even in the absence of clinically definable behaviors, it may be wise to consult a professional who can help confirm or deny your hunch. Your child's emotional issues deserve attention, whatever their nature. A problem defined is potentially a problem addressed.

## Activity Disorders

The term *activity disorder,* coined by Alayne Yates in her book *Compulsive Exercise and Eating Disorders,* describes an overinvolvement with exercise to the point of adverse consequences. Studies have reported that as many as 75 percent of eating disordered individuals use excessive exercise as a method of purging or of reducing anxiety.[4] They appear unable to stop exercising even when their extreme regimen results in injury, exhaustion, or other physical damage or otherwise interferes with their health and well-being. Individuals with activity disorders lose control of exercise just as eating disordered people lose control of food and dieting. The term *anorexia athletica* describes an EDNOS "for athletes who engage in at least one unhealthy method of weight control, such as fasting, vomiting," or using diet pills, laxatives, or diuretics.[5]

Eating disorders overall are more prevalent among athletically inclined subgroups in our society, such as dancers, skaters, gymnasts, equestrians, wrestlers, and track and field contenders. The demands of these activities parallel the demands of the disease. The rigors of achievement and performance require discipline, self-control, impassioned excellence, and the need to *make weight* and look good. The practice, practice, practice lifestyle involves such a commitment of time as to exclude ordinary amenities of life, such as mealtimes.

## A Case Study

Todd, at seventeen years old, was an all A student and a gifted pianist as well as an accomplished skater. Having grown up in a loving family, he had good values and a strong sense of responsibility and discipline, which allowed him to hold an after-school job despite spending over twenty hours a week at the rink. Soon after he moved away to college, he was overcome by extreme anxiety. Suddenly paralyzed by fears, he found it difficult to concentrate and to sleep. He envisioned his parents divorcing and his own terminal illness. During the first week of school, he became nauseated whenever he ate and so began refusing food. At the same time, he became too anxious to skate in competitions.

Todd's lifestyle had been quirky and extreme during his high school years. He stayed up till all hours of the night, and as a result his father had difficulty waking him for school. Because Todd generally missed the bus, his father drove him to school, frequently making himself late to work. Todd never ate breakfast, claiming that he wasn't hungry in the morning. After school he snacked continually before, during, and after work and skating until dinnertime, when he was no longer hungry for a meal. When the family went out together for dinner, he generally begged off, feeling fatigued after skating practice, having a stomachache, or not being "in the mood to eat." Though his mother tried to set limits on his out-of-control snacking, she felt that "what he puts into his mouth is really none of my business." Because he was "old enough to make his own decisions," his parents avoided discussing what was available for him to eat when the rest of the family went out to dinner leaving him behind. Feeling his emotional fragility, his parents kept news of other skaters' wins from him.

To the casual observer, and even to some psychotherapists, Todd would not appear to have an eating disorder, not even as a secondary diagnosis. His weight was normal and stable. His presenting problem was anxiety. His difficulty eating might have been due to nerves or depression. But with a history of addiction and depression in his extended family; of an excessive, imbalanced lifestyle as an athlete; of anxiety; and of personal issues about control, there is a likelihood that his eating quirks are signs of an eating disorder *in the making.* I would encourage parents to become sensitive to this possibility, particularly in light of the statistic that only 25 percent of individuals with eating disorders ever gain access to treatment.[6]

 **EXERCISE C Detecting Soft Signs of Predisease** To diagnose some hard-to-detect predisease signs, complete the following diagnostic questionnaire, circling the word that best describes the frequency of the behavior in your child: never, rarely, sometimes, often, always.

1. My child's eating lifestyle is unbalanced, extreme, or erratic and so are some of his other behaviors, such as his patterns of studying, talking on the tele-

phone, watching television, socializing, sleeping, shopping, gum chewing, drinking, cigarette smoking, or musical instrument practicing.

Never        Rarely        Sometimes        Often        Always

2. My child gets dizzy and has fainted in school, but claims this is "stress-related."

Never        Rarely        Sometimes        Often        Always

3. He seems anxious before eating, guilty afterwards, and is uncomfortable eating in front of others. Hiding food or empty wrappers is not unusual.

Never        Rarely        Sometimes        Often        Always

4. My child feels that I am too controlling, though I feel I give him lots of freedom.

Never        Rarely        Sometimes        Often        Always

5. He constantly seeks approval and avoids risks and confrontation.

Never        Rarely        Sometimes        Often        Always

6. He exercises too intensively, for too long and too often, and feels anxious and out of sorts if something comes in the way of his exercise routine.

Never        Rarely        Sometimes        Often        Always

7. He does not adapt well to transitions and changes.

Never        Rarely        Sometimes        Often        Always

8. He is a black-and-white thinker, catastrophizing life events; if he has a bad day, he feels as if he's blown the whole week.

Never        Rarely        Sometimes        Often        Always

9. He thinks people create and reinforce problems when they discuss them openly.

Never        Rarely        Sometimes        Often        Always

10. He always has good excuses for not eating a meal. Either there is no time, he is not hungry, he has already eaten, he doesn't feel like it, or he'll eat later.

Never        Rarely        Sometimes        Often        Always

11. He often pre-eats dinner before going out to dinner so as not to look like he eats a lot.

Never        Rarely        Sometimes        Often        Always

12. He refers to fat as a feeling. He feels "fat," "huge," "big," and so forth, in place of feeling distressed, sad, anxious, or angry.

       Never          Rarely          Sometimes          Often          Always

13. When disappointed or upset, he engages in self-destructive behaviors.

       Never          Rarely          Sometimes          Often          Always

14. He feels he is "masquerading as a thin person." He believes he is a fat person at heart, despite his physical appearance or what the scale reads.

       Never          Rarely          Sometimes          Often          Always

15. He sometimes misses school because of "not feeling well." (This might be due to taking laxatives or to wanting to stay in bed so as to be away from, and not tempted by, food.)

       Never          Rarely          Sometimes          Often          Always

16. He needs to know the contents of foods before he'll eat them. He's been known to interview restaurant bakers and chefs before eating a meal, and he studies food package labels for fat content.

       Never          Rarely          Sometimes          Often          Always

17. He lives for the future, when "things will be better."

       Never          Rarely          Sometimes          Often          Always

18. He eats the same foods over and over again, at the same time every day and in the same order.

       Never          Rarely          Sometimes          Often          Always

19. He has left his diary or journal out in places where it has been easy for me to find it. It seems as though he wants me to notice what he is experiencing, despite his apparent secretiveness.

       Never          Rarely          Sometimes          Often          Always

20. He avoids reading books or newspapers because he has problems concentrating.

       Never          Rarely          Sometimes          Often          Always

Did any patterns emerge in your responses to these diagnostic questions? If most of your answers are *often* or *always,* you may be looking at signs of disease or imminent disease. It might be instructive to ask your child to respond to this questionnaire after you have completed it. Much can be learned from comparing answers. If there is a discrepancy in perception, what might be causing it? What can you do about it? How might you and your child go about discussing it together? These discrepancies can become a jumping off point for a dialogue between you and your child.

## We Are All a Little Eating Disordered

Of the many smoke screens clouding disease recognition, the most insidious is that we all, to some extent, straddle the fine line between normalcy and pathology. During times of great stress, people frequently lose their appetites. Who isn't on some sort of dietary vigil in this era of health and fitness consciousness? How many people have said, even with tongue in cheek, that they "wish they could be just a little anorexic," if only until the unwanted pounds come off?

New projections promise a life expectancy of 120 years for people who "take care" of themselves by eating less and staying fit. According to the American Dietetic Association, at any point in time 45 percent of women and 25 percent of men are on diets, driving an industry that sells $33 billion worth of weight control products and devices each year.[7] One might assume that it is a young girl's *distortions* that lead her to believe she will become more popular as she grows thinner. But then she explains that "everything *did* change for me when I lost weight. I started getting phone calls, boyfriends, party invitations. . . . It never happened before!"

Youngsters observe their camp counselors choosing to forgo lunch in the interest of looking good in their swimsuits. A teen camp counselor reported that her six- and seven-year-old campers routinely inspected the nutritional labels on the items in their lunch sacks before eating. Food restriction is becoming synonymous with glamour and fame; revered and emulated women such as Princess Diana are less reticent about discussing their disorders publically.

As our computer-oriented lifestyles make us increasingly sedentary, it becomes imperative to watch what we eat and engage in regular exercise routines to remain healthy. The behaviors that characterize eating disorders can in certain contexts be seen as healthful accommodations to a changing lifestyle. Typically, the transition from normal behaviors and attitudes to diseased ones is so subtle and gradual as to go unnoticed.

The true distinction between normalcy and pathology lies in the *quality* of behavior—its extent, its purpose—and in the *capacity* of the individual to exercise free choice in connection with that behavior. When behaviors that should be autonomous are no longer under your child's voluntary control and when once benign behavior begins to interfere with his life functions and roles, he is displaying the distinctive hallmark of pathology. As you look for such distinctions in your child's behavior, ask yourself if he appears to be using food for purposes other than

- Satiating hunger
- Fueling his body
- Fostering sociability

If so, it is a good bet that something is up.

## PREPARING YOURSELF TO DISCOVER YOUR CHILD'S EATING DISORDER

Gleaning a diagnostic hunch can be particularly difficult if your own attitudes and behaviors involving food get in the way. Behaviors that appear normal and even healthful in your eyes could be fueling an eating disorder in your child.

 **EXERCISE D** Analyzing Your Own Attitudes Toward Food   To reach a greater degree of self-awareness about your own attitudes toward food, consider the following questions, and write your answers in the space provided.

1. Has your child ever run out the door to school in the morning in a big hurry and without breakfast? If so, do you know his reasons why?

   _____

   _____

   _____

2. Consider your own views about the importance of meals, particularly breakfast. Do *you* eat breakfast regularly? If not, why not?

   _____

   _____

   _____

3. If your child is racing out the door without breakfast, he may not be remembering to take a lunch either. What is your policy about lunch? (Have you ever considered making it for him? Do you send him to school with money to buy lunches? Have you ever inquired about whether or how that money gets spent?) Is lunchtime simply not your concern? If not, why not?

_____

_____

_____

4. It would be a good idea to plan to ask your child about his breakfasts and lunches. Can you be persistent when you ask your child about the motivations for his actions? How aware do you think he is of his own motivations? Do you see your child as defensive?

_____

_____

_____

5. When confronting your child about potentially touchy issues, can you tell if he is being open and honest with you? (What if he were to turn those questions back to you to discover why *you* don't eat breakfast; how would you respond?) Do you feel your child values himself enough to make it a priority to do what is best for himself?

_____

_____

_____

6. Are you tuned in sufficiently to notice if he is fearful about becoming fat from eating nutritious foods that fuel the body? Does he become irritable at the very mention of food and meals?

_____

_____

_____

7. Might he be willing to eat if good food were more readily available to him at home or if you were to join him at the table for breakfast before his day begins?

_____

_____

_____

8. If you are typically absent during the morning routine because of your work, sleep, or exercise schedule, what could you do to make it easier for him to eat breakfast and lunch (such as making lunches or setting the breakfast table the night before)?

_____

_____

_____

## Your Own Resistance

Most parents feel unprepared to diagnose their child's eating disorder. Moreover resistance to acknowledging disease or participating in recovery can be as strong for some parents as it is for some children. Resistant parents may be responding to their own uneven problem-solving skills and capacities to handle difficult interactions, their varying tolerance for the expression and acceptance of conflict or anger, and their varying ability to accept responsibility to make personal changes. Parents may secretly (or not so secretly) envy their child's thinness and self-discipline, wishing themselves the same capacities. Many believe that issues not acknowledged or discussed may disappear by themselves. Another often-unsuspected form of resistance is a defeatist attitude about their own effectiveness, which prevents parents from intervening proactively.

The greatest reinforcement to parental resistance is today's confusion about what truly constitutes healthy eating. Is fat-free and low-fat eating invariably healthy? Parents often lose sight of the fact that even the healthiest food attitudes become unhealthy when imposed too stringently or carried to extremes. In moderation there are no bad foods.

The question of what constitutes _healthy parenting_ pervades this book. Misconceptions about what adolescents need and the myth that parents must defer to adolescents' requirements are destructive and all too commonplace assumptions that have the power to derail and undermine any parent-child relationship.

Much of what you will need to do to prepare yourself to recognize disease and mentor your child's recovery involves gaining an awareness of your own feelings and attitudes toward food and problem solving and understanding their significance for your child. Here are two exercises designed to give you further insights into yourself and your attitudes, how these attitudes came to be, and how they may skew your perceptions and responses to your child. These exercises will help you identify the areas in which you might consider making some changes. It is critical that you understand *yourself* before you try to understand or communicate with your child on this topic.

 **EXERCISE E** Assessing Your Attitudes About Food and Weight, Then and Now  How you were as a child affects who you are now. To review and assess your early childhood attitudes and experiences with food and eating, read the following questions and write your answers in the space provided. When you were a child:

1. How did you feel about your body?

    _____

    _____

    _____

2. Were you ever teased or criticized by others because of the way you looked? If so, why?

    _____

    _____

    _____

3. Did you live with rituals concerning food? If so, what were they?

    _____

    _____

    _____

4. Was food ever used as a device to threaten or motivate you? If so, how?

    _____

    _____

    _____

5. What kinds of eating behaviors and meal patterns did you see in your role-models (your parents, older siblings, camp counselors, coaches, and so forth)?

    _____

    _____

    _____

6. How did these childhood events affect your attitudes and values then? Today? (If food was used as a bribe or if you were threatened with a week of no desserts if you didn't eat your peas, there is a good chance that you might have some residual dysfunctional food attitudes.)

_____

_____

_____

**EXERCISE F Assessing Your Family Background**   The attitudes of your *family of origin* (the family you grew up in) continue to influence your attitudes today and how you interact with your eating disordered child in your *nuclear family* (the family you created together with your partner and children). To develop your insights and facilitate family discussions about these influences, complete the following two assessments.

*Assessing Your Family of Origin*

Read the following questions about your family of origin and write your answers in the space provided.

1. What messages did you get from your parents about how people were supposed to look?

_____

_____

_____

2. How did your parents perceive you physically? How do you know?

_____

_____

_____

3. Who made dinners for you as a child? Who ate with you?

_____

_____

_____

4. What were dinner times like? What kinds of things were discussed?

_____

_____

_____

5. Draw a picture of your family dinner table. Who sat where? Was anyone often absent?

6. What were your family's food traditions, rituals, and quirks?

_____
_____
_____

7. How were troublesome issues handled? Were problems resolved? Give examples.

_____
_____
_____

8. Could people express themselves honestly and openly? Explain.

_____
_____
_____

*Assessing Your Nuclear Family*

Respond to the following statements by circling the word that best describes the frequency of the behavior described: never, rarely, sometimes, often, always.

1. I tend to be an overly controlling parent. This leads to an out-of-control child.

    Never        Rarely        Sometimes        Often        Always

2. I tend to be an overly permissive parent. This leads to an out-of-control child. (Your answers to the first two questions may reflect the fact that parents may be overly controlling and overly permissive at once.)

    Never        Rarely        Sometimes        Often        Always

3. At times I give my child too many choices; at other times I do not give him enough.

    Never        Rarely        Sometimes        Often        Always

4. I am excessively conscious of body size. I praise or criticize my children for their appearance.

    Never        Rarely        Sometimes        Often        Always

5. My partner and I do not present a united front; we generally do not agree on how to resolve problems.

       Never      Rarely      Sometimes      Often      Always

6. The members of our family typically keep secrets from one another.

       Never      Rarely      Sometimes      Often      Always

7. I feel there is not enough privacy in our family.

       Never      Rarely      Sometimes      Often      Always

8. There is alcoholism or drug addiction or both in our family.

       Never      Rarely      Sometimes      Often      Always

9. There is abuse (verbal, physical, or sexual) in our family.

       Never      Rarely      Sometimes      Often      Always

10. The members of our family are always trying to make each other happy and to avoid conflict and sadness at all costs. In our effort to be the Brady Bunch, the truth goes by the wayside.

       Never      Rarely      Sometimes      Often      Always

The greater your number of *often* or *always* scores, the greater the likelihood of eating disordered attitudes and issues in your family. Further, it would not be unusual for you to see similar patterns in your nuclear family as in your family of origin .

**Activity** Thoughts to Ponder  Did you know that as individuals grow older, their basal metabolism rate drops 4 to 5 percent with each decade? That as estrogen levels drop, women need fifty fewer calories per day at age fifty than at age forty? That as you grow older, to maintain your weight, you may have to eat considerably fewer calories daily and exercise more? Did you know that after you give birth to a child, your set point weight (the weight your body tries to maintain) may change, along with your shoe and blouse size?

How do you feel about these normal changes as they occur in your own body now? How are you accommodating these changes? Could your personal responses be negatively influencing your child? Are you aware of any rules you may be following about food and eating? Are you aware of your child's rules? Are they similar to yours? (You may want to record your thoughts in your journal.)

### Self-Assessment

Having gotten to this point, don't be discouraged if you are not feeling entirely prepared yet to deal with your child or this disease. An increased consciousness of the issues involved and a heightened self-awareness will be sufficient to get you through. Bringing problems to light should be an incentive for problem resolution, not guilt. Your proactive problem solving will provide incomparable role modeling for your child, in recovery and in all aspects of his life.

Some of the potentially problematic qualities you may have uncovered in yourself, such as a need to be in control or a drive toward rigorous self-discipline, are in many respects *strengths,* not weaknesses, enhancing the quality of your life and your child's. It is only in their *extent* and in their impact on your child that they may need modifying. Though the nature of your commitment to care for your child changes as he grows into adulthood, you will never stop being your child's parent—and he will never stop needing you to be.

Once parents come to better know themselves, their children, and eating disorders, they are ready to take action to confront the eating disordered child. Chapter Three suggests practical ways to begin a dialogue with the child who needs a parent's help.

# Taking Action

Part Two is about reaching out to your child and to the community to find the best help available. The three chapters in this part will give you the tools you need to connect with your child and find the best treatment and the most effective professionals to work with her and your family.

*What Parents Can Do*

1. Set standards for a balanced eating and exercise lifestyle at home. Everyone in your household should be eating three nutritious meals a day.

2. Prepare meals and expect your family to enjoy them together as often as possible.

3. Discuss your thoughts, feelings, and values with your children. Speak until you are heard.

4. Understand how your own attitudes about food influence your child, and try to keep them separate from your child's issues.

5. Hear the *feeling* messages behind your child's statements; respond to your *child*, not to the food she consumes.

6. Learn as much as you can before reaching out for help. Knowledge is power.

7. Keep expectations realistic for yourself, your child, the treatment process, and the professionals. Remember that you are dealing with a highly imperfect science.

8. Set goals for yourself and meet them. They will keep you focused and productive.

9. Remember that there are many "right" ways to do things.

10. Begin your foray into the community of health care providers knowing that your child deserves the very best and that your purpose is to make sure she or he gets it.

# Beginning the Dialogue with Your Child

*We never know whether the words we use and others hear, convey the same meaning . . .*
*how much more so when it is your son.*

Elie Wiesel[1]

There is no single, definitive protocol or "correct" course of action for you and your child to follow that will guarantee a solution to her eating problems. This chapter will help you to initiate a many-faceted recovery process as you first confront your child.

## THE PARENTAL ROLE

Your attitudes and beliefs about children and teenagers and the role of parents affect the way you respond to your child. It is important to identify your attitudes and the many misconceptions about the parental role when it comes to eating disorders.

*Common Myths About Eating Disordered Children and Their Parents—And What the Facts Are*

Myth 1.   *Parents are the cause of their child's eating disorder.* As discussed in Chapter One, parents cannot cause their child's eating disorder.

Myth 2.   *Parents should always become involved in monitoring what their child eats.* It is sometimes, although not always, appropriate for parents to become involved in the refeeding process in eating disorder recovery, depending upon circumstances and the child's needs. It is always appropriate for parents to prepare meals, have a house that is well stocked with nutritious foods, and to expect their child to eat.

Myth 3.   *Parents should never become involved in monitoring what their child eats.* As mentioned in the discussion of myth 2, this depends on what the individual child requires at any given time. (Chapter Seven offers some information about practical food monitoring.)

Myth 4.   *All kids are rude and obnoxious to their parents during adolescence; it's a natural part of the separation process.* Anger is acceptable. Rudeness and inconsiderateness should not be. They are one sign of a self-centered child with poor self-esteem who is incapable of properly expressing what she feels. Your child's attitudes toward you tell you a great deal about the quality of your parenting and what she sees as acceptable behavior in your home.

Myth 5.   *By the time a child reaches her teenage years, it is too late for parents to have any influence on her.* It is never too late for people to have positive influences on each other. Parents err in thinking their adolescents have grown up beyond their reach. The opposite is true.

Myth 6.   *It is normal for siblings to fight a lot and be mean to each other.* Frequent fighting is not normal, and like rudeness and inconsiderateness (see the discussion of myth 4), this behavior signals a child who is facing problems. Hitting is communication through violence, not words.

Myth 7.   *The best way to guarantee a child's healthy separation from the family is to give her as much freedom as possible as early as possible.* The capacity of a child to separate healthfully from parents correlates directly to how healthfully *bonded* she is with them first. Children learn how to be successfully separate *only* after they have enjoyed a healthy and meaningful connection. Sending children away to overnight camp at age six, seven, or eight is no guarantee that they will separate healthfully later.

Myth 8.   *It is inappropriate for parents to purchase a health club membership for their recovering child.* It is very appropriate to exercise. The goal for the eating disordered child is to participate in life in a moderated and balanced fashion; extremes such as total abstinence should simply not be options. A health club membership could provide a helpful practice ground for setting self-limits, as long as the privilege is not abused.

## Making Contact

Communication between parent and child is a dynamic that is complex at best, and it becomes even more so when communication takes the form of discussion about an eating disorder. Consider the following case study.

Alice, a bulimic adolescent, sat together with her family in my office. Her mother, Joan, asked her to explain something about her eating disorder. Alice's internist had sent a note home asking mother to stop bringing *trigger foods* into the house. Having no idea what a trigger food was, Joan turned to Alice for an explanation.

" I don't feel comfortable talking to you," was Alice's response. "This has nothing to do with you. It's not your problem. The subject is closed."

Alice's defensive response prompted Joan's tearful description of how helpless she felt. "Here I am, expected to help you recover from something I do not understand, and no one will even explain it to me!"

"If Alice would discuss her disorder with you, what would you like to know?" I asked Joan. There was no hesitation in her response. "I would want to know about what the eating disorder is and how it got started, what drives it, and how she can address it. I would want to know why she is required to go to the internist's office every week, what triggers her problematic eating habits, and if what we are doing at home is making things better or worse. But most of all, I would want to know why she won't speak to any of us about her problem!" Turning to Alice, Joan said, "I've always known what to do in the past, but suddenly I feel lost. . . . It's as if I don't know who you are anymore, or who I'm supposed to be."

Alice had nothing to say on the subject—nor could she explain why. "Do you feel your mother is being intrusive by asking such questions or that she could simply be trying to express her concern and desire to be more helpful?" I asked. Alice said she *felt* her mother was intrusive although she *understood* that her mother was only trying to help. She did not *know* the answers to her mother's questions or how to begin accepting help from anyone. Under the influence of her eating disorder, Alice had become more remote from her parents than ever. Because she could not recognize and respond to her own feelings, she was helpless to attend to her own needs, let alone the needs of her parents.

Though parents must retain clear and appropriate privacy boundaries with their adolescent children and respect the child's remoteness under the influence of an eating disorder, this does not exempt parents from being parental and from learning what is essential for them to know. It is precisely when parents are feeling most helpless and lost that they will be called upon to be most forthcoming and persistent.

From the very moment of their children's birth, parents strive to prepare them to leave home as emotionally healthy and highly functioning adults. Parents are teachers. Lessons taught about life will influence their child's eating. Lessons taught about eating, food, and nutrition likewise teach children about life and how to live it. An eating disorder suggests that an adolescent's developmental tasks have veered off course. It is for the parent to get them back on track.

## Understanding Obstacles to Parental Advocacy

As the healthy child matures and internalizes family and cultural values and controls, her need for external controls diminishes. When emotional development is interrupted and veers off course, however, the individual lacking fully developed internal resources turns to external resources, such as eating disorders to fill the void. When a child is incapable of exerting self-control, it is the parents' responsibility to pick up the slack and to provide the emotional structure that is lacking, at least until the child is capable of exercising her own initiative and has no further need to rely on disease.

Too many parents withdraw their influence from their children's lives prematurely, precisely when their children are least able to make responsible judgments on their own and when they need parental guidance the most.

 **EXERCISE A  Avoiding Parent Traps**   Here are some parental behaviors and attitudes that act as obstacles, preventing parents from helping their children. To help yourself recognize such traps, read each statement. Does it resonate with your own thoughts and actions? Circle Y for yes, N for no.

1.  Y/N   I fear that becoming involved with my child's eating disorder will jeopardize my relationship with my child.

2.  Y/N   I feel that the best way to be supportive to my child is with hugs and acquiescence, eliminating emotional conflicts even when that means not being true to myself.

3.  Y/N   Because I feel guilt for causing, or at least not preventing, the onset of disease, I feel inadequate when approaching my child.

4.  Y/N   I sometimes interrupt my child before really hearing what she has to say, offering advice before I know what she needs and wants.

5.  Y/N   I remember my own behaviors as a teenager and wonder, "Who am I to offer advice when I was worse than she at that age?"

6. Y/N   Knowing that I have no power over my child's actions when I'm apart from her, I assume I have no influence at any time.

7. Y/N   Assuming that involvement connotes intrusiveness, I worry that my child will be angered and alienated by my interest in her.

8. Y/N   Because I believe that my eating disordered child is emotionally fragile, I hesitate to say anything that might offend her.

9. Y/N   Sometimes I forget that no response is a poignant response; it implies just about any meaning my child chooses to assign to it.

10. Y/N   I believe that substance use (alcohol, cigarettes, drugs) and fad dieting are a natural part of growing up. I don't mind if she engages in these activities at home.

These notions are all nonproductive and can hinder your efforts to partake effectively in your child's recovery.

**EXERCISE B Walking on Eggshells: The Delicate Dance of Fear**   Do you find that you are afraid to ask your child questions because her answers may uncover unpleasantness, arouse your anger or hers, disclose a secret, or reveal a problem? Read each of the following questions. If you could ask your child the question, circle Y for yes. If you would be afraid to ask, circle N for no.

1. Y/N   Are you eating the lunches I make for you every day?

2. Y/N   Why do you feel it is so critical for you to lose five pounds? What will it be like for you if it doesn't happen? If it does?

3. Y/N   Which are the articles that interest you the most in the magazines you are reading?

4. Y/N   What kinds of issues are of greatest concern to you and your friends?

5. Y/N   Do you understand what an eating disorder is? How would you explain it to someone else?

6. Y/N   Do you know how people behave when they have an eating disorder?

7. Y/N   If you had an eating disorder, what would be your greatest concern?

8. Y/N   You've been in the bathroom a long time; are you okay?

9. Y/N   I found all of these candy wrappers in the garbage. Do you know where they came from? (If the answer is no: Would you feel free to discuss this with me if they were yours?)

10.   Y/N   You seem agitated and upset. Are you aware of what might be bothering you?

If your answers indicate that you're reluctant to discuss such things with your child, think about what's holding you back. Could there be unspoken issues between you and your child that demand protection? Could your hesitancy or ambivalence about asking what you need to know be giving your child a sense of being too powerful? Ironically, the more parents walk on eggshells in an effort not to miff their child, the more overpowerful she feels, and the greater her need to rely on the eating disorder.

Here are eight additional common obstacles for parents to overcome as they approach their eating disordered children. You may be experiencing several of these obstacles at once.

**The Adolescent Mood Obstacle**   Adolescence is marked by the onset of puberty with its chaotic onslaught of hormones and role confusion. As one college freshman reported, "I know I'm not ready to be an adult, but I'm certainly not a kid any more, either." Because this life stage can be characterized by moodiness, impulsivity, rebelliousness, and wholesale alienation from adults, adults typically *expect* teens to ignore parents, to be rude, noncommunicative, and hostile. But when you see such extreme behaviors as normative, you often miss what your child is *really* trying to say through these attitudes. The distancing teen, faced with a laissez-faire parent, easily slips out of the family's reach—a prophecy self-fulfilled.

**The Professional Advice Obstacle**   Health professionals typically advise parents to back off in the interest of supporting their child's fledgling independence. There are certainly circumstances where this advice is appropriate, but each case is unique, and each circumstance must be analyzed apart from such sweeping generalizations.

**The Overweight Fear Obstacle**   In trying to prevent children from becoming overweight, parents typically *create* fears and misconceptions in them. There are more than twenty million (roughly 25 percent) overweight young children in the United States today.[2] Our children are being raised among the temptations of abundant and affordable food, fast foods, absent parents, and sedentary and convenience-oriented lifestyles. Car-pooled everywhere, our children have decreasing opportunities to use their bodies actively. What are parents to do if not to become vigilant about their child's fat intake, purchasing *lite,* low-fat, and no-fat foods in an effort to teach healthy eating? It is easy to misinterpret what healthy eating is and to confuse our children with these misinterpretations. *Healthy eating is the capacity to eat anything and everything, any time, as long as it is in moderation.* Unhealthy eating is restrictive, unbalanced eating of any kind.

**The Support Obstacle**     Being supportive is a learned skill. With eating disorders, your child may have an adverse reaction to your *knowing* about her problem, let alone to accepting your help. Supporting her in eating disorder recovery requires responsiveness tailored to her changing needs. Her behaviors, and it is to be hoped her words, will keep you abreast of these changes, alerting you to the times when you ought to back off (but never to the point of losing emotional contact) and when you must sally forth. It is for you, the parent, to straddle the thin line between interceding and interfering with precision and flexibility throughout your child's recovery—and indeed throughout her life.

**The Friend Versus Parent Obstacle**     One of the toughest obstacles of all is the temptation to behave like your child's friend, especially at those times when her goals for herself parallel your goals for her, when she is feeling strong and capable, or when she is feeling particularly weak and needy. Yet it is up to you to remain consistent and focused, never losing sight of the big picture. As a friend, you run the risk of losing your objectivity; in the role of parent, you do not. Don't let empathy with your child lead to your inadvertent support of her disease.

**The Burden of Proof Obstacle**     So many parents feel they have no right to *accuse* their child of what might or might not be a disease. One parent admitted that she'd known about her daughter's bulimia for two years but felt her "hands were tied" because she could never "prove it beyond a reasonable doubt." Her fears about destroying their relationship, compounding her daughter's pain, and becoming inappropriately involved in a "place" where she did not belong caused her such consternation that she did not sleep a wink the night before she finally confronted her daughter.

**The Miscommunicating Family Obstacle**     When considering the functional health of your family, that is, how members of your family relate to one another, remember that communication is as much about what *is not* said as it is about what *is* said. What is not said is *interpreted* and *felt.* Children simply fill in the blanks with their misconceptions. A father criticizes a television celebrity for being fat, and his child translates that as, "Dad doesn't love fat people. I'd better not ever get fat." A mother exercises religiously every day, spending much of her time in a leotard. Her nonverbal messages are not lost on her young daughters.

**The "I Can't Tolerate Controls Myself" Obstacle**     Parents of today's eating disordered children tend to be baby boomers, members of the generation that grew up during the sixties and made freedom from constraints their goal in life. Perhaps responding to their own feelings that they were parented oppressively, these individuals tend to be loath to provide discipline for their children. However, when offered freedom and power without rules, children will fabricate devices (like eating disorders) to make up for the missing structure.

> **Activity** **Understanding Your Parenting Style**     Discuss your parenting style with your partner. Does he or she perceive your style as you do? How do you perceive your partner's style? Does he or she agree? How do your styles complement each other? How do your differences compound your child's difficulties? How do you assess which styles work best in specific situations? Have you ever asked your child for her perspective on your parenting styles? When it comes to helping a child with an eating disorder, parents must agree on their values and philosophies and act consistently.

## What Is Good for the Goose Is Not Necessarily Good for the Gander

Yet another obstacle for parents attempting to assist their children is the fact that behaviors and lifestyles that serve a parent well may cause problems for a child. One mother confided in her bulimic daughter that she was about to "commit a sinful act" by eating a fatty dessert but that she had promised herself she'd "exercise like crazy tomorrow." She could not understand how her "healthy" exercise regime and fat intake vigilance could adversely affect her bulimic daughter, but it did.

Another mother encouraged her bulimic daughter to keep a tally of daily calories side by side with the mother's own tabulations. This woman never allowed herself more than 1,200 calories per day, approximately half the amount her daughter needed to maintain a healthy metabolism and eating lifestyle. For the mother, weight restriction offered a degree of self-control within the context of her shaky marriage; for the daughter, weight restriction became an out-of-control aspect of her eating disorder.

These parents managed to maintain a functional balance in their lives, but their disordered children did not. The parents' primary or secondary means for reducing anxiety and coping with problems fell short of making them clinically eating disordered. Biochemically they were probably not as vulnerable to disease as their children. In a similar vein, by offering a glass of wine to a nonalcoholic, one is providing a delicious, relaxing, and even medicinal enhancement to an evening meal; the same well-intentioned offer made to a recovering alcoholic may be construed as a less than benign invitation to fall off the wagon.

Well-intentioned parental communications can become confused and misinterpreted messages when offered to children outside of a context of values and greater meaning. Even when parents are supporting what they feel is best for their child, like the mother who never allows her children to have dessert, they can be creating obstacles to helping that child. It is important to know when short-term gains are best forfeited in favor of longer-term ones.

Whereas some parents impose too many controls, and others impose too few, both leave their children incapable of self-regulation. Establishing proper controls and withdrawing them when appropriate is key to developing your child's capacity for internal self-regulation and self-esteem. Moreover, when parents show no flexibility, the child has no room to learn self-expression and problem solving based on the requirements of the moment.

Remember that words and actions carry messages of tremendous power, especially in light of the particular sensitivities of eating disordered individuals. One purpose of this book is to empower you to harness the enormous power of words to accomplish *good*.

 **EXERCISE C** **Recognizing Your Own Obstacles**   Before approaching your child about what may be an eating disorder, you may find it helpful to anticipate the trouble spots, in a effort to prepare yourself to face these obstacles. You may also want to discuss them with your partner or a therapist before you talk to your child. To identify potential obstacles, read each of the following descriptions of what you will do to talk productively with your child and write down the difficulties you think you might have in carrying out these actions.

1. I can approach my child with empathy. I can help my child feel understood and accepted so she will partner with me as her ally.

   *Obstacles:*

   _____

   _____

   _____

2. I can concern myself with the *process* of problem solving rather than with finding specific solutions to specific problems. I can think things through aloud with my child ("I'm wondering if this *other* option might be a preferable alternative." "Can you talk to me about *how* you are thinking about this?" "Have you considered thinking this other way, or asking so-and-so for an opinion?").

   *Obstacles:*

   _____

   _____

   _____

3. I can keep conversations goal directed. My goals are to hear my child, to let her hear herself, to share my values with her, and to encourage her to accept assistance. It can't hurt to explain to her what I hope to accomplish by engaging in a specific interaction with her ("Here is why I am asking this." "This is what I have in mind.").

   *Obstacles:*

   _____

   _____

   _____

4. I can keep the conversational ball rolling. I will try not to take turns with my child in saying things but will focus specifically on what my child has said. I will not state what my child already knows as if it is new information. I will

try to remember that I do not have to accomplish my ultimate goal in the first conversation, and I do not expect my child to know or to say right away what she needs from me.

*Obstacles:*

_____

_____

_____

5. I will try not to succumb to such conversation stoppers as, "Dad, *no* teenager ever confides in her parents."

*Obstacles:*

_____

_____

_____

6. I will not fall into the gender gap by thinking that there is some natural law against females' confiding in their fathers and males' confiding in their mothers. The capacity to be open and above board in communicating is not gender based. All teenagers want and need privacy about specific issues but not necessarily about their eating disorders.

*Obstacles:*

_____

_____

_____

7. I will be clear with my child that I do not intend to control her life but only to live in harmony alongside it. My goal is not to have power over my child but to empower her.

*Obstacles:*

_____

_____

_____

8. I will use I-based statements to avoid giving advice and blaming ("I notice that you haven't eaten much dinner," rather than, "You didn't eat enough dinner.").

*Obstacles:*

_____

_____

_____

9. I will try to use objective rather than subjective statements ("I notice your clothes seem to be getting larger on you," rather than, "You are too skinny.").
   *Obstacles:*

   _____

   _____

   _____

10. I will learn to expect and respect my child's resistance to treatment and recovery, knowing that this response, though misguided, represents her best effort to take care of herself and to survive.
    *Obstacles:*

    _____

    _____

    _____

11. I will attempt to *create* occasions to interact with my child. I will make a point of wandering into her bedroom when she is not particularly busy and hanging out there, testing the waters for any inclination to chat.
    *Obstacles:*

    _____

    _____

    _____

12. I know that I may eventually need to use my authority as her parent, through ultimatums or force, to get my child to treatment, at least initially. I know I can rely on the therapist to negotiate the resistance and anger between us. If my child walks out on me and the session, I can always stay and get help for myself.
    *Obstacles:*

    _____

    _____

    _____

**EXERCISE D** **Recognizing What Your Child Considers Supportive** How do parents know what feels supportive to a child? How can parents feel confident that they are not overstepping the line between intervention and interference when offering support? Here are some of the things your child might say to you were she sufficiently self-aware and capable of articulating her needs. To help yourself overcome obstacles to communication, read each statement, and if you can imagine yourself doing what your child is asking, circle Y for yes. If you can't, circle N for no.

1. Y/N Don't tell me what to eat; ask me instead if something is wrong. Your policing my food intake is less helpful in the long run than my learning to control myself.

2. Y/N If you see me struggling, notice it, comment on it, ask if there is something you can do. Ask me if I want to talk about it, but respect my answer if I say no. Bring the issue up again in another way, at another time. It helps me to know that you are with me, that I am not alone.

3. Y/N Notice that *I* am struggling; your accent should not be on my food and eating, but on *me*. It's OK for you to wonder aloud what might be making things so hard for me.

4. Y/N Rather than supporting my decisions, it would feel more reassuring to me if you would ask me how I arrived at them. Ask me why I feel the way I do before commenting on whether or not you agree with me. Ask me if I have considered thinking about things differently. Remember you are supporting *me*, not my decisions.

5. Y/N Please take the initiative with me; don't wait until I come to you. Ask me whether I am feeling upset if I seem upset to you, even though I may not be aware enough of myself yet to be able to answer you.

6. Y/N Offer to make my lunch for school. That little brown sack of sustenance at the bottom of my book bag does a lot to say how much you really care about me.

7. Y/N Listen to hear me, not for an excuse to tell me what you think. Don't be impatient for me to be done speaking. I have a right to my opinions.

8. Y/N You think that by not saying certain things you are avoiding an argument, but when a conflict exists, it exists whether you and I discuss it or not; bringing it to light increases the odds that we can resolve it.

9. Y/N    Don't feel that it is acceptable for you to say insensitive things to me because I am overweight. I am not this way by choice.

10. Y/N    Refrain from commenting on my thinness; it sets off my anxiety and determination to become even thinner.

11. Y/N    Don't sit by passively if others make fun of the way I look. My feelings are easily hurt, and I need your understanding and support.

12. Y/N    Don't feel compelled to accommodate my requests to bring low-fat and lite food products and junk food into the house. These will not help me recover.

13. Y/N    Honor your own needs. Don't go out of your way to make me special dinners or to change the family's eating lifestyle to accommodate mine. I'll make my own meal if I do not like what you are eating. Expect me to sit down at the table with you for communal dining. If I go overboard and eat up all of a certain food before the rest of the family has a chance to partake of it, expect me to replace it.

14. Y/N    Don't try to take control of my life, my disease, and my recovery by disposing of trigger foods that I bring into the house. Don't take on my problems as your own; don't lose sleep, don't miss your vacation so you can stay home to watch over me, don't refrain from eating out at certain restaurants that may be a challenge for me, and so on. Such actions both impose and take away undue power, reinforcing my insecurity and my need for the eating disorder.

One of your goals as you learn more about eating disorders is to be able to answer yes to more of these supportive behaviors.

## CONFRONTING YOUR CHILD CONFRONTING DISEASE

What do you *say* about a problem that makes its own rules, one of which is that it is not to be discussed? What do you *say* to a child who drops hints then retracts them in the next breath? What do you *say* to a child who claims of her disorder, "As soon as things come together in my life, I'll get rid of it"? What do you *say* to an anorexic child who claims that she really doesn't have an eating disorder at all, now that she has enough self-control not to fall below ninety pounds again, or to a child who says, "How can I be sick? I ate out with you at a restaurant, didn't I?"

even though she fasted all day in preparation for the occasion? In confronting your eating disordered child, you can count on confronting resistance—to recognizing disease, to accepting treatment, and to engaging in recovery.

## Confronting Resistance

Resistance often appears as early in the recovery process as the stage of symptom recognition and disease acknowledgment, taking the form of disease denial. It accounts for the secretive nature of the disease and often looks and sounds like fear—of change, of failure, of success, of relying on oneself, of displeasing others. Resistance is about holding onto symptoms that work for the patient; the task of treatment is to find alternatives that serve the patient more effectively. In most instances the effort to resolve a problem begins with defining the problem. In the case of eating disorders, and as a result of resistance, efforts to resolve the problem often need to begin *before* the patient acknowledges that a problem exists. In fact the first goal of treatment is inevitably to help the patient understand that there *is* a problem.

Resistance appears too in the patient's difficulty with accepting and committing to the process of treatment. Patients may commit to treatment but then regress into ambivalence about recovery. One of the first requirements for confronting your child successfully is that you understand and recognize the many faces of resistance. Individuals resist giving up disease for a variety of "good" reasons. In one instance a teenager assumed that a diagnosis of eating disordered was forever. Concluding that her fate would be sealed with the admission of disease, she needed to remain outside the treatment process because she needed to live with the hope of being well one day.

Accepting recovery connotes accepting disease and, with it, accepting one's own failings and vulnerability. Some patients believe they cannot exist without their disorder. When the child's resistance is intense, treatment might initially focus on less threatening, more attainable goals, with food issues always present but perhaps tangential until trust is established in the therapy process. Particularly in those cases where resistance to food changes is high, regular monitoring by a physician is critical to watch for degeneration in the patient's physical health.

Parents may also be resistant to recognizing disease or assuming a role in recovery, and this can compound the child's resistance. Parents of today's adolescents, who are otherwise so accustomed to living proactive, entitled, and empowered existences, in too many instances seem all too ready to abandon their take-charge stance in the face of their children's eating disorders.

 **EXERCISE E Recognizing Deterrents to Getting Better** Here are some of the forces behind resistance to recovery, described in the words your child might use if she were sufficiently self-aware. To identify some of the forces behind your child's resistance, read each statement, and if you think it is something your child might tell you if she could articulate her resistance, circle Y for yes. If it is not, circle N for no.

1. Y/N Tomorrow I will undo the positive changes that frightened me today.

2. Y/N I don't need to gain back all of my weight in order to be recovered.

3. Y/N I will surely become fat if I eat normally.

4. Y/N I am afraid of food; as soon as I begin to eat, I feel completely out of control.

5. Y/N I am not responsible for the good things that have happened so far in treatment.

6. Y/N I can't live without my eating disorder.

7. Y/N Everyone will stop caring about me if I get well.

8. Y/N If I let go of disease, I will also have to let go of my self-control, self-discipline, good grades, nice appearance, being the envy of my friends, invitations to the prom, and many other great perks.

9. Y/N You may consider my eating disorder to be yet another indicator that nothing is right in our family.

10. Y/N This treatment may be too expensive for you to handle.

11. Y/N If you and Dad become involved in treatment, you might begin fighting with each other, which could lead to divorce.

12. Y/N My eating disorder is embedded in every cell of my body. It is as intrinsic a part of me as my hair and eye color.

13. Y/N I want to be "special," not just "average" and "ordinary."

14. Y/N Giving up my disorder would be like going through a death.

15. Y/N The therapist is encouraging me to accept "responsibility" for the part of my problem that is in my power to control, but what he really

means is that I am to blame for my disorder; he's trying to make me feel guilty.

16. Y/N   Someday, when I have a husband and kids, a job and financial security, then I won't need my eating disorder anymore, and it'll go away by itself.

17. Y/N   I can eat a meal, so I must be recovered.

18. Y/N   I consider myself to be living a wellness lifestyle.

19. Y/N   Any amount of failure feels total and irrevocable to me.

20. Y/N   If you don't look at a problem, it's not really there.

As you look back at the statements you thought your child might make, consider how you might help her to overcome these specific resistances.

### Recognizing Hidden Agendas

With as much nonchalance as she can muster, a daughter begins to interview her mother: "Mom, have you noticed that the entire bag of Snickers has disappeared?" It is likely that this child needs and is asking for something more weighty than a discussion about candy wrappers. What does she really want to say? What is her hidden agenda? My guess is that this youngster is attempting to say "Help me!" to break her silence about her disease in the only way she knows how—disguised and cryptic. She is probably asking her mother to take initiative and control where she cannot do so herself. Feeling tentative about putting herself in a position from which she cannot retreat, she probably feels safer asking for what she needs in the form of a riddle. She may also be fearful about broaching a topic that seems a shameful indictment of her character, suggesting that she might be "crazy" or out of control. She might be asking whether or not she is sick.

Her mother could respond in various ways. She might pretend not to know anything about the situation, pretend not to be concerned about the worrisome signs she *has* noticed, acknowledge that she is aware that something odd is up but express no curiosity to know more, or acknowledge that she has noticed and is all ears to hear what her daughter has to say on the subject.

If her mother plays dumb in this situation, it might say to the inquiring child that her mother not only doesn't know but doesn't *care* to know about the child's quandary or the unhappiness and fear she is experiencing. This would reinforce the misconceptions discussed earlier that having family secrets is preferable to knowing unpleasant things, that ignorance and denial are viable alternatives to assuming responsibility, and that if one does nothing to stir up a problem, it might simply disappear of its own accord. Moreover, playing dumb will give the child the sense that she has once again put one over on her mother, increasing her sense of being overly powerful, self-destructive, and reliant on her eating disorder to control her otherwise out-of-control existence. This child might also deduce that her disease is too profound or serious for anyone to provide assistance. She might even get the message that her mother *prefers* her to be thin.

The more open a parent is to hearing the truth, the greater the chances the child will respond truthfully. This interchange was about a child asking for help. The best offer of assistance would take the form of the parent seeking further information from the child in order to understand her needs and her dilemma as fully as possible. In asking for this information and understanding hidden agendas, parents must practice the skills of active listening.

## Active Listening

*The beginning of wisdom is silence; the second stage is listening.*

Hebrew proverb

If you want your child to be forthcoming with you about her disorder, you need to become a better listener. The parent with a genuine interest in listening to and understanding the things her child needs to share enables the child to look deeper into herself to observe and reveal additional thoughts or feelings. An active listening response also offers the child the assurance that she is not alone and that she has the parent's unconditional support in her every effort to find assistance. Active listening is a fearless and optimistic model for interaction that demonstrates the power of joining with others to bring about change.

*How to Listen Actively*

1. Hear the feelings underlying the child's statement.
2. Summarize the child's statement, making reference to her feelings.
3. Avoid criticism, contradiction, explanation, and judgment; reinforce conversational comfort through openness.
4. Describe what you see, feel, and believe needs to happen next. (This is not the same as advice giving.)

Here's an example of a mother using active listening with her child. Before you read the mother's response to the child's accusation, think for a moment about how you would be likely to respond.

MOTHER:   Good morning. How are you this morning?

CHILD:   Can't you ever stop watching me and questioning me every minute?!

MOTHER:   Wow! You seem jumpy this morning. What's going on with you? You know, it seems that you feel I've been interrogating you about things lately. I'm not sure what I have done wrong. I feel badly that I made you feel that way, but I can assure you this has not been my intention. Can you give me some examples of when I made you feel like this?

---

**Taking Stock** **Active Listening**   To use active listening with an eating-disordered child, the parent

- Offers an open-ended but contained response that reassures the child the parent knows his or her own limits and is respectful of them and of the child's personal boundaries.

- Implies that he or she is content to wait for cues about the best pacing and timing for the child to disclose concerns.

- Role-models the child's capacity to ask others for what she needs in life. This is also known as assertiveness. A parent's comments and questions needn't be succinct, thought through, or even to the point. All they need to be is *expressed*.

- Demonstrates a sincere, unconditional readiness to assume responsibility where he or she can. The child is not alone with her feelings.

- Offers relief and an outlet to the child who asks a simple question (perhaps about a bag of candy) that may be a disguise for her interest in making a confession. By providing an opportunity for self-disclosure, the active listener helps the child to understand what motivates her own attitudes, behaviors, and responses.

---

## Hearing What Has Not Been Spoken

Every communication is composed of two separate components: the *overt* (the literal content) and the *covert* (the unspoken feelings). An active listener tunes in to the covert, underlying feeling messages and responds to them in such a way that the original speaker comes to recognize and understand her emotions, intentions, and self more fully.

 **EXERCISE F Learning to Listen Actively**   The following scenario contains an interchange that occurred between a young woman who was a patient of mine and her father after they had lunch together at a country club. As you read, consider the overt and covert meanings, and in the space provided, write down what you think the daughter and the father might have been trying to communicate.

DAUGHTER:   Boy, did I do my share of eating today!
FATHER:         Oh, come on! You hardly ate anything.

1. *What might the daughter have been trying to express?*

   _____

   _____

   *What she wanted to express:* her pride about how she had handled the challenge of eating lunch, emotionally and nutritionally. She felt it had been a real achievement that she had kept her meal down, and she wanted her father to notice her accomplishment and share her pride.

2. *What might her father have heard her say?*

   _____

   _____

   *What her father heard:* recriminations and fear about how she had overeaten in contradiction to her anorexic drive not to eat.

3. *What might she have heard her father say?*

   _____

   _____

   *What she heard her father say:* that he had not noticed how well she'd done. She felt abandoned and alone in her recovery efforts.

4. *What might he have been trying to express?*

   _____

   _____

   *What he was trying to express:* support and reassurance that she had not eaten anything that should have caused her grief, guilt, or weight gain.

Despite this parent's good intentions, he made his daughter feel that she had failed. An active listening, and more effective, response might have been: "You feel as though you ate a lot today. Tell me about that. It seemed like a normal portion to me. So what is that like for you?" This response would help this young woman to better understand herself and then better communicate her feelings and thoughts to her father. The active listening dynamic would ultimately enable her father to be as supportive of his daughter as he would have liked to be.

> **Troubleshooting Tip** Identify Feelings   When a child has difficulty identifying her feelings, parents can offer some assistance by suggesting that she try to identify feelings through four major emotional categories: (1) mad, (2) sad, (3) glad, (4) scared. Parents can also give the child some insight into her feelings by telling her what *others* might typically feel under the same circumstances.

 **EXERCISE G** Recognizing the Feeling Content in Messages   As you read each of the following statements, try to separate the content from the feelings that underlie it. Then, in the space provided, write down, first, what the listener might have heard and, second, what the speaker might have meant. Appendix A contains some sample answers; however, other answers are also appropriate. The object of the exercise is not to come up with the specific answers given in Appendix A but to practice the art of active listening.

1. Parent to child: "You have an adorable little figure."

   *What was heard:*

   _____

   _____

   *What was meant:*

   _____

   _____

2. Parent to child: "I am relieved to see that at least you're not so sick that you are fainting in school anymore."

   *What was heard:*

   _____

   _____

*What was meant:*

_____

_____

3. Parent to child: "You're looking so much better."

*What was heard:*

_____

_____

*What was meant:*

_____

_____

4. Child to parent: "No. I won't eat dinner."

*What was heard:*

_____

_____

*What was meant:*

_____

_____

5. Parent to child: "You can eat your cake only after you've finished your beans."

*What was heard:*

_____

_____

*What was meant:*

_____

_____

6. Parent to child: "Should you be eating that? I thought you were concerned about gaining weight?"

*What was heard:*

_____

_____

*What was meant:*

_____

_____

7. Parent to therapist: "How is my child doing?"

*What was heard:*

_____

_____

*What was meant:*

_____

_____

8. Parent to therapist: "I would like to become involved in treatment with my child."

*What was heard:*

_____

_____

*What was meant:*

_____

_____

In all your conversations with your child, the closer your responses come to addressing the *feelings* underlying the discussion content, the more effectively you will communicate. *No point can be made effectively and no dispute resolved when underlying feelings remain unaddressed.* The feeling message behind your intervention with your eating disordered child needs to be: "We'll get through this thing together. We are behind you all the way. This is a fine time to begin recovery. We are respectful of you and your courage for sharing your feelings with us and for starting to deal actively with the problem."

## Coming Face to Face with Your Child

On a daytime television talk show, the audience was asked to suggest ways that parents might deal with their eating disordered youngsters. Many in the audience were able to mouth the right words, even without a clear understanding of how these methods would be effective. They knew not to "nag" their children by requiring them to eat or attempting to control their food. They knew that parents must offer their children "self-esteem, not food." "Just keep loving them," said one parent to the others. Yet can you just *love* your child back to health? Don't most eating disordered children first become disordered despite parents who genuinely and actively love them? And can a parent just swallow the frustration and fear of watching a starving child avoid putting food to her lips?

As you prepare to talk about eating disorders with your child, you are approaching a volatile and uncertain situation. Remember that no interpersonal barrier is unbreachable as long as your intentions are good and your relationship is soundly based in love and mutual respect. Human interaction, particularly between parent and child, allows limitless room for error and damage control. Easily amended, rethought, or restated, miscommunications can be repaired during follow-up discussions—immediately afterward or three days, three weeks, or three years later.

Try not to be put off by your child's off-putting responses, such as, "It's none of your business." It *is* your business, and you have a right to ask because she is your child and you are her parent. You might respond in turn with a question like, "What is going on with you? Is there something happening between the two of us that I am not aware of?" Learn to avoid conversational sudden death discussion-stoppers such as "fine" or "whatever." These are idioms meaning, "I don't want to discuss this, so I'm blowing you and the topic off right now." Whatever it takes, do not let the conversation go until you are satisfied that you have said what you need to say and what your child needs to hear. Successful communication does not end till all parties feel heard. When conversations appear to be dead-ending prematurely, take the initiative to carry them through to their natural completion. Don't let statements like, "I don't feel like talking now," "You're one to talk!" and, "I've got it all under control" stop the conversation. Don't cut the conversation off yourself with remarks like, "I give up. I don't care anymore. You're on your own"; "If you don't eat, I'm taking away the car"; and, "Do it for *me.*"

When you find you have slipped into a nonproductive communication pattern, make it your business to slip out of it. And as you interact with your child, keep in mind that you are under no obligation to be perfect or even correct. Your child needs to understand and respect that, as this concept is basic to her learning about herself as well. Furthermore, she is far more tolerant of mistakes and resilient than you might think and is becoming more so all the time in treatment. Whatever you ultimately can't change in yourself, she will need to learn to tolerate or accommodate as she matures through the therapy process. It is not critical that your child feels the way you do about things, as long as she remains open to seeing all options available to her.

### Sample Script for an Intervention

PARENT:  I'm concerned about you. Here is what I've observed [*describes his or her observations*]. My hunch is that you may be needing some help now. What's your take on this?

CHILD:  There's nothing wrong [*or,* You're imagining it, exaggerating; *or,* It's really none of your business; *or,* If there's ever anything to be concerned about, I'll let you know].

PARENT:  I understand what you think, but it would be helpful for me to know more about how you've arrived at this conclusion. Because we see things differently, and because this might possibly be a matter of your health, maybe a professional should help us determine what, if anything, might be going on here.

CHILD:  I'm not going to see anyone. I don't want to, and I don't need to [*or,* I can fix things myself whenever I choose].

PARENT:  It's only natural to feel reluctant to investigate a situation that scares you or makes you feel out of control. A lot of people who don't understand eating disorders think all kinds of scary things about them, like once you have a disorder you've got it "for life" or that you have to be "psycho" to have an eating disorder or to go into therapy. You know that these notions aren't true, don't you?

CHILD: Of course. I also know there's nothing wrong with me. I'm just trying to keep my weight down so I can look good. All I want to do is lose ten pounds.

PARENT: What is so confusing about eating disorders is that they *appear* to be about food and weight, but they are *actually* devices that help people solve problems, cope with anxiety, and take control—not only of food, but of life. The odds are that if you are out of control with food and frightened about gaining weight, you are probably feeling out of control and fearful about other things in life as well. Eating disorders reflect how a person thinks, acts, and feels in general.

By the way, have you thought about why you feel you must engage in such extreme behaviors in order to lose weight? And are you absolutely certain that you'd be content to stop losing weight once you lost the initial ten pounds?

CHILD: OK, so let's say I have a problem and I went for help. What if things didn't get better for me even then?

PARENT: It's understandable that you might be concerned about that, because eating disorder recovery can be a real challenge and can take time. But you're up to it, and I'm behind you. You've done a lot of tough things in your life—you'll do this one, too. The changes you will need to make won't require you to totally revamp who you are; they will simply be a matter of fine-tuning some of the strengths and resources that you already have in place.

CHILD: What if I have to leave college [*or,* school]?

PARENT: There's a good chance that you could work on your recovery while in school, through various supports on campus. If the problem is too intense for you to stay at school, it will make sense for you to take a semester off, because there's not a lot of learning that can go on anyway when all you can think about is food.

CHILD: I'm not ready to get help now. I'll take care of this next week. Just give me a little time.

PARENT: Do you believe that waiting will help the situation go away? Initially, an eating disorder helps a person feel better, but the longer the disease goes on, the greater the damage it does to the body and the harder it is to fix. If you'd like to try to make a few changes on your own for a week or so and then see what happens, that's OK with me. But let's plan to talk about it again in a week's time to see how things are going.

CHILD: I promise, I can do this myself. I don't need anybody's help.

PARENT: If you had diabetes and needed insulin, I'd be responsible, as your parent, to make sure you got the medical attention you needed. This situation leaves me no choice either. Why not take the week you are looking for, and let's say that if you haven't been able to make sufficient changes in that time, then I'll step in at that point to find help for you. That's the deal. I will offer you a hand temporarily, just until you are free to take control of things on your own again. So, what do you think?

CHILD: I guess that sounds fair. I just wish I could be good enough the way I am.

PARENT: You *are* certainly good enough. My intention is to help you *stay* that way.

Achieving an open exchange is the most important goal as you begin to dialogue with your child. Don't expect results immediately, but remain focused, confident that you are doing what needs to be done, and persistent.

### Getting Started

By now, you have the essential information you need to confront your child. Think of an appropriate time to bring up the necessary conversation with your child, or resolve to take advantage of the next opportunity that presents itself. Decide whether you want to be with or without your partner when you talk with your child. If the two of you are to do this together, determine the things you and your partner should discuss prior to the dialogue with your child. Be sure that you are both of the same mind and that your child does not feel ambushed.

## THE AFTERMATH

**EXERCISE H  Assessing How You Did**    After you approach your child with your concerns and statements of your position, an assessment of how the conversation went can be a helpful tool, giving you guidance for your continuing dialogue with your child. Answer each of the following assessment questions in the space provided.

1. Do you feel you chose a good time to engage in discussion? (What was right with it? What was wrong with it?)

_____

_____

2. How do you feel your child responded overall and were you surprised by her response?

_____

_____

3. Did your child's feelings change in any respect during your interaction? If so, how so?

_____

_____

4. What did you say that you felt best about?

_____

_____

5. What might you have done differently if you had it to do over?

_____

_____

6. Did you find yourself in what felt like a power struggle? (What was it about? How did you respond? What might have been a better response?)

_____

_____

7. If you were with your partner during the discussion, were you happy with who said what and when and how it was said?

_____

_____

8. Did you anticipate the trouble spots accurately? (Did your efforts to overcome these obstacles work for you? Did they backfire?)

_____

_____

9. Are you aware of changes in your relationship with your child following the dialogue? If so, what are they?

_____

_____

10. How are you handling these changes?

_____

_____

---

**Activity** **Journaling Intervention Effects** Record in your journal any indications that your intervention was in some way reassuring to your child. Keep track of power struggles that may develop so you can attempt to resolve them. Note whether anyone is getting angry now and for what reasons. Write down your ongoing assessments of the unfolding changes in the relationship between you and your child (and you and your partner) and your sense of whether or not you are responding to them effectively. What else might you do?

---

## HITTING THE WALL

*A king was saddened to learn that his beloved son, the prince, had decided it was time to leave the kingdom and make his own way. In bidding him farewell, the king said to his son, "Return as far as you can, and I will come the rest of the way."*

Talmudic tale

In this section, I discuss a couple of problems you may well encounter during the moments, days, or weeks following your intervention.

Parents who find themselves up against a wall must consider this an invitation and a challenge to begin taking that wall down, one brick at a time. Your child's symptoms may be communicating something to you that even she does not understand. The rockiest periods in treatment are typically the most productive periods, stimulating both you and your child to add techniques to her survival bag of tricks. If you notice that your child feels pain in confronting disease and treatment, keep in mind that her eating disorder is a metaphor for other pain that she has not yet been able to conceptualize and deal with. Uncovering pain is the first step in eradicating it. See if you can help her to comprehend this and to identify her pain—all of it; this knowledge will make the recovery process much more gratifying.

"Anger, like a deep breath, cannot be held indefinitely."[3] When you approach your child about an eating disorder, it is safe to anticipate some anger on her part as well as your own. Though unpleasant and often feared, anger can be a most empowering emotion when expressed effectively, as it leads to the definition and resolution of problems and personal needs. Author Terri Apter describes fighting between parents and children as parents' not learning what the child has to say.[4] So welcome your child's anger with facilitating responses like, "I see. What else? Tell me more." This will assist her to teach *you* a thing or two about what she lacks and craves from her relationship with you.

During the tough times, you can expect to be the target of your child's intolerance and frustration. Because parents' love is unconditional, children typically assume that parents are a safe haven and that the children will be wholly forgiven for their hurtful behavior—a dubious honor for parents but well worth recognizing and understanding. Where there is anger, you can be assured there are hurt feelings. By attending *first* to your child's hurt feelings rather than to the hostility, you will go far in reducing the depth of your child's defensiveness and rage. *The capacity to resolve conflict through an open expression of hurt feelings between parent and child can remove barriers to intimacy and deepen ties.*

Anger goes both ways; parents have the right to feel hurt and anger too. Don't be afraid to express honest anger toward your eating disordered child, communicating your needs and making appropriate demands, although always making it clear that your anger is with the eating disorder, not the child. This will help you be less critical and help her to feel more embraced and fully accepted. Anger and love coexist quite happily, though one might momentarily obliterate sight of the other. Active listening is a superb way to resolve anger.

Some professionals advise parents to let go of their own anger in an effort to avoid power struggles, to simply ignore their child's raging and refuse to fall into the *tantrum trap.* Emotional distance can be helpful momentarily; it can allow the parties to simmer down and think through why the problem occurred, how it might best be resolved, and how such a situation might be avoided in the future. I contend, however, that anger in any form *requires resolution* eventually, later if not sooner, and that resolution entails the mutual satisfaction of all parties involved.

Don't be fooled into believing the myth that your child's refusal to eat is her way of saying she is mad at you. Anger does not cause disease. It is cause for concern when your child's anger, among other feelings, *cannot be expressed freely and openly.* When an individual cannot recognize and express her feelings, her needs cannot be met, her problems cannot be effectively resolved, and she feels out of control and unable to cope with life.

Remember that anger is a real, legitimate, acceptable, and very human feeling. Modeling the honest and fearless expression of human feeling, even if it means raising your voice, can only benefit your child—who will be learning to do the same through treatment.

**Activity  Reversing the Errors of the Past**   Think about any incident that has occurred between you and your child where you aroused her anger inadvertently. In hindsight, do you know why she became so irate? What might you have done differently? What can you do now, to reverse the errors of the past? What might you watch for as clues that the mishandling of anger is threatening to sabotage your relationship with your child? How can you prevent such problems from occurring?

If you regret some incident in the past between you and your child that slipped by without discussion, consider taking action now. It is never too late to undo such an event, to say: "You know, I have been thinking about something you did [or said] three weeks ago. It occurs to me, as I rethink the situation, there may be more to what is happening with you than I realized at the time. I'd like you to think back with me for a moment. Perhaps you could help me understand something that still puzzles me."

## Rethinking Power Struggles

It is important to understand that the real struggle for power exists between the patient and her disease, not between patient and parent or patient and therapist. Nonetheless, by sacrificing their values on the altar of peacekeeping in their fervent efforts to avoid power struggles with their children, parents typically put too much emotional distance between themselves and their offspring or they create emotional distance too soon. In actual fact, *there is nothing wrong with engaging in struggles with your child if those struggles are part of a process leading to anger and conflict resolution.* By butting heads and locking horns, children find out who they are and where they stand in relation to others. They learn how to face and resolve problems constructively, thereby putting their eating disorder out of business.

**Troubleshooting Tip** Don't Participate in No-Win Situations   When you believe a battle is being fought to achieve control rather than a negotiated resolution, disengage from the struggle. R*ecognize what the power struggle is designed to achieve* (your child's sense of power), and respond to *that.* Why is your child feeling powerless in regard to you? Asking, "Do I look fat?" is a typical means your child may use to rope you into a power struggle where you are defeated before you begin. It is a forgone conclusion that what you say will be misconstrued. If you respond affirmatively, your child will not forgive you. If you respond negatively, she will either distrust both you and your answer or feel elated that this is how you see her. You might explain your decision not to participate in this no-win bantering, however, and ask what she really wishes to accomplish by asking that question.

*Soft power,* the exertion of power over another by getting him or her to want the same thing as you do is always the better way. Obviously, no one can make another person eat. When your child digs in her heels and says no! when you have run all the bases and are still striking out, having done what you can to educate, persuade, and set clear limits, it may be time to play hard ball. Exerting your power and authority as a parent is always a legitimate option when it is based on the expression of a clear, appropriate and consistent system of values. Remember, while your child is still at home, you remain her primary means of support, providing the roof over her head, the bicycle she uses to overexercise, the car she drives, her tuition for college. Your child is sick. Do not be afraid to treat her that way. Through tough love and a united front, in these particularly difficult situations, you and your partner may begin to evaluate options you would have preferred not to consider. Though you cannot demand wellness, you certainly can hold out for a substantive and ongoing communication with your child—if not about the disease, then about other issues of great consequence to you both.

In the end, however, you cannot get around the now familiar formula: take control where you can and let it go where it is beyond your reach. Express your feelings, then back off and let reality enforce its inevitable consequences. If your child becomes weak enough, she will collapse and find herself in the nearest emergency room. If she refuses help long enough, she will be forced to take a leave of absence from college or make some similar accommodation. But in the meantime, don't stop talking, no matter how defeated you feel. Your continued concern is worth more than you know.

**Activity** Liberating Yourself from the Need to Control    In letting go of situations that are beyond your control, you will find yourself feeling liberated. Feeling a need to control people or life situations beyond your reach can cause great anxiety and despair. Think of other areas in your life where you feel pressure to be in control (you may wish to use your journal for this activity). How might your efforts in these other areas affect your need or wish to be in control of your child's disease? How much of your need to be in control is really about fear? How much is about anger? Helplessness? Powerlessness? Understanding these aspects of yourself can help you gain some perspective about your own struggles. Observing your own need to assume control helps you to better understand your child's motivation to remain involved with her disorder.

## When Nothing Else Works

In the event that your resistant child becomes harmful to herself or others (that is, she attempts suicide or self-injury or she drives under the influence of drugs or alcohol), you must be prepared to remove her forcibly to a safe environment. If she resists, it is appropriate to call the police to assist you in committing her to a hospital setting. But such forcible commitment, though it can mark the acceptance of disease and the start, renewal, or commitment to recovery, is never in itself more than a temporary solution.

Bringing your child to a readiness to accept treatment is a major step toward her recovery. The next chapter presents the complex dynamics of eating disorder treatment itself.

# Understanding Treatment Options

*Give a man a fish, and you feed him for a day. Teach a man to fish, and he will not go hungry.*

Proverb

In order to choose wisely from the many options that eating disorder treatment offers, you need to be as knowledgeable as you can be about the various styles, modes, and milieus of treatment available to your child and family. It is particularly essential to understand the cornerstone of the treatment process, psychotherapy. Shrouded in an aura of mystery, the therapy process is as much an art as a science. Misconceptions about what happens in therapy have caused more than one parent to make treatment decisions that have not served his or her eating disordered child well.

## WHAT EATING DISORDER TREATMENT AND PSYCHOTHERAPY ARE ABOUT

Successful treatment for eating disorders puts an end to food restriction and to bingeing and purging behaviors. It normalizes food intake as it resolves the underlying emotional issues driving the dysfunctional behaviors.

*Common Myths About Eating Disorder Treatment and the Psychotherapy Process—And What the Facts Are*

Myth 1.   *A person can recover from an eating disorder through willpower alone, through behavioral changes alone, or through self-esteem work alone. A* person recovers from an eating disorder through behavioral and emotional changes, made simultaneously.

Myth 2. *People in therapy are mentally ill or emotionally weak and are generally at an advanced stage of disease.* In fact, people in therapy are seeking an opportunity to define and solve problems. This is a demonstration of strength, not weakness. Moreover, people who enter therapy early in the disease, before habits have a chance to become ingrained, have a better chance for a quick and complete recovery.

Myth 3. *Eating disorder treatment never leads to complete recovery.* Eating disorder treatment can lead to varying degrees of recovery, including complete and total recovery.

Myth 4. *You can determine whether the therapy process has the potential to be successful only after months of treatment or by how your child feels about the therapist.* The first meeting with the therapist should suggest the potential for success. Other indicators of productive treatment are the emotional and behavioral changes your child makes.

Myth 5. *When a child is dealing with several therapy issues at once, it is not necessary to deal directly with food behaviors; they will improve as emotional issues are resolved.* The dysfunctional food behaviors should be treated simultaneously with the emotional issues. They are intractable habits that will not disappear unless specifically addressed.

Myth 6. *By bringing an eating disorder out in the open, one risks making the problem worse and the child more unhappy.* As discussed earlier, confronting problems can create productive controversy and can give clarity and definition to an already existing issue, increasing the chances for problem resolution.

Myth 7. *A truly strong family never has fights and should not have problems that require therapy.* All families have disagreements and problems. A strong, successful family is one in which family members can discuss anything together without fear, resolving problems as they arise.

Myth 8. *The therapist best qualified to treat an eating disordered child is one who has recovered from an eating disorder herself or himself or who has psychoanalytic training.* The therapist best qualified to treat an eating disordered child is one who works actively, purposefully, and with deep caring, experience, and expertise in this area.

Myth 9.    *In family therapy the child's therapist runs the risk of breaching the child's confidence if she or he also works with the family.* The therapist who works effectively with both individual and family strengthens and quickens the recovery process. She or he can avoid breaching anyone's confidence by enforcing clear boundaries, understanding the parental role in recovery, and promoting family therapy.

Myth 10.    *In family therapy there is one patient only—the person with the eating disorder.* Because family members typically share issues with the patient, their needs and responses also must be addressed; otherwise everyone stands to lose. Every family member is of equal importance in the context of family therapy and the family systems approach.

Myth 11.    *In family therapy the child's dependence on his parents becomes greater.* When this is the case, it is temporary. The security, bonding, and trust developed in family therapy increases the child's ability to *separate* healthfully and comfortably from the family and ensures his desire and capacity to return to the family with the same degree of comfort. Therapy teaches your child the skills he needs to become an independently functioning adult.

Myth 12.    *Your relationship with your child may not survive the jolt of bringing him to treatment against his will. If it does survive, it may become more hostile later, as family treatment brings problems to light.* In fact, family therapy improves family relationships by reinforcing sound communication and increasing mutual trust. Bringing problems to light is a prerequisite to solving them.

Myth 13.    *The best time for your child to enter treatment is when he feels ready, when his physical health is compromised, or when you've reached your wit's end.* The ideal time for your child to begin therapy is as soon as either of you detects a hint of an emotional problem that needs resolving or of an eating dysfunction of any kind.

Myth 14.    *The eating disorder treatment should continue until your child begins to eat normally or the insurance runs out.* There are several cues for concluding the therapy: your child's weight returns to normal, his dysfunctions with food subsides, and either all the emotional issues driving the disease are resolved or you and he are capable of resolving the remaining issues without assistance.

Eating disorder therapy helps the patient to manage his symptoms as he regains sufficient control of his life to ultimately outgrow and eliminate his need for those symptoms.

### Therapy Is About Making Changes

Change develops out of ferment and signifies the breaking apart of an old system. A potent diagnostic and treatment tool, change indicates where the patient has been and where he is going; its rhythm sets the pace of treatment. The process of change need not be disruptive if it takes on the simple and gentle quality of fine-tuning certain aspects of the patient's existence. The goal of change is not to be right but to be flexible—not to take control of external forces but to accommodate and adjust to them—in other words, to roll with life's punches.

The mark of a successful treatment process is change in behaviors and thinking, whether in the form of an epiphany or a tweaking perceptible only to the patient. All change, from the least significant to the largest and most dramatic, begins with one small step. The cumulative impact of small steps may not be apparent at once, though you and your child should see changes of various sorts and degrees almost immediately with the advent of treatment. Behavioral changes will generally be easier to discern than those confined to emotional expression. With patience you will see your child's small steps grow into big ones.

You may also see that even small changes may evoke big anxieties in your child—these minor alterations may lead to potentially enormous and unsettling consequences. Your appreciation and support of the changes he has made can be extremely important to your struggling child.

 **EXERCISE A** **Making Changes: Tiny Steps, Limitless Opportunities**   Here are some typical changes that occur during therapy. If you are at an early stage of getting help, the odds are that you have not seen any of them yet. But watch for them. They will appear ultimately and, when they do, will signify great accomplishment. Read each description. Does it portray a change you see in your child? Circle Y for yes, N for no. Use the space provided at the end of the exercise to write in any other changes you may have noticed.

1.  Y/N   Change in the time of day my child eats.
2.  Y/N   Change in the variety of foods he consumes.

3. Y/N    Change in the sequence of foods he eats.

4. Y/N    Increase in portion sizes.

5. Y/N    Introduction of a new food.

6. Y/N    Increased daily intake of a specific food group.

7. Y/N    Decreased need for daily weigh-ins.

8. Y/N    Less feeling of shame after eating.

9. Y/N    Decrease in eating breakfast foods (yogurt, cereal, bagels) throughout the day.

10. Y/N    Elimination of typical anorexic foods (frozen yogurt, egg white omelets, diet pop) from his diet.

11. Y/N    Increased comfort in eating in front of others.

12. Y/N    Fewer excuses about why he can't eat.

13. Y/N    Less moodiness.

14. Y/N    Greater ability to commit to decisions about what to eat and how to behave.

15. Y/N    Demonstration of ability to make any *one* of the preceding changes at least one time over the course of a week.

16. Y/N    *Other changes I have noticed include*

_____

_____

_____

_____

This is one exercise in particular that you may want to return to over and over as your child's work progresses. You may never see all of these changes nor is that necessary. As your child begins to recover, *any positive change sustained over time* will be a signal that good things are happening. Even the smallest change can represent a battle hard fought.

## How Change Happens in Therapy

Therapy is about change; change is about learning. Moshe Feldenkrais, scientist, philosopher, and inventor of the potent Feldenkrais Method for functional and neurological integration, has discussed why it is difficult for people to learn, commenting, "Sometimes we are unable to enact certain motives because we want them only too vaguely."[1] He explains that "learning is not the training of willpower but the acquisition of the skill to inhibit parasitic action and the *ability to direct clear motivations as a result of self-knowledge.*"[2] And Feldenkrais argues that "most of the limitations we encounter are imputable to the personal experiences we are subjected to rather than to inheritance. . . . That which is formed through personal experience is essentially alterable and a priori, capable of being influenced by a new personal experience."[3]

Psychotherapy can be just such an experience. We use but a fraction of our latent capacity in most of our actions; psychotherapy increases that use. Through therapy, we learn how to learn. In psychotherapy, previously unrecognized or undefined thoughts, feelings, needs, and fears take form and are recognized (learned). Like an engine running on all cylinders, a person who knows himself fully becomes capable of integrating disparate elements (both successful and unsuccessful) of the self to achieve increased responsiveness and emotional versatility. Feldenkrais advocates learning to achieve not perfectability but a state of "unstable balance" in a life of risk and uncertainty, alternating between the improper and remediated use of ourselves.[4]

He contends that emotional versatility (which arises out of emotional integration) is the mark of emotional maturity. Past personal experience is broken into its constituent parts, and these parts form new patterns to fit the present circumstances of the environment and the body.[5]

You can expect changes in the behavioral and the emotional spheres to be uneven, with changes in eating behaviors typically lagging behind emotional improvements. Change in either sphere will affect change in the other. Though attention to emotions alone will not resolve food dysfunction, emotional issues must be addressed before food dysfunction will be repaired. Similarly, *inter*personal change will beget and reinforce *intra*personal change and vice versa; so, by recognizing and accommodating your child's changes and integrating your *own* changes, you stand to make a substantive investment in his recovery.

Though the therapy and change process is not easy, in most cases it is enjoyable; one patient described the therapy dynamic as "chocolates for the mind." Although psychotherapy is problem centered, one of its primary functions is to help the patient recognize and validate his *strengths,* assessing and mobilizing internal resources wherever they lie.

### The Therapy Relationship

The patient-therapist relationship, or *therapy relationship,* a prototype for all healthy relationships, gives your child the opportunity to experience, practice, and master the full gamut of relationship and problem-solving skills. Through this empathic therapeutic relationship, your child learns to risk turning to human beings for comfort and nurturance rather than to a disordered relationship with food, ultimately depriving his disease of a place to land and take root.

In the early stages of treatment, disease and patient are virtually indistinguishable, and the therapist is forced to straddle a fine line between patient advocate and disease adversary. By creating a working partnership with your child, the therapist aligns with your child's *strengths,* respectfully acknowledging the purpose of his symptoms and the need he feels to retain them.

The therapy relationship must not ever be developed at the expense of, or become a substitute for, the patient's other significant relationships. Outpatient therapy happens for forty-five or fifty minutes once or twice a week; for the rest of the time the patient must continue to be responsive to the greater environment, especially to his parents and family.

### Goal Setting

Therapy provides the opportunity and emotional environment necessary for resolving problems. Eating disorder work is unique, as we have seen, in that eating disorder problems typically must first be *defined* in treatment, then acknowledged, then understood—and all this must occur *before* the patient can make a decision to even attempt a resolution. Treatment goals must accommodate all these initial steps and stages.

Goal setting is the primary vehicle for therapeutic change. Long-term and short-term goals coexist, overlap, and vary from session to session. Whether changing goals are implicit or explicit, they determine the direction and purpose of every therapeutic session. When goals are neither expressed nor recognized, the patient runs the risk of losing sight of the purpose of his work, subsequently experiencing a sense of futility and failure that though unwarranted can derail even the most earnest treatment efforts.

It is not uncommon for therapist, child, and parents to approach the same therapy session with altogether different goals: the therapist may want to bring about cure; one parent may want the child to lose or gain weight; the other parent may want him to stop vomiting. The child, meanwhile, may want nothing more than to cling to the disorder for dear life and to become the best anorexic possible. One father asked his resistant daughter, "If every grade you ever got had to be an A, why are you content to accept something less than an A in recovering from this disease?" The answer lay in their goal variance. "I want A's in thinness, not in recovery," she explained. A patient who vomited after every meal stated that because she wanted to vomit less, her recovery goal was to eat only one meal a day.

It is essential to begin the treatment process at the point where your child is. Once you have gotten him to treatment, you may need to put your own goals on the back burner for a time to accommodate his needs, capacities, and treatment pacing. You are now in a position to invite, not force, him to see what you see and to want what you want. Ultimately, people's various goals will converge and then dovetail, guiding the process to a successful end.

Breaking goals down into their component parts is key to successful problem resolution, making every step eminently achievable. Gaining twenty pounds may seem a Herculean task; adding a pat of butter to a slice of bread once or twice a week will seem more within reach.

 **EXERCISE B** **Setting Goals to Resolve Problems**    To begin defining appropriate goals and taking steps to realize them, complete this exercise. In the first column ("Problems: . . ."), list problems your child faces in the areas of food and eating, emotions, and personal relationships. In the second column ("Possible Goals"), identify one or more goals to achieve in order to begin resolving each problem. In the third column ("Goals Breakdown"), divide each goal into smaller, more easily accomplished goals.

Here's an example:

| Problems: Food and Eating | Possible Goals | Goals Breakdown |
|---|---|---|
| Fear of eating fat | Introduce fat | Purchase butter |
| | Use spread on bagel | Do so once a week |
| | Use salad dressing | Use lite dressing to start |

Write your answers in the space provided.

| Problems: Food and Eating | Possible Goals | Goals Breakdown |
|---|---|---|
| | | |

| Problems: Emotions | Possible Goals | Goals Breakdown |
|---|---|---|
| | | |

| Problems: Personal Relationships | Possible Goals | Goals Breakdown |
|---|---|---|
| | | |

Now, how might you define your own problems as your child goes through the therapy process? Using the same format you used in the first part of this exercise, identify your problems with understanding the disease, finding your role in recovery, and interacting with your child; establish your goals; then divide them into smaller goals.

Here's an example:

| Problems: Finding Your Role in Recovery | Possible Goals | Goals Breakdown |
|---|---|---|
| Insufficient meal preparation | Make family dinners | 3 times per week |

Write your answers in the space provided.

| Problems: Understanding the Disease | Possible Goals | Goals Breakdown |
| --- | --- | --- |
| | | |

| Problems: Finding Your Role in Recovery | Possible Goals | Goals Breakdown |
| --- | --- | --- |
| | | |

| Problems: Interacting with Your Child | Possible Goals | Goals Breakdown |
| --- | --- | --- |
| | | |

Setting realistic goals is a way of enabling yourself to put one foot in front of the other so you can move forward and maintain a momentum.

## Learning How to Resolve Problems

Individuals with eating disorders typically operate under the misconception that life is supposed to be easy and problem free and that competent people have it all together, a notion as defeating as it is untrue. The task of eating disorder treatment is to allow the patient to discover, accept, and accommodate to life's less than perfect reality. Therapy provides the patient a practice ground for learning by doing. *The process through which problems are resolved must be recognized and owned by the patient,* so that he can reproduce this same process in the face of problems that arise in other contexts.

## Two Case Studies: Relating Food Use to Emotions

Making connections between food use and emotional issues is a crucial function of the therapy process, as the following example shows.

A recovering bulimic college senior had not been able to figure out why she impulsively quit her summer job, what she wanted to do after she graduated from college, and what her interests were. She was following her friends' lead about where to live and what to do after graduation. Not knowing if she should work or play (travel) after graduation, she could not even begin to entertain the option of doing some of both. Through eating disorder treatment, she made progress on food-related issues and these accomplishments spurred broad-based emotional development.

- Through her efforts to strive for more "good eating days," she learned about intention and goal setting in other life spheres.
- Through her increased self-awareness about food, she came to understand the role of self-awareness in problem solving.
- Through her efforts to deal with food issues, she learned how uncomfortable it could be to face her own limitations; at the same time, she learned that she could tolerate this discomfort and work through it.
- Through her attempts to regulate the amounts and kinds of food she ate, she learned to find a moderated balance between recreation and work, both in her college life and in her postgraduation plans.
- Through her treatment, she learned that by hoping her problems would work themselves out by themselves she was putting faith in that which was beyond her control. The idea that *she* could fix her own problems put power back into her hands.

Our attitudes toward food and eating are barometers measuring how we function in our lives. This notion is important to your understanding of critical aspects of your child's eating disorder, treatment, and recovery. Here is a second case study to illustrate further the connection between food use and abuse and general life function.

Samantha, an anorexic young adult, broke up with her boyfriend quite suddenly one day, finding him at his place of business and breaking her disruptive news to him while he was on the job. Leaving him no opportunity to respond, she made her proclamation, turned on her heel, and left.

This was not unusual behavior for her. Samantha was used to turning her back on problems, to avoiding conflict and unpleasantness, even at the risk of compromising her relationships with others and being unfair to herself. By controlling the dynamics of this breakup as she did her food, she was able to bury her hurt feelings, which then remained unrecognized and unresolved, exacerbating her need for her eating disorder.

Samantha's capacity to care for herself and others is disordered. The emotional versatility required to maintain strong and healthy relationships is directly correlated to versatility in the areas of problem resolution, food, and eating. People with eating disorders are problem-avoidant and relationship-impaired.

## When Therapy Needs an Eating Disorder Focus

When your child is clearly suffering from an eating disorder, there is no question about the kind of treatment that is needed. The difficulty arises when the problem is not clearly defined. When eating problems coexist with other problems that may be more highly visible or may take a greater toll on daily function, ambiguity about the treatment focus is inevitable. Should eating disorder treatment be the treatment of choice in your child's case?

Take, for example, the case of Todd, the young man described in Chapter Two. Todd displayed separation problems, excessive fears and anxiety, and some mildly oppositional behaviors, and in this mix his quirky eating habits were seen as incidental. Anorexia would not be his primary diagnosis, but that does not mean that eating disorder treatment would not be the most appropriate treatment for this young man. In light of his emotional issues and his need to understand his eating behaviors as extensions of his feelings, *eating disorder therapy could have helped him create a framework for healthy eating that could have served as a model for moderated living.* As discussed in Chapter Two, if an emotional syndrome behaves and feels like an eating disorder, disturbing the individual's life quality as does an eating disorder, what does it matter if the dysfunction is not considered a clinical eating disorder? If the issues are those of an eating disorder, so should be the treatment protocol.

Parents must learn to understand the nature of the treatment they are purchasing and to recognize to what end that treatment leads. Eating disorder treatment, with its multifaceted bent and its attention to both behaviors and emotions, offers unique qualities. It treats the person as a whole even as it addresses the eating disorder specifically. Nonspecialized psychotherapy may overlook food-related dysfunction, leaving it untended for months or even years. Parents of eating disordered children must be careful to distinguish general psychotherapy from eating disorder therapy; they are not the same thing.

## PREPARING FOR TREATMENT

Don't expect to put your head on your child's shoulders in an effort to force him to see things as you do. His treatment choices must be his own, but this does not mean you should be without a voice. Your child needs to hear from you about your ideas, your concerns, your values, and how *you* might approach this problem, even as he makes his own decisions and determines his own course of action. He will need your input now so that he can learn to function well without you later.

### The Eating Disorder Treatment Team

Eating disorders are most effectively addressed by a collaborative, multidisciplinary team of professionals. Depending on your child's needs, the outpatient eating disorder treatment team may include you, an individual and a family therapist (who may be the same person), a nutritionist, an internist, and a medicating psychiatrist. School personnel and hospital staff may also be helpful additions to the team. The participation of these various disciplines will vary from case to case and from stage to stage of treatment and recovery.

There are times when the full complement of team members will be required as early as the diagnostic stage. In one instance a patient needed to be seen by a psychotherapist, individually and with her family, by a nutritionist for assessment and education, and ultimately by an internist before she realized a problem existed that was worthy of her attention. Though certain disciplines may not be active at a particular point in treatment, this does not minimize their potential for influence and involvement later, should the need arise.

Parents typically express concern that involving several professionals will be costly. In reality the team approach is so comprehensive and effective, it invariably proves to be the least time-consuming and most cost-effective form of treatment. A treatment team is more likely to get results and to get them faster. (Further discussion of financing your child's treatment can be found in Chapter Five.)

### "It's His Treatment, Not Yours."

You've probably heard this warning before: "It's his treatment, not yours." "Stay out of your child's affairs, disease, treatment, food," you might have been told.

"You'll only make things worse." One parent testified to me that things did get worse when she discussed eating with her child. "I needed to back off totally," she said, "and refrain from ever mentioning food to show my son that he could be in control of himself and to let him know that what he does, he does for himself, not for me." Backing off is not necessarily incorrect. But neither is it applicable to all children throughout all (and particularly the early) stages of recovery. When your child is responsive to recovery, he will need emotional space to accomplish his goals independently. However, if you opt for a hands-off posture *prematurely,* before your child is capable of responding appropriately to and for himself, you may be doing him a disservice. Without your input he may choose not to recover or may flounder about in the recovery process.

Even if your input does little more than evoke opposition, at least you will have stimulated some self-awareness and perhaps helped him face certain issues, whereas a passive response to an active disease can only make matters worse.

## What the Therapist Does

Just as there are myths and misconceptions about eating disorders, there are myths and misconceptions about the professionals who treat them.

*Common Misconceptions About Therapists*

| | |
|---|---|
| Misconception 1. | The therapist is responsible for getting my child to eat, to stop purging, and so on. |
| Misconception 2. | The therapist is responsible for getting my child to lose weight (or to gain weight). |
| Misconception 3. | The therapist is supposed to make my child more responsive to me. |
| Misconception 4. | The therapist is supposed to bring about a cure. |
| Misconception 5. | Both my child and I are supposed to be comfortable with everything the therapist says or asks of him or us. |
| Misconception 6. | The therapist is supposed to tell me what goes on in the sessions with my child. |
| Misconception 7. | The therapist is supposed to tell me what my child has said about me. |
| Misconception 8. | The therapist has the final say on whether or not my child sees an internist. |

Misconception 9.  My child is supposed to be happier as a result of his treatment.

Misconception 10.  The therapist has no responsibility to me, as I am not her or his patient.

The adept psychotherapist creates a safe emotional environment in which an empowered patient can make changes. "I'm an introspective and extremely intelligent and open person," stated one of my patients. "How is talking to you going to be any different from confiding in my parents or close friends?" The value of the therapeutic interchange lies less in the specific information that the therapist shares with the patient or in how the therapist listens and more in the therapist's ability to get the patient to *use himself* maximally in response to the therapy relationship, himself, the disease, and life itself. It is not enough that your child feel good about his therapist. The requirements for the effective eating disorder therapist are quite specific.

In conducting a process that is active, directive, and informal (I recommend that patients, even young children, use the therapist's first name), the therapist juggles

- Issues and needs of the moment with those of the past
- The needs of the body with those of the psyche
- The patient's wish to remain sick with his need to recover
- The patient's need to focus on food to the exclusion of emotions with his need to focus on emotions to the exclusion of food
- The patient's need to discuss *why* the problem exists with the therapist's need to discuss *how* the patient can set about to improve things
- The goals of each party with the diverse goals of the other interested parties
- The need to invite problem disclosure with the need to create a safe emotional environment
- The need to be authoritative with the need to be nurturing

**Activity** Setting Realistic Expectations  In your journal, prepare a list of what you hope your child's therapist can and will do for your child. Then compare your list to the following descriptions of the therapist's role in treatment, in order to determine how realistic your expectations are for your child's treatment. Identify the specific points where your expectations diverge from the therapist's functions.

## The Therapist's Roles

This section describes the functions your child's therapist should perform, which will help you keep your expectations and demands on target. As you read these descriptions, you will notice that the therapist is your child's teacher in many of the same ways you are. Much of what the therapist does with your child mirrors what you do with and for him. Keep in mind, however, that there are some major distinctions between the role of therapist and that of parent; no matter how much the therapist cares, no matter how deep his or her emotional involvement, it is not the same as yours. The anguish and frustration of living side by side with eating dysfunctions in one's own child cannot be overestimated. One desperate parent I know of was driven to throw all the food in her house down the garbage disposal. This behavior was motivated by love and her need to protect her vulnerable child. Give yourself permission to feel your feelings deeply.

The therapy process is a gentle dynamic of guiding the patient's observation, self-awareness, and choice making. These requirements pale by comparison to parents' requirements on behalf of their children, which are much more rigorous and emotionally demanding; nothing can be left to chance, not a stone left unturned, when your child's health and happiness are at stake.

*As a gatekeeper, the therapist*

- Requires a medical evaluation to rule out organic causes for what appear to be emotional problems.
- Controls the direction of the work, not the patient.
- Assesses if and when inpatient work should become an appropriate alternative to outpatient treatment.
- Retains a focus on weight-related issues as they connect to underlying emotional issues.
- Reaches out to the patient who appears to be prematurely disengaging from treatment, increasing the patient's staying power.
- Coordinates the efforts of the treatment team, facilitating treatment by keeping lines of communication open and active between various parties.
- Prepares the patient to outgrow the need for treatment.
- Communicates with parents as needed.

*As an interpreter, the therapist*

- Explains how the disease diminishes life and how the therapy process enhances it.
- Unmasks the cover-up functions of abnormal eating.
- Keeps treatment expectations realistic: things will feel worse before they feel better.
- Anticipates, embraces, and discounts the patient's negations and distortions, reframing unrealistic ideas and beliefs.
- Helps patients and families understand the connection between family functioning and the health of the individual.
- Listens to parents' questions with an ear to the issues that underlie the inquiries: Why is the parent asking now? What might these questions indicate about the parent's own feelings and needs?

*As a teacher, the therapist*

- Teaches alternative approaches to coping and problem solving.
- Educates the patient and parents about nutrition and eating.
- Role-models by offering her or his own thought processes: "Here is what I am thinking . . ."; "This is why I ask . . ."; "Here is what I am wondering about and why . . ."
- Teaches the patient to tolerate free-fall sensations in recovery (and in life).
- Teaches the patient his right and responsibility to ask for what he needs in treatment and in life.

*As a collaborator, the therapist*

- Allows the patient to define problems and set the pace of the psychotherapy work.
- Joins with the patient: "How might you do things differently were you the therapist or the parent?" "Help me think about what you just said."

*As reality tester, the therapist*

- Keeps food issues clearly in view as they relate to feelings and to coping.
- Keeps goals realistic (vomiting three times as opposed to four may be an achievement).

- Offers the possibility of being thin (in control) without being anorexic or bulimic.
- Recognizes, uncovers, and defines resistance to treatment, offering up these findings as therapeutic issues to be discussed and understood, not as invitations to engage in power struggles.
- Starts where the patient is emotionally. The therapist must avoid conveying "I am on your side" in lieu of providing honest commentary on the inappropriateness of the patient's thinking.

*As a liberator, the therapist*

- Grants permission for the patient to feel his feelings and experience his needs and then express them both.
- Facilitates the development of healthier defenses, increasing the likelihood of discarding familiar, less functional ones.
- Invites the patient to use his intra- and interpersonal power benignly and effectively.
- Reframes confrontation as a realistic and productive relational process.
- Encourages the expression of complaints or disappointments with therapy and therapist, bringing such problems to resolution.
- Challenges the patient without overwhelming and discouraging him.

*As a parent figure, the therapist*

- Maintains an unconditional positive regard for and acceptance of the patient.
- Sets loving limits; maintains unconditional honesty in communication.
- Teaches the patient about life and how to live it most effectively.
- Simultaneously connects with, yet individuates from, the patient, preparing and inviting him to function as a separate and autonomous individual.
- Ultimately releases the patient, with pleasure and pride in his accomplishments.

*As coach and mentor to parents, the therapist*

- Teaches parents to listen to and to hear their child.
- Reinforces positive parental values and roles.
- Is responsive to parents' needs as well as to their child's needs.
- Educates, normalizes the disease and recovery processes, reality tests, and role-models communications with the child.

- Includes parents in the process of making changes.
- Facilitates communication between parents and child.
- Supports parents and their functions in the eyes of the child.

### A Word About Confidentiality

The therapist's need to maintain confidentiality is real; it protects all parties and must be respected. But it should not preclude the therapist's relating certain pivotal information to you, about you, and for you. In situations where the patient is in danger of doing harm to himself or others, the therapist is legally bound to inform you and other necessary people of what the patient has said in confidence about doing such harm. In every other situation *the artfully handled family session is the best way around any conflict between the need to be informed and the protection of confidentiality. In an atmosphere that is open and above board, where trust is facilitated not violated, family sessions can eliminate conflicts of interest as they benefit all parties through the free exchange of previously close-kept information.*

## UNDERSTANDING TREATMENT APPROACHES AND PHILOSOPHIES

The three most successful approaches to eating disorder treatment are (1) the psychodynamic model, (2) the cognitive-behavioral model, and (3) the disease-addiction model (twelve step). All need to be conducted within the framework and context of the family systems theory approach. The most effective therapists know and can use all these approaches, going outside the single-model box for the treatment methodologies that most closely accommodate the patient's needs and particular learning style. This integration of the best of the available styles and techniques is called *eclecticism.* What works best, *is* best. A patient who feels constrained unless he can move about may need to begin a session by taking a walk around the block with his therapist. A patient struggling to eat in front of others may benefit from sitting down to a meal together with the therapist. A patient going away to college may find it helpful to remain connected and accountable to someone back home in his effort to sustain his gains; in this instance, faxing food journals to the hometown therapist or nutritionist might be a helpful tool for making a smooth transition.

## The Psychodynamic Model

The psychodynamic approach to treatment views behaviors as derivatives of internal conflicts, motives, and unconscious forces. The belief is that if behaviors are discontinued without addressing the underlying motives driving them, relapse will occur. Symptoms, seen as expressions of the patient's underlying needs and issues, supposedly will disappear with the working through of these issues. This is not the case, however. The psychodynamic model is not by itself sufficient to overcome the complexity of the food-related symptoms and behavioral rituals of eating disorders. Thus the need for the cognitive-behavioral model.

## The Cognitive-Behavioral Model

Despite the fact that eating disordered patients are generally bright and highly sophisticated, they tend to lack an accurate cognitive understanding of themselves and eating, subscribing instead to distorted ideas about their bodies and how the world works. The cognitive-behavioral approach challenges distortions and faulty knowledge. This model, used in conjunction with the psychodynamic model and the family systems framework, has proved to be most responsive to the emotional, perceptual, and behavioral needs of the eating disordered patient.

Addressing the relationship between thoughts, affect, and behaviors, cognitive-behavioral therapy turns down the volume on the emotions driving dysfunctional behaviors, freeing the individual to hear the dictates of his rational mind. By reinforcing more objective cognitions, the patient overcomes the relentless emotional demands of his personality and of disease. The recovering patient ultimately feels a greater sense of self-control, becoming more highly aware of himself and his disorder and more capable of arriving at problem solutions on *his own*, independent of the guidance of the psychotherapist.

> **Taking Stock** **Understanding Cognitive-Behavioral Therapy** Cognitive-behavioral work is based on several assumptions:
>
> - Life beliefs, attitudes, and values are acquired through learning.
> - People continue to learn and change throughout their lives. Though early learning is particularly difficult to eradicate, there is always room for *new* learning, emotional and intellectual, to exist *alongside* the old.
> - People learn best in a trusting and secure environment.

Exhibit 4.1 illustrates how cognitive-behavioral therapeutic change works. Behavioral change results in feeling change; feeling change results in attitude change; changes in attitudes and feelings result in changes in behaviors. And so the circle is complete. It is inconsequential which change comes about first; whatever the changes and wherever within the system they are initiated, they reinforce each other.

An eating disordered child seeking change can successfully enter this process anywhere, though cognitive behavioral change may offer the easiest access to progress initially. Though feelings cannot be completely harnessed, beliefs, knowledge, and behaviors can be. When a recovered bulimic was asked, "What would you be if you could be anything in the world?" her immediate emotional response was, "Skinny." An instant later, she was able to tap into her cognitive reservoir to remind herself that when she was skinny, she had never been as miserably unhappy. She corrected herself: "I would want to be me."

 **EXERCISE C Changing Via Many Routes**  To aid your understanding of the psychodynamic, cognitive, and behavioral therapy philosophies as routes to change, read the following scenario and, in the space provided, write in your answers to the questions about it.

An eating disordered young man stopped at a fast-food buffet restaurant to binge eat each day on his way home from school. He would then purge, feeling relieved and content for a short time. In an effort to change this pattern, he could have

1. Made *behavioral* changes, such as not using his car for transportation, not bringing bingeing money to school with him, or changing the route that he took to get home.
   *How might changed behaviors have been helpful to him?*

   _____

   _____

2. Tried to understand *why* he behaves as he does and *how* these behaviors work for him. In so doing, what *cognitive* realizations would he gain about
   *His relationship with food?*

   _____

   _____

**Exhibit 4.1. Cognitive-Behavioral Therapeutic Change.**

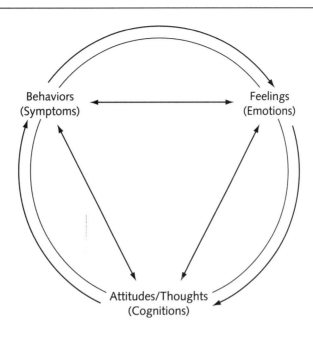

*His relationship with his parents?*

_____

_____

*His performance at school?*

_____

_____

*His capacity to cope with adversity?*

_____

_____

3. Tried to grapple with and change the uncomfortable *feelings* (the psychodynamic) that first propelled him toward these dysfunctional behaviors.

   *What might these feelings have been?*

   _____

   _____

As you consider your answers, you will see how diverse are this young man's options for making changes and that a change in any one sphere would have had a bearing on each of the other two spheres.

### Brief, Task-Centered Therapy

Brief therapy is often a requirement of insurance programs with managed care. Short-term, educative, and reality-based, brief therapy uses task assignments (homework if you will) that make the intervals between treatment sessions as significant for learning and growth as the sessions themselves. It relies on the cognitive-behavioral model but applies it in a new format, with a highly pragmatic, directed, and independent focus offering time-efficient and time-limited cognitive decision making and action. By asking the patient, "What will you *do* about this problem now?" brief therapy can be motivational. After the initial series of six to twelve sessions, the patient is invited to return to treatment for brief interludes only at such time as he experiences the need for additional therapeutic input.

Achieving success through brief and task-oriented methods requires a self-sufficiency and a motivation that are rarely seen in the eating disordered patient. By deemphasizing the therapy relationship and focusing mainly on symptom extinction, this technique produces changes that for some individuals are often superficial and transitory. Nevertheless, with so many children needing care beyond the capacity of insurance coverage, parents must begin to direct themselves to the sobering realities of resources available. Acting as child advocates, parents are left with the option of making appeals for additional services (see Chapter Five). In addition, they can support recovery at home through their own mentoring activities, through various means and to varying degrees (see Chapter Seven).

**Taking Stock  Defining Brief Tasks**  Whether eating disorder treatment is brief or long term, a task orientation sets a pace and maintains a direction for treatment. Concrete tasks are particularly helpful in heightening self-awareness and regaining control over out-of-control behaviors. *Task contracts* between patient and therapist might stipulate such behaviors as these:

- Wear an elastic band on your wrist and snap it when feeling the urge to purge.
- Wait ten minutes before purging.

- Journal daily food intake and fax these records to the therapist.
- Binge with a pencil and paper next to you. Make a notation about your feelings every few minutes. Which of your efforts work best for you? Which are not successful?
- Add (or delete) one dessert a week or fried food twice a week.
- Create a written plan for structuring your day, addressing tasks, food, and meals.
- Exercise ten minutes a day.
- Change what you bring for lunch one day a week.

**Activity** Defining Tasks for Your Child   In your journal, write down some tasks that might be useful to your child and that could be broken into easily accomplished *task bytes*.

## The Family Systems Approach

All treatment approaches should be carried on within the context of family systems theory, a technique which fully appreciates the role of parents and families in a child's recovery. It affirms that every member of a family system has an impact on every other member. Change in one part of a system affects change in every part of the system. Individual changes made within a static or resistant family system are bound to meet with extinction, whereas changes which take place within a fluid and responsive family system are generally potent and lasting.

## The Twelve Step Disease-Addiction Model

The twelve step program of Alcoholics Anonymous (AA) as adapted by Overeaters Anonymous (OA) can be an effective supplement to cognitive-behavioral and psychodynamic therapy, though not recommended as the sole treatment. It can also be an effective means of relapse prevention. This technique works best when there is a *dual diagnosis*, that is, when the eating disordered patient is also diagnosed with other addictions, such as to alcohol or drugs.

Free twelve step group meetings are available nationwide, providing a network of support that is strengthened by the dynamic of human interconnectedness, empowerment, trust, and interdependence. The twelve step approach envisions the patient as a victim of a disease that renders him powerless. He must come to grips with this notion as a prerequisite to finding support for healing outside himself, through a *higher power*. The higher power may be seen as a superhuman spiritual element or as the strength derived from the interconnectedness of people caring about one another. Sponsors and mentors are available for ongoing consultation, monitoring, and support, typically offered in service to the mentors' own recoveries. Group support is the strength of this approach, making the technique particularly useful in treating bulimics, who benefit most profoundly from group therapy experiences during and after recovery. The sustaining principles of the twelve step approach are optimistic, based on the belief that people can and do change, regardless of how great their obstacles.

Eating disorders are not true addictions, as we have seen, so some of the twelve step principles may not apply. Your child's participation in these programs should be monitored by his therapist, with OA concepts accommodated to his specific needs. Craig Johnson, Ph.D., has devised a model for specifically adapting the AA and OA methodology to the treatment of eating disorders.[6]

Some OA and AA groups may not fully understand or accept individuals with eating disorders. If for any reason your child is not comfortable with a particular group, he should not hesitate to try another or to talk with someone who might be able to guide him to a more appropriate group. Each group has its own flavor, which may change from session to session based on membership and participation. Be aggressive in going after what feels good and right to you and your child, relying on your instincts, and making changes when things aren't going as well as they might.

**Taking Stock** **Considering a Twelve Step Program**   Here are a few indicators of when it might be appropriate for you and your eating disordered child to consider an affiliation with a twelve step group.

- He is addicted to alcohol or drugs or both.
- Alcoholism or another addiction runs in your family.
- He thrives on support and personal attention from others.
- He feels so alone with his disease.
- He needs ongoing monitoring and accountability to sustain his gains.

- He has not benefited sufficiently from the cognitive-behavioral approach to treatment.
- He would find it helpful to learn from the experiences of others who are going through or have been through this ordeal and who are in recovery.
- He believes he is a hopeless case and needs a lot of encouragement.

## UNDERSTANDING TREATMENT MODES

The various modes of eating disorder treatment present you with options, not all of which may be appropriate or necessary for your child at every stage of his recovery. It is important that you understand these fully so that you can make wise decisions as you guide your child's treatment.

### Individual Treatment

In a treatment sequence that offers nutritional, behavioral, and physiological interventions, individual eating disorder therapy is the central element that assesses and treats the fundamental emotional disorders that underlie the dysfunctional behaviors. Research has shown family treatment to surpass the benefits of individual treatment for the recently stricken anorexic child living at home.[7]

### Family Treatment

*Adolescence is something that happens to a family, not just an individual.*

Nathan Benn[8]

The mother of an anorexic teenager felt that family therapy would be a "distraction" from her child's individual issues. "These are *her* issues," she explained. "They have little to do with us . . . and especially because of her age, *she needs* her privacy and separation from us now." This mother is correct in thinking that her child has unique personal issues that require privacy and a degree of separation from the family. She is sadly mistaken, however, in her thinking that family and individual therapy preclude, rather than enhance, each other and that individual issues develop in a vacuum. A child's individual issues take shape through family interaction; the family is the child's holding environment throughout life. Family therapy honors the child's right to privacy as it also addresses family values, secrets, and patterns of noncommunication.

The most timely and effective eating disorder recoveries happen in the context of loving families whose members are willing to assume responsibility for aspects of the recovery work, be it through providing a willing and sympathetic ear, offering an empathic and realistic understanding of the treatment and recovery process, demonstrating a willingness to accept their own contribution to disease, or assuming the responsibility for making their own changes to facilitate cure. Your process of attempting change alongside your changing child will make his job easier and will make you a more effective mentor; the recovering individual in a family system where he alone is working to create change typically hits a wall of resistance. The child at greatest risk for leaving therapy precipitously and prematurely is the one who has never been accompanied to treatment by a parent.

It is not unusual for eating disordered children to at once invite and rebuff the attentions and assistance of family members—seeking recognition for their accomplishments then feeling resentment at being scrutinized, asking for parental support in meal planning or food preparation then resenting what feels like "policing." Parents and siblings need to increase their tolerance of the inconstancies of recovery's emotional roller-coaster. Simulating the dynamics of life at home, the family treatment mode allows children and parents to practice problem resolution through problem negotiation. Keeping all parts of the family system in alignment and up to speed, it takes the onus of illness and change off the patient.

The way a child interacts within his family of origin is a clear indicator of who he is and how he relates to the world at large. Family treatment keeps parents and children abreast of each other's changes, maximizing the effectiveness of everyone's responses to change. Families with children in treatment should meet together in therapy sessions periodically, if not regularly, even if only once or twice a year. The younger the child the more pivotal regular family treatment is to a successful outcome.

 **EXERCISE D** **The Family's Response to Treatment**   Sometimes looking at your own and other family members' reactions to your child can give you the clearest picture of how your child has changed, what he has accomplished, and what remains to be done. To become more aware of changes in family dynamics resulting from changes in your child, read the following descriptions of a series of family attitudes that are changing over time. In the space provided, write down examples of these attitudes that have appeared in your own family.

1. The family's initial refusal to admit that the problem existed.
   *Examples in our family:*

   _____

   _____

   _____

   _____

2. The family's fear of what such an admission might imply and what it might require in terms of response from each of them.
   *Examples in our family:*

   _____

   _____

   _____

   _____

3. The family's coming to understand that eating disorders are not about food and that the issues underlying the individual's disease affect each family member's life.
   *Examples in our family:*

   _____

   _____

   _____

   _____

4. The family's feeling of losing hope and running out of patience as both disease and recovery drag on and make life difficult.
   *Examples in our family:*

   _____

   _____

   _____

   _____

5. The family's recognition that progress ultimately is a global improvement reflecting upon all family members' lives. Improvement means that the patient regains trust in himself and in everyone around him and that family members

experience a growing trust in the disordered individual and in themselves; they understand and accept him, his disease, and the recovery process.

*Examples in our family:*

_____

_____

_____

_____

You may want to return to this exercise after a time to clarify for yourself how the fears, concerns, expectations, and other feelings of all family members continue to evolve. It will also help you remain aware that the issues of an eating disorder are rarely exclusive to the symptom carrier.

## Families Share Issues and Responsibility

In family therapy, if there is a tendency to find that one person or another is largely "to blame," it's a cinch that the therapist has failed to point out an essential tenet about families—no single individual is *ever* wholly culpable within a family because *a family is a system, with every element affecting every other element.* If a mother is seen as overly controlling, it is because the family needs and wants her to assume responsibility for filling a vacuum they have created. If a child is overly controlling, it is because the parents fear confrontation and actively choose passivity as an alternative. Identify the *mutuality* of relationships in your family or you will come away having missed the very essence of family treatment.

Do not be afraid of bringing sensitive issues into the open in front of your children. Family therapy offers limitless opportunities for self-expression and the sharing of information and therefore for change and growth. One mother feared that if she and her husband expressed any anger toward each other, the marriage would surely end and the children would be scarred. This fear (not the conflict itself) might well have contributed to their daughter's anorexia. Discussing and resolving issues you fear might feel embarrassing or risky often proves empowering. If you and your partner do come upon any issues in treatment that are not relevant to the workings of the greater family system but that pertain solely to the two of you, a few sessions for you and your partner can be an invaluable adjunct to the wider family treatment process.

**Taking Stock** **Considering Family Treatment**    Here are the circumstances in which family treatment is *not* an appropriate addition to your child's individual treatment.

- The family members are not respectful of each other's privacy and personal boundaries.
- The family is chaotic, impulsive, and at time abusive, communicating through actions, not words. With such families it may be preferable for multiple therapists to treat the disordered individual and the rest of the family separately, though in a single facility, such as a community mental health clinic, so that the therapists can easily share necessary information and findings.
- The family members are incapable of forming healthy attachments with each other. Their attachments are either overly enmeshed or nonexistent.
- The eating disordered individual has become old enough and financially secure enough to move out of the family home and live independently. This patient enjoys the option of working effectively on family-based issues in the family's absence (although even here an occasional family session may be valuable).
- The parents do not want to become involved because they are fearful or otherwise reluctant or not interested.
- The parents do not have the financial means to be involved.

If parents, for whatever reason, are not actively involved in their offspring's recovery, it is imperative that they not purposefully or inadvertently sabotage their child's efforts. Moreover, if it is not possible for your family as a whole to be involved in your child's treatment, long-distance conference calls can create valuable connections. It can also be quite effective for individuals in the family to get individual help for themselves. There are many routes to fostering constructive changes in your family and your child.

## Group Psychotherapy

One of the most meaningful and nonthreatening eating disorder treatment tools is group work, in which individuals interact to learn about themselves, their disease, the recovery process, and communication skills. Groups can serve as a bridge into treatment, an adjunct to individual or family treatment, or an aftercare alternative to prevent relapse. Because the single most significant factor in maintaining recovery strides is the patient's resolve to remain in some form of treatment following recovery, group participation is one of the best and least expensive ways to stay in treatment and stave off regressions. Groups that are free of charge, open ended, educative, and have a varied membership week to week are called *self-help* or *support groups*. They are either peer-run or professionally assisted.[9] *Therapy groups* have the same participants week to week and are run by a professional. Whether long- or short-term, therapy groups are more conducive to delving into deep emotional and relational issues than are open-ended support groups.

Support from fellow group members can be a potent source of self-esteem and an impetus to change. The greatest fun in group work is that it focuses on what happens in the here-and-now. Issues are not simply discussed; they are lived, acted out, palpable, and ongoing right before the participants' eyes. Benefits may be gleaned through active or passive participation. To secure the greatest benefits from group work, it is essential to participate regularly and fully.

The multifamily group is a marvelous therapeutic tool that serves parents, other family members, and friends as well as patients. An adjunct to most eating disorder hospital day programs, this group provides a vehicle in which you and your family can interact with other families even after your child's discharge from the program. Typically a professionally run, open-ended support group, it allows you to see how others have survived and handled the issues and to recognize that you are not alone as you learn about yourself, your child, the disease, and recovery.

 **EXERCISE E** **Judging the Benefits of a Support Group**    If you choose to attend a family group, with or without your child, here is a tool to help you judge the value of that experience. Read each of the following statements. Does it resonate with your observations? Circle Y for yes, N for no.

1. Y/N    The group experience taught me important information about eating disorders.

2. Y/N    The group offered me the chance to assess where I stand on a variety of parenting issues and how effective I have been in communicating my values as a parent.

3. Y/N  The group made me feel embraced by a community of others going through similar experiences.

4. Y/N  I recognized feelings that I never knew I had.

5. Y/N  I had goals for the sessions and those goals were met.

6. Y/N  The therapist was evenhanded, giving everyone a chance to speak and not letting anyone monopolize the group's attention.

7. Y/N  I found it helpful to observe other families interacting with each other.

8. Y/N  I left the group feeling optimistic about recovery.

9. Y/N  I left the group understanding some additional things about my child.

10. Y/N  The experience increased my understanding of how families function.

11. Y/N  The group gave me practice in communicating with my child and with others. I got good feedback about the way I communicate.

12. Y/N  The group has helped me establish connections with some potential friends. I want to go back for more sessions.

If your group experience was beneficial, most of your responses should have been yes.

## The Medication Alternative

It is not unusual for parents to be skeptical of drugs and reluctant to consider the medication option for their child. However, although there is no medicine known to cure an eating disorder, there is increasing evidence that medication can be a highly beneficial treatment option for eating disordered individuals when used in conjunction with some form of therapy and monitored by a physician. A disturbance in the balance of a brain neurotransmitting chemical called serotonin has been implicated in biological psychiatric illnesses such as depression, obsessive-compulsive disorders, hypersensitivity, anxiety, and impulse disorders. Eating disorders, which may coexist with any of these psychiatric disorders, are also indicative of abnormalities in the serotonin system.

The recently developed selective serotonin reuptake inhibitor (SSRI) drugs have revolutionized the treatment of anxiety and depression during the past decade. Though often called *antidepressants,* SSRI drugs have also been described as *brain tonics* for their positive effects on so many mental and emotional functions, including concentration, memory, impulse control, self-confidence, compulsions, obsessive thinking, premenstrual syndrome, migraines, and physical pain reduction. Research has shown that Prozac helps anorexics maintain weight gain, decreasing the incidence of relapse once there has been clinical stabilization. Such results may eventually be proven for other SSRI drugs as well. SSRIs may also reduce appetite and promote weight loss. Contrary to earlier concerns, they do not appear to cause problems for anorexics. Bear in mind, however, that the medication alternative may have limited efficiency in patients with inadequate nutrition. In addition, if purged, medications obviously will have no effect.

New SSRI medications that are more specific in their actions are rapidly entering the market. With fewer side effects, easy tolerability, and a wide margin of safety, SSRI drugs are being prescribed readily. Death from an overdose of these drugs is rare, another reason that they are widely prescribed.

**How SSRIs Work**     Serotonin is available to us only through food. SSRI drugs do not create serotonin but make the serotonin that is present in the body more available for use by inhibiting (stopping) its reuptake (reabsorption) into the brain. Diminishing the intensity of compulsive thoughts and feelings (not eliminating them), these benign and nonaddictive drugs enable the patient to respond and make changes more effectively throughout the therapy process. Medication-induced attitudinal and feeling changes stimulate behavioral changes, and eventually, these lead to the patient's feeling better enough to stop needing the medication. There is increasing evidence that the way we think and feel actually creates neural pathways in the brain; the powerful combination of cognitive treatment with medication allows the depressed patient to think his way through to new, remediated brain patterns as he also chemically induces them.

**How Medicating Is Done**     Medicating is an art as well as a science, requiring some degree of trial, error, and adjustment in response to the patient's self-observation and self-reporting. Individuals may do well on one type of SSRI medication yet not be able to tolerate another. Drugs can be used in various combinations to customize their effects to the patient's needs. Individuals on SSRI drugs must be encouraged to be patient because results are not immediate; it takes anywhere from three to eight weeks or longer for the maximal effect to become apparent. Those who discontinue their medications or their treatment prematurely because they feel better on medication are at risk of relapsing. In depression, treatment with antidepressants should last at least a year, and if there have been multiple relapses, treatment may be lifelong. The same is suspected to hold true for eating disorders. The possible emergence of other symptoms following eating disorder recovery has implications for additional benefits of continued medication as well. When the patient does discontinue an antidepressant, it is important that he notify his physician first, as some medications need to be tapered off to avoid withdrawal-like syndromes of anxiety or gastroenterological distress.

SSRI drugs improve quality of life without altering the individual's personality and with minimal, if any, side effects; headaches, sleep disturbances, dizziness, and upset stomach are typical and generally fleeting consequences that appear and subside after a week or two. Extreme fatigue, tremors, or increased agitation may contraindicate the continued use of a particular drug. In this instance, another serotonin reuptake blocking drug might be a more compatible choice. The conscientious physician prescribing medication will first require a baseline blood chemistry evaluation to rule out the possibility that an organic dysfunction is responsible for bringing on the symptoms being treated.

Compliance with medication is often a problem for people with eating disorders. They voice fears that the medicine will "control my mind," "take away my thinness," or "make me drug dependent." Often families support such misconceptions. You can help your child understand that medication is an important part of his treatment, restoring a normal brain chemical balance and alleviating symptoms. Though medicine does not bring about a cure, it makes a cure more attainable, getting your child where he wants to go and getting him there faster. Exhibit 4.2 lists medications and typical dosages commonly prescribed for eating disordered individuals.

**A Word About Dysthymia**     In considering the option of medicating a child with an eating disorder, it is important to be aware of a condition called *dysthymia,* a low-level depression or heart-heaviness that never gains enough potency to disturb one's role functions, only one's quality of life. Many patients and therapists consider such low-level depression not worthy of pharmacological intervention, and many patients become aware of having had this condition only retrospectively, after drug therapy for the eating disorder also alleviates the dysthymia, and they grow to appreciate what a relief it is to actually feel good.

## Exhibit 4.2. Medications Used in Eating Disorders.

| Category | Drug Name | Dosages (mg/day) | Comments |
|---|---|---|---|
| Selective serotonin reuptake inhibitors (SSRIs) (antidepressants) | Prozac | 20–80 | 60 mg/day may be instrumental in interrupting the binge-purge cycle for bulimics. |
| | Paxil | 10–60 | |
| | Zoloft | 50–200 | |
| | Luvox | 50–300 | |
| | Celexa | 20–40 | |
| Newer SSRIs | Remeron | 15–45 | Antidepressants that are designed to have fewer side effects and that interact with neurotransmitters in addition to serotonin (each of these drugs has a specific profile; the physician tries to target the medication to symptoms). |
| | Effexor | 75–375 | |
| | Serzone (nefazodone) | 100–600 | |
| Tricyclic anti-depressants (TCAs) | Norpramine | 100–300 | Older but still valuable drugs. |
| | Tofranil | 100–300 | |
| | Pamelor | 50–200 | |
| | Anafranil | 100–250 | |
| | Elavil | 100–300 | |
| Monoamine oxidase inhibitors (MAOIs) | Parnate | 20–50 | |
| | Nardil | 45–90 | |
| | Wellbutrin | 150–300 | Not used for bulimia because it may potentiate seizures; also marketed as Zypreza, used for smoking cessation. |
| | Trazodone | 200–600 | Often used to enhance sleep. |

| Antianxiety agents (benzodiazepines) | Valium | 2–40 | Anxiety is a typical consequence of eating more normally and gaining weight. SSRIs are the preferred antianxiety agents for children. |
|---|---|---|---|
| | Ativan | 0.5–10 | |
| | Xanax | 0.5–4 | |
| | Buspar | 15–60 | Often useful for patients who abuse substances. |
| | Klonopin | .01–.03 mg/kg | |

*Note:* Dosages listed are those typically used for depression.

**Nutritional Supplements**    In their book *Zinc and Eating Disorders,* Schauss and Costin report that most anorexics and many bulimics are zinc deficient.[10] A deficiency in zinc causes loss of taste sensitivity and appetite, reducing the desire to eat. What may start out as a diet motivated by a reasonable desire to lose weight may turn into a physiological desire not to eat because of a resulting zinc imbalance, although zinc therapy has been discarded by most physicians who have tried it with their eating disordered patients. Multivitamins, calcium tablets, and protein drinks also fall into the category of supplements that may be beneficial. Be aware, however, that no supplements should be taken without the knowledge and consent of a physician.

## DETERMINING THE BEST TREATMENT MILIEU

The *treatment milieu* is the environment in which your child will be working. Should it be inpatient or outpatient? And if it begins as outpatient, at any point should it become inpatient? And if your child does need inpatient treatment, where is the best place for him to go, when, and for how long? A sequencing of treatment milieus is often most efficacious, though only 5 percent of eating disordered patients become inpatients during their recovery treatment.

**Taking Stock** Choosing a Treatment Milieu

*Guidelines to Follow*

- When you have a choice of effective treatments, always choose the least radical.
- Try to keep your child in the mainstream of normal outpatient living for as long as possible.
- Recovery, like disease, never stands still. Continually assess the appropriateness of your child's current treatment milieu, allowing the status of his evolving recovery to determine whether a change is needed.
- The need for inpatient work is not determined by the severity of symptoms, but by the degree of physical damage, the loss of life role function, and the depth of resistance to change in outpatient work.
- Recognize that outpatient care is not lesser quality care; it is simply less intensive. The elements of inpatient and outpatient treatment are in most respects the same, varying in intensity and comprehensiveness.

*Information to Gather About a Treatment Setting*

- The services provided
- The requirements for admission
- The program's treatment philosophy
- The personnel who will attend to your child
- Daily activities and protocols
- Means of transitioning from one milieu to another
- The average length of stay
- Financial arrangements
- Aftercare opportunities and facilities
- The number of patients on an inpatient unit (if your child is the only eating disordered patient on a unit, he will miss a major source of recovery incentives: socialization with other recovering patients).

**Activity** Examining Treatment Options   After reading each of the following descriptions of treatment milieus, consider its applicability for your child, and note your thoughts and questions in your journal.

## Outpatient Treatment

Outpatient treatment involves considerably less expense, life disruption, and intensity of care than does inpatient work and cannot provide as comprehensive or rigorous a treatment experience. Outpatient care permits recovery to happen in the context of daily living, as the patient attends school, works, and interacts with family and friends. Taking place weekly or biweekly, both in the psychotherapist's office and other settings, outpatient treatment coordinates diverse services as they are needed. These may include medical, psychological, psychopharmacological, and nutritional care. The danger in outpatient treatment lies in the possibility that the patient may not receive enough of the right supports in this relatively structureless milieu or may find it hard to comply with required lifestyle changes. For example, when an outpatient therapist asked that a patient cut back on her excessive participation in her favorite sport, the patient asked, "Why are you punishing me?" But it was a needed behavioral change, not punishment, that the therapist had in mind. Outpatient work needs to replicate within the context of daily living the behaviors imposed by the more restrictive inpatient setting.

## Inpatient Treatment

If outpatient work is not sufficient to bring about recovery progress, the patient may qualify for inpatient care, either hospitalization or extended residential treatment. The inpatient setting should be seen as a short-term booster to the long-term outpatient effort. Inpatient settings offer a complete roster of services; art therapy, dance therapy, sand therapy, psychodrama groups, locked bathrooms, and constant availability of professional services are generally among these programs' offerings. The patient's transition from an outpatient setting to an inpatient one and back again to outpatient care must be carefully orchestrated to avoid undue turmoil and stress and to ensure a meaningful division of professional labor. Your inpatient child should be allowed to continue seeing his outpatient therapist so that he does not lose his established, productive therapy relationship.

**Residential Care**     Residential care provides a long-term, nonhospital, comprehensive milieu away from home for the patient's treatment and recovery in the company of other individuals working toward similar goals. Because it provides comprehensive eating disorder care outside a hospital, this alternative is generally somewhat more affordable. However, insurance companies may be less likely to fund a treatment program in a place that is not primarily a medical facility. It is preferable, when possible, for a child to recover in his own home environment, surrounded by his family.

**Hospitalization**     Determining the need for hospitalization as an alternative to outpatient eating disorder treatment is an ongoing diagnostic task. If your child meets any of these four criteria, his condition may warrant hospitalization:

1. He displays signs of being in physiological danger.
2. The disease has adversely affected his capacity to function adequately in his life roles (as a student, family member, friend, and employee).
3. His outpatient work has not brought about sufficient or timely progress toward recovery.
4. He feels his behavior is so out of control that nothing short of hospitalization can contain it.

An interim experience only, hospitalization for an eating disorder is a temporary but valuable prelude, adjunct, or alternative to the outpatient eating disorder treatment effort. Hospitalizations do not cure patients with eating disorders. They stabilize or reverse these patients' deteriorating physiological condition through refeeding or they jump-start patients who are stalled in their outpatient work or who are unsuccessful in accomplishing required changes. *Having to hospitalize your child is not an indication that he is too sick to recover completely. Nor does it imply that he has not already made substantial progress along the recovery continuum.* The hospital experience will renew and reinforce what he has already gained in recovery. Some hospitals offer services to eating disordered patients through general psychiatric programs. Avoid this alternative where possible, selecting programs that specialize in the care of eating disordered patients.

## Hospital Day Treatment Programs

In this age of limited insurance coverage for hospital care and mental health services, overnight stays in hospitals are fast becoming an anachronism. When they step down to less expensive day treatment programs, patients participate on a hospital eating disorder unit for a part of every day, returning home to sleep; this is the primary distinction between inpatient care and day treatment. Day programs may be partial (four to six hours a day) or extended (7 A.M. to 7 P.M.), the latter providing three square meals and snacks. Both enforce weight restoration, use behavior modification devices (such as locked bathrooms and exercise restrictions), and employ a full complement of staff and peers who dialogue with patients in the context of various treatment venues including meals, educative and support groups, and recreation therapies. If your child spends time as an inpatient or day patient on an eating disorder unit, the hospital will provide academic tutoring so that he will not fall behind in school. By reducing the number of hours he spends on a day unit, the recovering patient can remain part of the program while enjoying an ever-growing degree of independence from that program.

**Taking Stock** Understanding What a Hospital Program Can Do for Your **Child**   A hospital program, inpatient or day, brief or extended, can

- Save your child's life if force-feeding or other medical attention is essential to keep him alive (though force-feeding is rarely required). The hospital setting ensures your child's renourishment at a safe and prescribed pace, stimulating weight gain at a rate of anywhere from one pound to three pounds per week (one pound is the norm).
- Clarify and focus treatment goals for him and the professionals helping him.
- Orchestrate his behavioral changes and deal with their aftermath.
- Expose him to others in similar situations (this can promote self-awareness and the development of social skills, marking the beginning of friendships and camaraderie).
- Put him in closer touch with his feelings.
- Give him permission to speak out about his disease and his needs.
- Foster his reality orientation.
- Increase his capacity for introspection.
- Handle his anxiety over the weight he gains.
- Give him a better sense of his strengths and thus more self-confidence.
- Prepare him to transition to a more productive outpatient experience.

 **EXERCISE F** Choosing a Treatment Program   To begin the process of thinking about the best milieu for your child, read each of the following descriptions and before each one write in the letter that corresponds to the most appropriate treatment milieu: (a) outpatient treatment, (b) hospital inpatient treatment, (c) hospital day program treatment, or (d) residential care treatment. In some cases, several settings may be appropriate. (See Appendix A for suggested answers, but remember that it is the *extent* of your child's problem that will determine your best treatment choice. Answers will vary depending on how severe the symptoms are, their duration, and how amenable your child might be to making changes.)

1. My child has progressed nicely in his short hospital stay but needs to continue treatment.
2. My child has lost too much weight in too little time.
3. After years of hard work, my child is recovered. He wishes to ensure his gains by continuing treatment.
4. My child is approaching a dangerously low weight after months of outpatient treatment.
5. My child is starting to relapse into anorexia after being recovered for one year.
6. My child is unable to stop purging. He feels completely out of control.
7. My child has started experiencing heart problems.
8. My child has been told by our insurance company that his hospitalization coverage is about to end.
9. My child does not want to (or cannot) get out of bed in the morning.
10. My child spends a minimum of three hours a day exercising.

In any treatment setting, you and your child are likely to work with many professionals. The next chapter will help prepare you to deal directly with these important people in your child's recovery.

# Reaching Out for Professional Help

The voice at the other end of the phone belonged to an inquiring mother. "I guess I should be asking for your credentials." she said. "I'm so new at this, I don't even know *what* to ask." This mother was frightened and confused, not knowing if what she saw in her child was an eating disorder. Compounding this, she was too embarrassed to share her concerns and feelings with relatives and friends. This mother was performing one of the more courageous parental acts: reaching out to a professional for help.

## GETTING STARTED

In searching for the best professionals to work with your eating disordered child, your first task is to network in your community, using every personal and professional connection available to you: family doctors, local hospital eating disorder units, friends, relatives, friends of friends, friends of relatives, school personnel, the Yellow Pages, and so forth to find the best assistance. Eating disorder support organizations such as ANAD (National Association for Anorexia Nervosa and Associated Disorders) are also excellent referral sources.

> **Activity** **Gathering Resources**   List those referral sources who might provide some guidance and support for you in your search for professional help. Use the chart provided in Exhibit 5.1 for your notes as you create a web of contact possibilities. Ask your resources what they know about the professionals you are considering, how they know this, and if they know of anyone who has been helped by these individuals.

**Exhibit 5.1. Sample Referral Sources Chart.**

| Name | The Professional She or He Knows | How She or He Knows of This Professional | People This Professional Has Helped | Comments from These People |
|------|----------------------------------|------------------------------------------|-------------------------------------|----------------------------|
|      |                                  |                                          |                                     |                            |

**EXERCISE A** **Evaluating Referrals**   As you seek the right professionals for your child and family, use the criteria in this exercise to decide which individuals to speak with. Read each of the following criteria, and if the individual meets it, circle Y for yes. If he or she does not, circle N for no.

1. Y/N   Has extensive experience in this field.
2. Y/N   Has a philosophy of eating disorder treatment that focuses on both the dysfunctional behaviors and the emotions driving them.
3. Y/N   Includes parents in various aspects of treatment.
4. Y/N   Has connections to other skilled collaborating professionals.
5. Y/N   Is in reasonable proximity to your home.
6. Y/N   Has affordable fees (perhaps a sliding fee scale) and may be covered by your health insurance.
7. Y/N   Has a track record of success and a reputation of excellence.
8. Y/N   Has received good recommendations from people you respect and trust.
9. Y/N   Has a caring attitude.
10. Y/N   Develops a good rapport with patients. Is engaging and knowledgeable.
11. Y/N   Has the capacity to recognize medical issues that may be serious and require immediate attention.
12. Y/N   Is willing to work as part of a treatment team, including a nutritionist, physician, and family therapist, should you require this.

It is not unusual for recovered eating disordered individuals to go into the profession of helping others with the same problem. But the common notion that the best person to treat an eating disorder is one who has recovered from the disease himself or herself is a myth. You need not be a horse to be a horse doctor—need I say more?

## When to Begin the Search

In determining when to begin reaching out, on the one hand be aware that *the sooner you act the better.* The longer you wait, the greater the opportunity for dysfunctional behaviors to become entrenched, resulting in body chemistry imbalances, weight changes, interpersonal problems, and role dysfunctions. On the other hand, once parents learn that their eating disordered child has been purging, they typically fear that if help is not in place *immediately,* these behaviors will cause irreparable damage. This is not the case. Unless your child has become too weak to function or is experiencing other medical problems, you have adequate time to go through the process of finding good professionals. With a disease as long term as an eating disorder, taking a week or even a month to get recovery started will probably make no significant difference in your child's overall health.

### How to Begin the Search

In determining whom to contact first, keep in mind that you can start your search anywhere. It is inconsequential whether your first contact is with a teacher, a therapist, a nutritionist, or a pediatrician; all roads should eventually lead to the same destination. Also, it is not necessary to begin the treatment process with a hospital program. An initial assessment of your child's needs can be done adequately by an experienced outpatient professional. Your child's evaluator will determine whether a hospital placement is the preferred milieu at this point, which is most likely not the case.

Wherever you start, it is important to be clear about your goals for phone conversations with the professionals you choose to contact.

 **EXERCISE B Conducting the Initial Telephone Contact**  This exercise will help you track your needs and requirements *before, during,* and *after* each phone call you make to a professional. You deserve to have these needs met—*all* of them. Keeping them clearly in mind will help you make that happen.

*Prior to the Telephone Conversation*
You probably have very specific questions and issues that you want addressed. List them here in the spaces provided.

1. *What questions do you need to ask?*

   _____

   _____

   _____

   _____

2. *What issues do you need explained?*

_____

_____

_____

_____

*During the Telephone Conversation*

As you talk to the professional, you will begin to develop an impression of him or her. Answer the following questions by circling Y for yes, N for no. The professional may need to give you some unhurried, quality time as you have a great many criteria that must be met. Ideally, all your answers will be yes.

1. Y/N  Does this person help you formulate and define your questions and concerns for this conversation?

2. Y/N  Does this person anticipate and guide your questions and concerns about your child's treatment?

3. Y/N  Does this person have a firm grasp of the disease? Can he or she explain eating disorders? Can he or she describe what eating disorder treatment entails and how it works?

4. Y/N  Does this person understand that eating disorder problems are broad based and integrative?

5. Y/N  Does he or she have a working relationship with collaborating professionals? If not, will he or she cooperate with other professionals you may want to bring in?

6. Y/N  Can this professional describe how he or she works (the therapeutic philosophy and style)?

7. Y/N  Is this professional willing to start where you are, focusing on your immediate needs at the time of the conversation?

8. Y/N  Can this professional perform the family therapy as well as the individual therapy if need be? If not, can he or she appreciate how important the connections between patient and family are?

9. Y/N  Does this professional consider himself or herself a specialist in eating disorder treatment? Do your concerns sound legitimate to him or her?

10. Y/N Does this professional have a backup person who stands in for him or her in emergencies? Does this professional refer patients to a reputable hospital eating disorder program? Which one?

11. Y/N Does this professional discuss eating habits, food quirks, and meal patterns with patients as a matter of course during the evaluation and throughout the treatment process?

12. Y/N Does this professional seem warm and friendly and genuinely concerned?

13. Y/N Is this professional knowledgeable about nutrition?

14. Y/N Does this professional regularly work with a nutritionist?

15. Y/N Can you work out a fee and payment plan that is suitable for you? Is there a sliding scale for fees if you need one?

16. Y/N Does this professional inspire confidence that your child can make a full recovery?

*After the Telephone Conversation*

After your conversation, consider your impressions of the professional. Answer the following questions by circling Y for yes, N for no. Again, ideally, all your answers will be yes.

1. Y/N Did this professional appreciate that you needed her or his time and consideration now, and that you will continue to need a voice and a role in the treatment process?

2. Y/N Did this professional appreciate the impact of the family on the child and vice versa? Did she or he respect how important your family is to you?

3. Y/N Did this professional speak with empathy and have an ear for your feelings, values, priorities?

4. Y/N Did this professional accept and give legitimacy to all of your feelings?

5. Y/N Did this professional believe that an eating disorder can be overcome, or did she or he see it to be like alcoholism, something your child will deal with throughout the rest of her life?

6. Y/N Did you get some notion of the approximate length of time recovery could take? Six months, two years, five years?

7. Y/N  Did this professional return your call promptly? Were your concerns important to her or him?

8. Y/N  Most of all, did you feel better after having spoken with this professional? Did you get a feeling of reassurance, optimism, and hope for recovery?

9. *Write down your other impressions:*

_____

_____

_____

As the current manager of your child's case, don't hesitate to follow through with as many calls to professionals as you need in order to feel convinced that you have found the best person for you and your child. It is absolutely imperative that the professionals you choose welcome you into the therapy process as a member of the treatment team.

## Notify Your Insurance Company

Before you do another thing, I would advise you to notify your insurance company, describing the treatment you anticipate you will be needing and asking the insurer to inform you about what your policy covers. Get this information from the company in writing. Here's what you need to know:

- What types of professionals are covered under your insurance plan?
- How many counseling sessions is each family member allowed for the calendar year?
- How many sessions currently remain for the year for each person?
- How many marriage counseling and family therapy sessions are allowed?
- How many inpatient days are allowed in a psychiatric or eating disorder unit? In a medical unit?
- How many days are allowed in an outpatient day program?
- Is nutritional gastronomic tube-feeding covered?
- How many visits to a physician for monitoring of the eating disorder are covered?

If you find you are not feeling emotionally up to the task of dealing with financial details right now, find a reliable person to pick up the slack for you until you are able to handle these matters yourself. Someone needs to track insurance benefits in order to alert you when they are close to being exhausted so you can determine how to proceed. (Dealing with your insurance company as treatment progresses is discussed later in this chapter.)

## THE TREATMENT TEAM

As I discussed in Chapter Four, your child's treatment team may include a number of specialists. This section defines and differentiates these professionals.

### Finding a Psychotherapist

Many people begin their professional search by contacting a psychotherapist to provide individual therapy for their child. You will find you have various therapist options.

**Psychiatrists**   Psychiatrists are medical doctors specializing in mental health treatment; they prescribe and administer drugs and may or may not perform psychotherapy.

Psychiatrists who specialize in administering medication are referred to as psychopharmacologists. Medicine checks with these specialists are generally fifteen- to twenty-minute sessions geared solely to the discussion of the effects of medication, not to psychotherapeutic issues. It is standard practice for a patient to see different professionals for her therapy and her medication.

**Psychologists**   Most psychologists have a Ph.D. degree. They are trained to practice psychotherapy, conduct scientific research, and administer psychological tests, IQ tests, learning disability evaluations, and the like. However, these kinds of tests are in most instances irrelevant to the treatment of an eating disorder. Some psychologists have a Psy.D. degree, a doctorate in clinical psychology.

**Social Workers**   Social workers have master's (M.S.W.) or doctor's (D.S.W.) degrees, depending on their number of years in training. Social workers are usually generalists in the practice of psychotherapy, with their training based primarily in clinical practice. They work with individuals, families, couples, and groups. They may also perform milieu-specific work, such as hospital social work, school social work, or social welfare case work. Because social workers generally train formally for less time than either psychologists or psychiatrists, they generally charge less and are more accessible to you through programs supported by tax dollars and public funding. Your child typically has wide access to social workers on the staffs of most public schools, community mental health clinics, public service agencies, and so forth, places that provide services free of charge or on a sliding fee scale for individuals with limited financial means.

**Others**      Other individuals trained to practice psychotherapy include licensed clinical professional counselors (LCPCs), marriage and family counselors, and psychiatric nurses, to mention a few. Their degrees vary from bachelor's to master's and Ph.D.'s, and their training includes the clinical practice of psychotherapy.

People often wonder if therapists from different disciplines work differently and if the quality of their work varies depending on their level of training, with a greater number of years in training correlating to better treatment. In my experience, this is not the case. I have found that a professional's training and academic degree are less significant indicators of how that person works than are his or her personality, warmth, personal value system, breadth of general education and interests, capacity for empathy and self-awareness, and life experience. Formal training is just the beginning of what it takes to become a good psychotherapist. Talented practitioners transform knowledge into wisdom, intuition into judgment, and experience into confidence.

Listen and respond to your intuition as you choose a practitioner for your child. Trust yourself and go with your feelings. If your choice is not entirely successful, you can always make accommodations or changes later on.

## Rounding Out the Professional Team

Beyond your child's individual psychotherapist, you and your child may need or choose to use some or all of the following members of the interdisciplinary eating disorder treatment team.

**The Family Therapist**      Family therapy can be conducted by the child's therapist or by a collaborating family therapist. The choice to employ the child's therapist lies in part with the child and in part with the therapist. Some believe that the relationship between patient and therapist is inviolate and not to be contaminated by family members' coming into the process. Some patients may feel threatened by the prospect of a parent-therapist alliance. Others, however, understand that having a common therapist for both patient and family can simplify and integrate information gathering and dissemination. A major factor in the decision is the skill and comfort level of the therapist with family work, the quality of his or her relationship with the patient and family, and his or her philosophy of treatment.

There are essentially two forms of family treatment that you need to be aware of. In *conjoint family therapy* the entire family comes together in the treatment sessions; in *family counseling* the therapist sees the parents together and the child alone. This technique allows the therapist to advise parents about the best way to manage their child's eating problems at home.[1] It is imperative that the therapist make clear to patient and parents alike that parental sessions are not designed to divulge private information, betray the child's confidences, or make executive decisions behind the child's back. Typically, and especially when there is even the slightest chance that meeting with parents alone may infringe on the rights of the child, it is preferable for the family to meet conjointly.

An effective family therapist promotes family changes that *parallel and strengthen the child's changes.* Here is a typical example:

- As the parents, through family work, demanded more respect for themselves, their child began to treat them with greater civility.

- As the parents became better listeners, their child became more expressive.

- As the parents made more demands, the child became more responsible and cooperative.

- As the parents expressed more interest in understanding her anger, the child became less hostile.

- As the parents no longer needed to walk on eggshells with her, the child became more candid and forthright.

*Write down some of the ways your family could benefit from the work of family therapy:*

_____

_____

_____

_____

**The Nutritionist**    By fostering balance and moderation in the act of eating, the nutritionist helps the patient take her first steps toward establishing balance and moderation in other life spheres. This professional requires the patient to take responsibility for feeding and becoming accountable to herself. A nutritionist's perspective is both specific regarding food and global regarding lifestyle.

Your child will approach her nutritionist in search of far more than a weigh-in, a food plan, or simple advice about what to put in her mouth. Typically, she seeks a relationship with someone who understands eating disorders and sincerely cares about her. The nutritionist should teach your child general techniques of self-care. Compare the responses of two nutritionists to an emaciated and starving patient. One advised her to drink ice cream sodas and eat candy bars; the other attempted to correct her perceptions about herself by explaining: "You know, you are abusing yourself. I wonder if you are aware of that." Which person would you prefer to have working with your child?

The nutritionist is not another therapist, but in many respects she owes it to the patient and to the eating disorder recovery process to act like one. She can be both an interpreter and educator. If the child says, "I am feeling fat," the nutritionist's response should be along the lines of, "You realize that is a tip-off to you that you are actually feeling something else; what might that be?" If it is not, then she has missed an important therapeutic opportunity.

Nutritionists may facilitate self-appraisal and accountability through the use of tools such as food journals and meal plans. Neither should be considered a test of the patient's ability to succeed and perform but a diagnostic aid, a barometer of her strengths and weaknesses, of things that are working and things that are not, of the pace and direction of progress. Food journals should include adequate space for entering feelings and insights so they can be used to set the direction for future efforts. Written plans and journals create a sense of security, safety, and predictability within the unsafe spheres of food and weight. What makes these devices more than just another set of rules is their planned obsolescence. Like training wheels on a bike, they are mere props that will be shed as soon as the patient is able to find her own balance.

As educators and motivators, nutritionists help regressed patients get back on track through goal redefinition. They make eating safe and weight control possible by suggesting the right foods, in the right amounts, in the right frequency, and at the right pace. In discussing food, the effective nutritionist offers the patient a context for self-observation and self-appraisal, for problem definition and problem resolution, all of which apply to making changes in *areas beyond food,* furthering the recovery process as a whole.

*Write down some of the ways your child might benefit from work with a nutritionist:*

_____

_____

_____

_____

**Taking Stock** **Making Sure You Have the Right Nutritionist** *Beware* the nutritionist who

- Sets out a rigid food plan that your child must adhere to and that does not take into consideration what your child likes to eat.
- Threatens to give walking papers to your child if she resists this food plan.
- Attempts to *fix* your thin child by fattening her up.
- Prescribes additional calories or a diet rather than a healthy eating lifestyle.
- Sends your child on her way without scheduling a follow-up visit to assist and support her nutritional efforts.
- Does not connect food-related behaviors to your child's emotional issues and feelings.
- Implies that there are *good* foods and *bad* foods and that healthy eating involves staying away from the bad foods.
- Is not interested in understanding and interpreting for your child *how* and *why* her dysfunctional eating habits occur and the dynamics behind her efforts to make changes.
- Is not genuinely committed to eating disordered patients, especially those who are obstinate and oppositional to the point of being hostile.
- Does not speak the truth because it might make her unpopular with your child.
- Teaches about food groups and nitpicks exchanges and calories to the exclusion of discussing healthy eating and lifestyle choices.
- Tries to motivate your child through fear or her need to please.

**The Medical Doctor: Internist or Pediatrician**     Usual standards of physician evaluation are only one issue in assessing a medical doctor's capacity to treat an eating disorder. It is critical that your internist or pediatrician also know enough about these disorders to recognize which physical symptoms need immediate intervention and which can safely be watched for a time. A patient's need for her doctor's input will vary from daily or weekly to semiannually, depending on her medical requirements and stage of recovery. Internists and pediatricians may initiate or facilitate an eating disorder diagnosis and monitor weight gain or loss. By assuming a policing role, the physician may help to contain out-of-control behaviors, making firm nutritional demands of the patient, then holding her to them. Should food- or weight-related ultimatums become appropriate during a course of treatment, the internist should be the one who enforces them, thus protecting the more fragile patient-parent and patient-therapist relationships.

If someone other than a physician makes the eating disorder diagnosis, it is imperative that an internist or pediatrician be brought into the case very early in treatment to evaluate the physiological status of the patient, ruling out organic dysfunction as the cause of the problem and establishing a baseline record of the patient's blood chemistry, weight, and vital signs. Only a medical doctor can admit the patient to a hospital if that step becomes necessary. Referrals to medical specialists may be obtained through the American Medical Association or the American Academy of Pediatrics.[2]

**Taking Stock** **Assessing Your Child's Doctor**   These are some key traits you should look for in your child's physician:

- The physician should have a great deal of experience and sensitivity in handling eating disorders.

- The physician should not be put off by the fact that eating disorders can be emotionally demanding and time-consuming cases. She or he must be prepared to understand and respond to power struggles, denial, resistance, and volatile feelings.

- The physician must be comfortable not only in treating the disease but in maintaining an ongoing dialogue with your child and, in some contexts, with you.

- Even though the vast majority of patients recover without hospitalization, the physician should be affiliated with a hospital or with other professionals from a hospital that has an eating disorder unit.
- If the physician is without much experience with these disorders, she or he should be willing to refer more complex cases to eating disordered experts.
- The physician must be prepared to expend time and energy collaborating with other professionals, because your child's evolving state requires continual evaluation and goal revisions.

*Write down some of the reasons your child needs the input of an internist:*

_____

_____

_____

_____

**Hospital Personnel**     Depending on the circumstances of your child's case, the professionals who work with her while she is hospitalized may remain part of her postdischarge team. Nurses, dietitians, or social workers who lead body image, meal therapy, or multifamily groups may continue to offer these services to your child on an outpatient basis. It is not uncommon for those children who do need hospitalization to have several short hospital stays during the course of a recovery. (Hospital care and criteria for hospitalization are discussed at length in Chapter Four.)

*Write down reasons your child may need to maintain contact with hospital staff:*

_____

_____

_____

_____

**School Personnel**     Schools can play a highly significant role in eating disorder education and prevention. They provide services for troubled students through professionally run peer support groups, drop-in centers, individual and group psychotherapy, coaches and mentors, health classes and health fairs, and personal tutoring. Do not hesitate to garner the insights, support, and feedback of a favorite teacher, guidance counselor, or coach. If your child has begun to slip in her academic standing, teachers will appreciate and benefit from your input about why this is happening and may have insights of their own to offer. If you know your child's needs and can make a case for assistance, your child's school is prepared to partner with you to enhance your child's capacity to learn and to perform optimally.

*Write down the names or titles of the people you might talk with at your child's school and what you might want to accomplish through these conversations:*

_____

_____

_____

_____

The roles of all members of the professional team will overlap to one degree or another but should never contradict or interfere with one another. The responsive internist, for example, in treating the whole person, provides emotional support and addresses nutritional issues. In less complicated cases it is also perfectly appropriate for the internist to prescribe and monitor psychotropic medications. The nutritionist, like the physician, does not perform a therapy function, but hears and highlights therapy issues, reinforcing the work of the therapist. The therapist talks consistently and openly about nutrition and eating patterns, connecting food-related behaviors to underlying feelings.

## WHAT TO EXPECT AND DEMAND FROM PROFESSIONALS

Hungry for connectedness as well as food, the eating disordered patient approaches professionals with many levels of needs. To accommodate the diverse and often covert agendas your child brings with her, the effective therapist or other eating disorder professional blends knowledge with an expansive heart to make connections that are soul to soul.

### Watch Out for Professionals Caught Up in Weight Traps

A patient cannot benefit maximally from the psychotherapy process until she reaches 85 or 90 percent of normal body weight. Beyond that, food and weight issues in recovery warrant attention *only* insofar as they indicate food abuse, potential physiological damage, or significant behavioral change. *How* and *why* weight is being gained and lost, by what means, and at what rate, determines the significance of weight as a diagnostic tool. A low weight may or may not indicate the failure of a recovery process for an anorexic, and a stable or increasing weight may or may not indicate a movement toward health. There is no magic in numbers on the scale; the magic, instead, exists in the emotional resiliency and the quality of behavioral self-regulation underlying weight changes.

## Your Child's Professionals Should Be Listening to You

Deferring to their child's or her therapist's demands for treatment privacy, parents typically feel disempowered. As I discussed in Chapter Four, you are entitled to understand and participate in your child's treatment, and the therapist should include you in various aspects of it. The therapist cares for the patient by caring for her parents too. It is that simple.

> **Troubleshooting Tip** **Ask Appropriate Questions of the Therapist**   As a parent, you have the right to ask questions pertaining to yourself and your needs, to your own role in the recovery process, and to the functioning of team members. Specifics about what is said between your child and her therapist must remain confidential unless and until your child chooses to share this information with you. The first example in the following list shows inappropriate questioning. The second and third examples illustrate acceptable information seeking.
>
> - Mother to therapist: "I want to discuss Joan's depression with you. What did she tell you about it?" This question oversteps Joan's personal boundaries.
> - Mother to therapist: "I am very concerned about the extent of Joan's depression, and am hopeful that she has chosen to discuss it with you. I am wondering how I might best respond to her." This question asks for information to meet the parent's *own* feelings and needs.
> - Mother to daughter [*in a family session*]: "Joan, it was hard for me to watch you be as sad as you were this week. Do you have any objection to

discussing what made you so sad?" In this interaction, the issues are aired openly so that everyone has simultaneous access to the concerns and the opportunity to respond to them and to the person who feels and expresses them.

**Taking Stock** **Assessing the Therapist's Willingness to Treat You as a Participant** Do you feel comfortable asking your child's therapist the following questions? You should. You need to ask such questions periodically throughout your child's treatment.

- What do I have the right to ask and to know about my child's treatment?

- Is treatment working? Is my child responsive and making sufficient headway?

- Can something be done to make her treatment more effective? Are all the necessary adjunct treatments in place—nutritionist, internist, and so on?

- Am I responding appropriately to my child's changes? What might I do to reinforce treatment changes?

- Are you on top of how my child eats and how she thinks about and feels about food and weight? Do you check in with her about this regularly?

- Can things be made any easier for the family? How? Might we come in for family treatment occasionally?

- How might I be of assistance to my child regarding her eating?

- How freely can I share my thoughts, fears, and feelings with my child?

Your child's therapist should be willing to coach you about how to behave at home with your child to facilitate her treatment process, and to discuss what the recovery process has been like for you. Family therapy, as described earlier, is a perfect forum for such discussions, particularly when your questions might warrant answers from your child.

In addition, the good therapist hears what you say between the lines and responds to your spoken and *unspoken* emotional needs. In this respect, she or he listens to you in the same way that you listen to your child. Here are some examples of typical parental questions and the frequently unspoken questions they also contain:

| Question Asked | Questions Requiring an Answer |
| --- | --- |
| How is my child doing? | Am I doing the right thing for my child? |
| | Is there something more I could be doing? |
| | I wonder if my child has been sharing the hard realities of our home life with you lately? |
| How much longer till she is cured? | Is therapy as effective as it might be? |
| | Will our finances be sufficient to carry us through this process? |
| What does my child think of me? | I am worried that I am behaving badly. |
| | Could we talk together in family treatment? |

 **EXERCISE C  Having All Your Questions Answered**  In the space provided, write a question that you have asked or would like to ask your child's professional. Then write the *real* question(s) that underlie your original question.

Question Asked                                            Questions  Requiring an Answer

_____          _____

_____          _____

_____          _____

                                                                 _____

                                                                 _____

                                                                 _____

An astute professional should answer both your spoken and unspoken questions. If she or he does not, you should feel empowered to re-ask the question in another way, as in the exercise, in order to get the response you need. The therapist's responses should confirm that your concerns are legitimate and welcome. Take note of the practitioner's attitude. You can be assured that the therapist who is open to listening actively to you listens competently to your child as well. The therapist who holds you at bay is possibly encouraging your child to do the same thing.

Aside from answers to your questions, you deserve reassurance from the therapist when things are going well. You also need to know what you are doing *right*. Parents need encouragement and bolstering as much as their children do to get through this crisis. A parent's renewed strength and optimism can go a long way to sustain a child through treatment and recovery.

## PROBLEMS WITH PROFESSIONALS

You are in tune with your own child as no one else can be; trust your instincts and respect your own insights even when they are at odds with the most proficient treatment team professionals.

Your child's doctors and therapists do not live with her—you do. At least initially, they may not know as much about who she is and how she behaves as you do. Moreover, even professionals make mistakes. Here are some typical problems. If you have had these problems, make notes about them in the space provided. Recognizing these problems is the first step toward problem resolution.

**The Professional Will Not Share Information with You** Some professionals err in believing that for ethical or other reasons, they cannot give you any information. They do not envision treatment as a partnership among patient, professionals, and parents, nor do they understand the impact of the family system on the individual. They may not know how to perform family therapy and may feel ill equipped to involve the family in a constructive way. Some professionals mistakenly assume that encouraging geographical or emotional distance between parent and child will promote the child's capacity to separate from the family as a healthfully functioning adult. They misinterpret a parent's need to be included in treatment as an intrusion that threatens to undermine their work. Or they may simply not be familiar with eating disorder treatment protocols.

*My child's therapist has the following problems with supplying information:*

_____

_____

_____

_____

**The Professional Has Not Yet Recognized the Disease**     Some of the professionals treating your child may not be aware that an eating disorder exists. They are at the mercy of what the patient tells them, as eating disorders are unlikely to be brought to light through a physical exam, cursory evaluation, or laboratory tests. Eating disordered individuals are reticent to expose the bizarre and destructive behaviors around which their lives center, as these provide their primary source of identity, invigoration, confidence, and self-control even as they create a sense of shame and disgrace.

*My child's professionals may not be fully informed about her condition, as indicated by the following problems:*

_____

_____

_____

_____

**The Professional Does Not Encourage Disclosure**     Some professionals lack the experience or ability to help patients talk about their disorders. Eating disordered individuals fear that admitting disease to a professional might obligate him or her to wrest it away from them. When one mother spoke to her daughter's pediatrician about her hunch that her daughter had bulimia, the doctor made it clear that she would do her best to make the appropriate diagnosis, hoping to evoke a confession in the medical evaluation. However, she warned the mother not to count on any definitive answers. "If your daughter chooses not to tell me, there is no way I can get her to 'fess up,'" she said. However, a savvy professional with a practiced ear knows how to listen to what has *not* been said and how to ask for what she or he needs to know. From a description of values, attitudes, and emotional issues, a medical doctor and certainly a therapist should be able to infer the existence of an eating disorder in the past, intuit it in the present, or foresee its likely onset in the future. Even the most discreet patients are invariably relieved to be found out by someone who can help them.

*My child's professionals may not be skilled enough to help her disclose her disorder, as indicated by the following problems:*

_____

_____

_____

_____

**The Professional Isn't Knowledgeable or at Ease in the Situation**     Professionals sometimes do not feel comfortable dealing with what they consider bizarre and inexplicable disorders. By refusing to acknowledge them, some may inadvertently enable problems rather than eradicate them. One physician prescribed laxatives for a young bulimic patient who claimed she was constipated; another prescribed diuretics for a bulimic patient's self-described "menstrual bloating." An eating disordered woman confessed that she had been seeing her psychiatrist for seven years about other problems without admitting to him that she vomited twenty to thirty times per day. She chose to keep this knowledge from him for fear of risking his rejection. This therapist should have been able to read signs of a predisposition to disease, thereby anticipating and inviting disease disclosure.

Professionals trained prior to the emergence of literature on eating disorders twenty years ago may not have dealt with this illness as part of their training. One such physician, speaking with an eating disorder therapist, asked, "Do you really think these patients actually *do* these frightful things to themselves?" Others err in assuming that treatment techniques that apply in other situations will work for eating disorders as well; they assume that any competent and effective medical or mental health practitioner can adequately perform the tasks of eating disorder treatment. As a result, too many patients remain under the care of physicians and psychotherapists for months or even years without specifically addressing eating disorder issues or working toward effecting a cure.

*My child's professionals may not be comfortable or forthcoming in treating this condition, as indicated by the following problems:*

_____

_____

_____

_____

**The Professional Tries to Handle the Case Singlehandedly**     Some professionals believe that their expertise is all a patient needs, failing to recognize the diversity of skills required to manage the recovery process. Each eating disorder practitioner needs to view his particular role as only one part of a more comprehensive treatment structure. Mental health professionals are certain to be less familiar than internists with the impact of disease on physiology and less familiar than nutritionists with the fine points of nutrition; doctors of medicine may not fully understand the impact of disease as it bears on a patient's emotions and personal interactions.

*My child's therapist or doctor may not see the bigger picture, as indicated by the following problems:*

_____

_____

_____

_____

**The Professional Dominates the Patient**     Therapists and other practitioners who are not aware of their personal biases and vulnerabilities may exert undue control over the patient. A hospitalized patient who requested a modicum of flexibility with her daily menu was told, "Food is medicine. There will be no exceptions." Reminiscent of strict parental controls, this response won the battle but lost the patient, who walked out of the program. Therapists who are not on top of their own feelings and beliefs can inadvertently discourage the patient's freedom of expression. A young anorexic woman in psychotherapy for depression failed to discuss her eating disorder in treatment because, whenever she began to allude to it, her therapist's eyes would well up with tears. The therapist had been anorexic at one time herself.

Beware the therapist who has a personal ax to grind, who imposes erroneous theories or solutions on patients. By taking sides or imposing undue personal biases, therapists may *foster* problems and *create* rifts between family members that may develop into chasms. For example, patients and parents may long for connectedness but the therapist may nevertheless advocate separateness, denying families the opportunity to work together. Beware too of the therapist who sets up a competition in which he or she strives to be seen by the patient as all-nurturing and to paint a picture of the parent as unjust or malicious.

*My child's therapist has demonstrated emotional bias or subjectivity as indicated by the following problems:*

_____

_____

_____

_____

**The Professional Is Unresponsive**    In an effort to remain unbiased and objective, some professionals feel they must act as a clean slate for their patients. One of my patients complained of a former therapist who contributed little more to their sessions than, "Oh, really?" "Uh, huh," or, "How did that feel?" This patient, learning nothing and going nowhere, came to dread going to therapy and left treatment with that professional after three sessions.

*My child's therapist may be so passive that he or she is not giving direction or focus to the work, as indicated by the following problems:*

_____

_____

_____

_____

**The Professional Will Not Negotiate Fees**    Some therapists feel it is unethical to reduce a fee so that treatment can be more affordable, assuming that nothing short of full payment will demonstrate that the patient values the treatment appropriately. But eating disorder treatment can be extremely costly. Especially if your child hasn't the benefits of insurance coverage, it would be helpful to know that your therapist will consider accommodating your financial needs now or in the future as a way of accommodating your child's continuing therapy needs. A fee reduction is typically based on family income, but you might also support your need for a fee accommodation by bringing in a record of your medical expenses to show that they are beyond usual and customary.

*My child's therapist is unbending when it comes to finances, as indicated by the following problems:*

_____

_____

_____

_____

## A Case Study

Janet was anorexic. Her therapist told her parents to stay out of their daughter's affairs and intentionally kept them in the dark about her condition. At one point the therapist left town for three weeks, and during that time, Janet's pediatrician informed the parents that their daughter's weight had dropped precipitously, making her a candidate for hospitalization. This couple then faced the responsibility for making this critical decision. Undereducated and uninformed about Janet's condition, they did not know if they had time to wait for the therapist to return, if intensified outpatient work would be a sufficient alternative in the meantime, if a day treatment program would answer Janet's needs, or if she might die or be permanently injured if not hospitalized immediately. Because the professionals treating Janet had never formed a unified team, these parents were unable to get much help from the physician either.

"We were flying blind," they explained later. "Our daughter's very life was in our hands. In seven months of treatment, her therapist had communicated with us only three times, all of which were at our initiative. She refused to involve us in the therapy process, and then wouldn't disclose any information about Janet's condition when we asked, for fear of breaching her confidence. Everything rested on our decision which we were obviously in no position to make. It was a nightmare."

Yet this problem could have been unequivocally and easily avoided through proper communication, professional to professional and professional to parent.

 **EXERCISE D** Hearing What Professionals Say  Like everyone else, professionals miscommunicate. The most common error is not communicating completely enough. Incomplete comments are particularly prone to being misconstrued and therefore can be dangerous. Incomplete thoughts provide opportunities for listeners to project their own biases, to hear what they want or need to hear. Read each of the following statements made by professionals and, in the space provided, write down, first, what the listener might have heard and, second, what the speaker might have meant. Appendix A contains some sample answers, but other answers are also appropriate. The goal is not to come up with the exact answers given in Appendix A but to gain some appreciation of how easily miscommunication occurs and how critical it is to listen carefully and ask clarifying questions.

1. Therapist to parent: "Don't bug her about her food. Mealtimes should be free-choice times."

*What was heard:*

_____

_____

*What was meant:*

_____

_____

2. Pediatrician to patient: "You'd better stop putting on weight, or we may have to send you to see a nutritionist."

*What was heard:*

_____

_____

*What was meant:*

_____

_____

3. Pediatrician to patient: "If you want to lose weight, let's put you on 1,200 calories a day."

*What was heard:*

_____

_____

*What was meant:*

_____

_____

4. Internist to patient: "You must gain five pounds in order to return to college in the fall."

*What was heard:*

_____

_____

*What was meant:*

_____

_____

5. Internist to patient: "If you continue to refuse to eat properly, you can forget about playing softball anymore."

*What was heard:*

_____

_____

*What was meant:*

_____

_____

6. Pediatrician to parent: "Leave it alone for now. If the problem gets bad enough, you can always hospitalize her."
   *What was heard:*

   _____

   _____

   *What was meant:*

   _____

   _____

7. Internist to parent: "He's sixteen—it's time to let him make his own decisions."
   *What was heard:*

   _____

   _____

   *What was meant:*

   _____

   _____

8. Internist to patient: "Great job! You haven't lost any weight."
   *What was heard:*

   _____

   _____

   *What was meant:*

   _____

   _____

9. Internist to patient: "You look really good. No need to come back for a checkup for six months."
   *What was heard:*

   _____

   _____

*What was meant:*

_____

_____

10. Internist to parent: "Beware of monitoring by a physician. It could make your child feel like an invalid, or frighten her."

*What was heard:*

_____

_____

*What was meant:*

_____

_____

11. Therapist to parent: "If we can take care of the emotional issues, the food issues will straighten themselves out."

*What was heard:*

_____

_____

*What was meant:*

_____

_____

12. Therapist to patient: "If you lose any more weight, I'll stop working with you."

*What was heard:*

_____

_____

*What was meant:*

_____

_____

13. Therapist to parent: "When she's ready, she'll respond to you."

*What was heard:*

_____

_____

*What was meant:*

_____

_____

14. Nutritionist to patient: "It's okay to eat the same foods over and over as long as you keep eating."

    *What was heard:*

    _____

    _____

    *What was meant:*

    _____

    _____

The complexity of communication can be either a deterrent or a boon to human connectedness, depending on the quality of the skills that people bring to their interactions. Good communication skills are not difficult to learn. Discussions in family therapy and diligent practice at home provide two opportunities to improve these skills. (Active listening skills are described in Chapter Three.)

## Managing Your Own Biases in Choosing Professionals

Your personal biases and issues could lead you to make poor professional choices. Parents with little tolerance for candor, conflict, or the difficult issues that recovery engenders may seek to avoid dealing with their own emotions and confronting those of their child; they may view their child as fragile and unable to endure the rigors of effective and purposeful treatment. In either case, parents may seek out professionals who enable the child to follow the path of least resistance, doing what is most comfortable for themselves, rather than what is most productive for the child.

**EXERCISE E Choosing Unwisely** Here are some descriptions of parents making poor choices in choosing or dealing with their child's professionals. As you read each item, consider whether you have ever fallen into any of these or similar traps with your own child. In the space provided, note your similar situation and how you have already resolved it or how you are planning to resolve it.

1. The mother of a young boy was told by his pediatrician that he had anorexia. Incensed, and probably frightened about implications for the family, she sought out another pediatrician. This one told her that her son's diet and precipitous weight loss were "fine" and to leave him alone. She chose to stay with

the second pediatrician, preferring his diagnosis despite the evidence that her child had a problem.

_____

_____

_____

_____

2. Just as a young man began to make recovery headway, his parents suddenly took the initiative to find a new therapist for him, one who would be less "disease oriented." They found the "perfect person," a therapist who told the patient that he "needn't worry anymore about having to gain weight." All he would need to do now was "what was right for his body." When this new therapist contacted the nutritionist on the case, she said she wanted to discuss the patient's "little problem with food." "*Little* problem?" the nutritionist responded. "Are we talking about the same patient?"

_____

_____

_____

_____

3. The parents of an anorexic young adult were very happy to abide by a therapist's advice to stay out of their daughter's treatment as they hated confrontation and preferred to leave the problem to the therapist to "fix." They were happy not to be asked to engage in family treatment.

_____

_____

_____

_____

4. A parent who called a psychotherapist to make an appointment for her child warned the therapist not to talk about food with the girl. "It's a loaded issue," she said, "and will only put her on edge. Better to leave that one alone."

_____

_____

_____

_____

## PARENTS ARE TEAM PLAYERS

As the first manager of your child's case, you have responsibility for gathering the treatment team together and coordinating its initial efforts. The professional you contact first may recommend a ready-made team of individuals already accustomed to working with each other. Otherwise the task falls to you to find individual players who are competent, experienced, and willing to cooperate with each other. You and they become part of a team, working together mutually and openly to achieve a common purpose.

Once the team comes together, its management is generally passed to the primary therapist or internist, who will take responsibility for coordinating team efforts thereafter. Still, you will want to be watchful that treatment does not veer off course. Even with an active and proficient team, you will need to continually communicate to them the changes that are happening at home. Professionals who are genuinely concerned will be grateful for your input.

 **EXERCISE F Advocating Within the Treatment Team**   Your intervention and feedback may be needed to inform, motivate, or hold accountable the professionals in charge or to otherwise tweak their behavior. Read each of the following actions parents of a recovering anorexic teenager might think of taking now that their daughter, though appearing to eat well, has begun to lose weight again. If the action is appropriate and productive, circle Y for yes. If it is an action parents should avoid, circle N for no. (See Appendix A for the answers.)

1.  Y/N   Begin to monitor what the child is eating, and take privileges away if she can't regain control of herself.

2.  Y/N   Mention the weight gain to various team members.

3.  Y/N   Discuss with team members why the gain is worrisome to the parents.

4.  Y/N   Threaten to replace the team members if they cannot reverse the child's weight loss.

5.  Y/N   Ask to be told what gets discussed in therapy or other professional sessions.

6.  Y/N   Ask for team members' support or to be included in a team meeting.

7.  Y/N   Ask if team members have been in touch with each other about this problem.

8. Y/N  Request that team members communicate more regularly with each other.

9. Y/N  Request that team members get back to the parents with their ideas and suggestions.

10. Y/N  Ask team members not to mention to the child that the parents have been in touch with them.

## A TEAM APART: YOUR HEALTH INSURANCE COMPANY

Parents have the potential to become powerful child advocates with the insurance company financing their child's mental health treatment. This is the age of managed care, of restrictions in services provided and number of sessions allowed. Insurance agencies are reluctant to fund treatment for diseases that resist cure within the prescribed six to twelve sessions. Obviously, eating disorders fall into this category. Severe cases that would once have been given two to seven months of inpatient care now are offered two days to two weeks. Seventy-pound patients are now told they must be sicker before they can be helped. Every third case that needs hospitalization is denied access to this form of care today.[3] The parent whose sole motivation is the well-being of her or his child often has a better outcome in educating these companies and lobbying for the child than professionals do. However, when hospital and medical office personnel specialize in dealing with insurance affairs, do not hesitate to use them to take advantage of their services.

Remember that insurance companies are profit driven. If you are seeking personal growth for your child, their goals differ from yours. Insurance companies are not inclined to cover conditions other than those that are clearly defined, concrete, and reparable in a finite number of sessions. Although most companies will not cover eating disorders per se, they will generally cover medical complications of the disease and limited treatment of the accompanying emotional conditions. It is the highly knowledgeable parent who approaches the company with diagnoses, goals, and strategies in hand, who is most likely to convince an insurer that the most efficacious and comprehensive treatment is also the most economical treatment. If you are refused access to extended services or denied services from additional professional disciplines, it is your privilege to make an appeal demanding a forty-eight-hour resolution. Professionals working with your child should be happy to support your arguments with records and documentation. When appeals fail, seek legal counsel.[4] Do not hesitate to cite biological and genetic evidence of eating disorders to ensure that your case receives the same insurance reimbursement as other medical and biological psychiatric disorders. (This is known as *parity.*)

Typical outpatient recoveries can cost $100,000 or more over the years. Hospitalization can cost between $570 and $1,400 per day.[5] If, after all the lobbying efforts and appeals have been made, your coverage runs out, you may need to seek out other ways to accommodate your child's needs. You might become more active in guiding your child's recovery yourself. You might consider transferring the therapy work to a public or subsidized mental health clinic that offers a sliding fee scale determined by the patient's (or patient's family's) capacity to pay. Ask your child's current therapist to make a personal referral for you to an experienced eating disorder therapist at such a clinic. Remember that hospitals have sliding fee scales and budget plans. Some states have insurance programs designed specifically for the hard-to-insure individual. You might check out these alternatives. In some cases, it might be appropriate to apply for public assistance. You may be dealing with this recovery over the long haul and must realistically plan for that eventuality in terms of accessing and sustaining both emotional and financial resources.

**Activity Preparing to Talk to Your Insurer** Before contacting your insurance company, you will need to do your homework. Plan how you will make your case. Consult with your team, first, for advice and suggestions. Your child is sick. She has a disease, and medical insurance covers illness. In making your appeal, speak directly to a psychology liaison or other higher-up. Ask to speak to that person's supervisor if you still are not getting satisfaction. Keep a record of the names of the people you have spoken to and of those you might still need to contact. Don't stop until you have spoken to all who have the power to help you. Be prepared with the following information:

- What your child has accomplished in treatment.
- What more she needs to accomplish.
- How effective her current team is.
- Why the next step is critical in your child's recovery.

- The corroborating evidence from team members.
- Why it will be more cost effective in the long run to have your child engage in treatment and recovery *now.*

## EVALUATING THE FIRST SESSION

There is much to be gleaned about the potential for treatment success in the first therapy session and about the person with whom you and your child will be working. In the first session, the patient and possibly her parents, face to face with the prospective psychotherapist, assess whether or not the chemistry is good. It is important for you to interpret the events of that first therapeutic hour correctly, for it is here that problems are defined and choices are laid out about what must be done. You may not always be in a position to play an intrinsic part in these choices, but more often than not, you will have some influence in bringing child and health professional together.

 **EXERCISE G** **Assessing the Quality of the First Therapy Session**   The therapist should accomplish most, if not all, of the following tasks in the first therapy session. (You would do well to request a double session for your initial meeting. You will need the time.) Read each of the following items, and if it was addressed in the session, circle Y for yes. If it was not, circle N for no. The more yes answers the better. You can complete this exercise yourself in response to the first family therapy session and ask your child, if she is agreeable, to complete it in response to her first individual therapy session (substituting *I, mine,* and *me* for *we, our,* and *us*).

*With regard to the dynamics of the moment, the therapist*

1. Y/N   Started where we were, acknowledging and responding to our feelings about being at the session.

2. Y/N   Questioned and responded to our feelings about facing disease and its recovery.

3. Y/N   Reassured us and gave us hope for recovery, minimizing fears and defensiveness that could otherwise have sabotaged our progress.

4. Y/N   Helped each individual define his or her agenda (hopes) for the meeting and for treatment and was responsive to these diverse agendas.

*With regard to family dynamics, the therapist*

5.  Y/N   Noted family attitudes, patterns of interaction, distortions, values, and myths.

6.  Y/N   Rectified our distortions.

7.  Y/N   Recognized strengths in the family.

8.  Y/N   Determined how each person's individual goals and problem perceptions differed.

9.  Y/N   Allowed us to define our mutual problems and goals as a family.

*With regard to the eating disorder, the therapist*

10.  Y/N   Educated us about what an eating disorder is and what it signifies, its impact on the body, mind, and family relationships.

11.  Y/N   Listened to our questions about the disease and cleared up confusions.

12.  Y/N   Explained the intention of disease to promote survival and thereby created an atmosphere of optimism about the patient and about her prospects for recovery.

*With regard to treatment, the therapist*

13.  Y/N   Helped us anticipate the patient's ongoing ambivalence toward recovering.

14.  Y/N   Explained what to expect from treatment, describing how treatment goals will be addressed, assessed, and updated on a continual and mutual basis.

15.  Y/N   Informed us about treatment options.

16.  Y/N   Introduced the concept of the treatment team, interpreting the roles of the various participating professionals and describing how the treatment team functions. Nutritional services and family therapy were recommended as important adjuncts to individual treatment.

17.  Y/N   Obtained signed releases for the transfer of confidential therapeutic information among team members.

18.  Y/N   Required a prompt appointment with a medical doctor for a physical examination. Discussed the benefits of medication (if a medication alternative appeared appropriate).

*With regard to recovery, the therapist*

19. Y/N   Educated us about the unique nature of eating disorder recovery.

20. Y/N   Defined appropriate roles for each of us to play in recovery.

21. Y/N   Offered everyone permission not to be perfect. Described how stumbling blocks can ultimately lead to emotional growth.

*With regard to the therapy relationship, the therapist*

22. Y/N   Invited the patient and family members to contact the therapist whenever necessary, with or without appointment and gave instructions for therapeutic emergencies.

23. Y/N   Encouraged the patient and family members to discuss, rather than act out, any ambivalences about continuing treatment.

24. Y/N   Laid the foundation for a fulfilling therapist-patient relationship, establishing enough trust that the patient feels liked and supported and is willing or even eager to return.

As you came away from the session, did you feel satisfied that you had gotten much of what you needed? Though the foundation for treatment may not yet be completely set, you should feel a firmness of footing. Note that cumbersome in-depth histories and details about early life should take a back seat to establishing a trusting working relationship and meeting the patient's and family's pressing needs at the moment.

 **EXERCISE H** Assessing Your Child's Response to the First Few Therapy Sessions   To evaluate your child's initial reaction to treatment, read each of the following possible reactions. Does it apply to your child? Circle Y for yes, N for no. Most, if not all, of the answers should be yes. Go ahead and ask your child some of these questions if you aren't certain about what you have observed.

1. Y/N   My child likes the therapist, and will return for additional sessions willingly.

2. Y/N   My child has begun to learn about herself; specifically, she is beginning to assess where else in her life, besides eating, there may be inflexibility and extremism; she is beginning to recognize her fears, her anger, and her misconceptions.

3. Y/N  My child has come away from therapy recognizing her strengths.

4. Y/N  My child has come away from therapy knowing what to expect from treatment. She knows it will keep her on track.

5. Y/N  My child understands that everything said in confidence will remain in confidence, short of her intending to do harm to herself or others.

6. Y/N  My child feels accepted, legitimized, and cared for by the therapist.

7. Y/N  My child understands the masking role of abnormal eating habits and knows that she is not crazy.

8. Y/N  My child recognizes her own ambivalence about treatment and knows the consequences of not recovering.

9. Y/N  My child understands that treatment choices are essentially hers to make if she can make them responsibly.

10. Y/N  My child has begun to grasp the ironies of this disease: the less frequently one eats, the slower one's metabolism, and the more one gains weight; the more frequently one eats, the more normal the metabolic rate, and the less weight one gains.

11. Y/N  My child can see that the need to control food represents the need to establish controls in other life spheres.

12. Y/N  My child understands that therapy is a place where food will be discussed without shame and for a good reason.

13. Y/N  My child is respectful of my feelings, needs, role in treatment.

14. Y/N  My child understands that she must rethink what constitutes failure.

Having the best professionals in place is a major step forward. Chapter Six explains what you can expect in the recovery process upon which you and your child have now embarked.

# Recovery

As you face your child's recovery, keep in mind that eating disorders fulfill important, even noble, functions for their victims, making them particularly difficult to dislodge. Do not expect recovery from this disease to be synonymous with feeling better—not immediately, anyway. By letting go of disease and the security it provides, your child can expect to come face to face with his own imperfection in a less than perfect world. At the same time, he will discover strengths he never knew he had, enabling him to arrive ultimately at a recognition and acceptance of himself as a total person. There is no *right way* to recover; there are, however, guidelines that can make the recovery process more effective. Eating disorder recovery is based on two premises: People can and do change, and in the search for solutions, if one thing doesn't work, something else will.

*What Parents Can Do*

1. Understand that you can play a significant role in your child's recovery.

2. Mentor the treatment process, supporting and facilitating it where possible.

3. Be openly curious about what might make the process more effective.

4. Keep talking, asking questions, and expressing what you think and feel.

5. Remember how good your intentions and goals are.

6. Don't back down in the face of intimidating professionals or your child's hostility.

7. Monitor your own attitudes. Parents' fear of fat can lead to dieting in children.

8. Lead by example; live your values. Role-model a lifestyle that avoids excesses.

9. Educate your child, but do not unfairly prejudice his choices regarding treatment. Know your limits and maintain your boundaries.

10. Consider making your own changes, and get help for yourself if you feel you need it.

# Understanding the Recovery Process

Groping one's way through the uncertainty of the recovery process provides superb practice for dealing with life. The task at hand is not about tidying up a recovery, which is naturally disorderly, but learning instead to navigate through the disarray, making corrective adjustments as one proceeds, confident of one's capacity to stay afloat.

## WHAT EATING DISORDER RECOVERY IS ABOUT

*Habit is habit . . . and not to be flung out the window by any man, but coaxed downstairs a step at a time.*

Mark Twain

I found this a surprisingly tough chapter to write, a testimony to the obscurity and ambiguity of the recovery process. It is often difficult even to discern what the patient is recovering *from*. Is it from a poor self-image? From obsessive thinking about food? From destructive eating behaviors? Once his eating habits are corrected, must his thinking about food be changed before we can say recovery has occurred? If the recovered individual harbors a remnant of fear about food or becoming fat after his eating habits and attitudes are healthy, has he really recovered? One young mother who seems totally recovered from her eating disorder nevertheless worries that her healing may not be complete enough to guarantee that none of her old, distorted attitudes about food will be communicated to her young children.

How do people recover, and how do they stay recovered? Why do they relapse? Is it because they need more of what worked or because they need something different? Even from the therapist's vantage point I cannot honestly *know* what each individual's unique personal recovery experience has been and exactly how these experiences differ one from another. There are no medical tests that definitively confirm when recovery has happened or how. Indeed much of the recovery process occurs in the course of daily living after the patient has left treatment. Self-reporting of recovery is a highly subjective process as well, dependent on the patient's capacity to be self-aware and expressive of his inner experience.

I was in the middle of the dance floor at a friend's child's bat mitzvah celebration one evening, when a beautiful young woman came running up to me and threw herself into my arms. My mind flipped frenziedly through the hundreds of sessions I had conducted over the years with countless young patients in an attempt to place this lovely young woman. The face and body, though familiar, in no way matched the gaunt and sunken appearance I knew when I had been treating her.

Frannie was almost unrecognizable now for the robust and glowing health that she exuded. In treatment with me for anorexia before she had moved out of town, she had been through several hospitalizations in a long-term battle with a disease that at times seemed to be winning out. After her family moved away, she continued treatment in her new location. If not for this serendipitous meeting, would I ever have surmised how magnificently she had survived?

Though the majority of people who recover from an eating disorder typically stay recovered, some individuals feel themselves to be *in recovery*, actively and continually through time, like those with addictions. As it is unrealistic and countertherapeutic for a person to remain in treatment indefinitely, assessing recovery results as people continue to live out their lives remains a perpetual challenge for surveyors. There is nothing as gratifying for a therapist as being contacted years later at the time of a former patient's college graduation, first job promotion, marriage, first child, and so on.

## Why Recover?

When an eating disorder takes over, it saps the life of its host. It limits emotional resourcefulness, flexibility, personal comfort with self and others, and the capacity to assume control and take initiative in most if not all spheres of existence. Moreover, eating disorders result in damaging physiological changes, such as electrolyte imbalances and arrhythmias that can lead to cardiac arrest and other organ dysfunctions to mention a few.

## How Recovery Happens

Recovery happens when the patient wants to become healthy, and when he achieves a healthy body weight with some degree of emotional comfort around sustaining this weight. Behavioral recovery signs are normalized eating, a sustained abstinence from the binge-purge cycle, and in women, the restoration of menstruation; emotional recovery signs include the patient's capacity to deal with feelings and problems more productively, using devices other than food for coping. Eating disorder recovery is inspired through the therapist's capacity to connect with the patient's individual strengths. There is no one definitive formula for success that all patients can follow to get from point A to point B. The recovery process is one of emotional and behavioral growth, plateaus, and breakthroughs, dotted with recurring regressions that become less significant as recovery proceeds (see Exhibit 6.1).

During therapy, the patient gives up a sustaining partnership with disease to find authenticity in an intimate healing partnership with the therapist. This in turn spurs the development of the patient's alliance with his own maturing self. By relinquishing the dysfunctional behaviors that mask true emotions, the patient ultimately comes to know and accept all his feelings fully, becoming an emotionally integrated person and thereby maximizing his options for solving life's problems. The answers and solutions he seeks lie within himself; the well-schooled patient, through his self-encounter—like Dorothy, the Tin Man, the Scarecrow, and the Cowardly Lion in Oz—eventually comes to appreciate that there is no wizard as powerful as the resourceful self. Therein lies the dramatic variability of recovery experiences.

Recovery tends to take a long time because it requires so many changes, choices, and commitments:

- A cognitive understanding of the problem.
- A cognitive acceptance of the problem.
- An emotional acceptance of the problem.
- An understanding of how food and exercise imbalances are part of a bigger picture of life imbalances.

## Exhibit 6.1. Behavioral and Emotional Growth Happen Concurrently but Not Necessarily at the Same Rate.

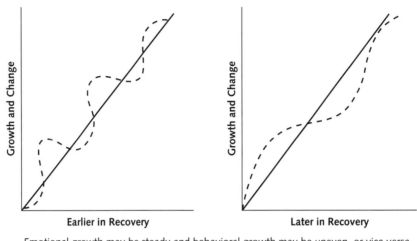

Emotional growth may be steady and behavioral growth may be uneven, or vice versa.

- - - Behavioral growth ——— Emotional growth

- A capacity to *name* his feelings rather than respond to them behaviorally.
- An active choice to let the disease go.
- An active choice to find alternative, less damaging coping tools.
- An active choice to find the strength and courage to take the risks required to recover. (These risks take the form of behavioral changes and emotional risks.)
- An emotional versatility that allows him to accept, tolerate, and move beyond discomfort.
- An active choice to restore weight.
- An improved trust in self and others; improved self-esteem.
- A capacity to sustain a forward momentum in a sometimes slow and difficult process.

Eventually, the newly developing coping lifestyle defined by these changes and choices begins to feel like the better lifestyle. Understanding how much your child has to do to achieve recovery puts you in a better position to mentor his progress.

## Triggers to Recovery

What inspires a person to feel ready to let go of an eating disorder? The answer to this question is as hard to discern as the reason why a person initially succumbs to disease. It is often difficult to identify a specific event or point in time. Sometimes, timing and maturational life circumstances make the difference; at other times, resolve or fear may be motivational forces. Factors that touch off recovery never occur in a vacuum; as the well-prepared garden yields the healthiest blooms, the ultimate *leap into health* is founded on an accrued sequence of therapeutic and nutritional achievements.

Recovery preparedness includes the patient's *developing cognitive* capacities to understand and accept resistance and then develop strategies to counteract it. Recovery begins with his ability to recognize the sensations of recovery (the extreme discomfort of feeling "huge," for example) and his choice to stay with those feelings. Recovery begins with the patient's choice to assume control of that which is truly in his control—himself.

## Case Study

In recovery for six years, a young, anorexic woman who worked well in treatment but who could not commit herself to eating better and gaining weight, took a job in the "real world" after college. As a schoolteacher she found herself to be a superb educator and capable of developing loving relationships with her students. She became romantically involved with a fellow teacher, and meals became very much part of their relationship as they spent more and more time together.

She began to make plans to move out of her parents' home. She could begin to see herself now in a different light, imagining herself a married woman with children. She understood that her ability to handle food without fear would be critical in creating a wholesome life for her future family. It would lie at the heart of making a home, of nurturing her children, of bringing family and friends together, of religious ceremony and rootedness in her ethnic culture. Food preparation and consumption would be important mechanisms through which to teach her own children to take care of themselves as balanced, choice-making individuals with judgment and control.

Functions that once had been challenging were becoming second nature. Her initiative and success in her job and her newfound feelings of intimacy and normalcy ultimately were transferred to a new initiative with food. "Before, I would simply not have tolerated taking risks with food," she reported. "Now, I am getting so used to taking risks of all kinds and doing so well with them, eating is becoming just one more of my many victories." She also made certain to begin some very focused work with her nutritionist at this pivotal time in her recovery, after having been away from that process for some time.

 **EXERCISE A** **Becoming Inspired to Recover**   Recovery rarely if ever takes the form of epiphany, but is instead a gradual and subtle coming together of growth factors over time. The young woman in the case study had worked hard and accomplished much in eating disorder treatment, but life circumstances completed her recovery. To gain a further understanding of the factors, or triggers, in recovery, answer the following questions about the case study in the space provided.

1. What do you see as the contributing factors to this woman's eventual recovery?

   _____

   _____

   _____

2. How might things have been different for her had she not had the benefit of her previous emotional and nutritional growth through eating disorder recovery?

   _____

   _____

   _____

## Setting Recovery Goals

Defining and refining both long- and short-term treatment goals is a primary task throughout recovery. Far and away your child's most significant goal is to take responsibility for his accomplishments in treatment—to recognize what personal success is made of, how it feels, and how his initiatives have brought it about. He must comprehend that improvements in recovery, as in life, do not happen through chance, luck, or magic; things get better because the individual makes the choice and commitment to take purposeful action.

A full and complete recovery may prove to be a goal too threatening for your child to aspire to at the start of the treatment process. So even if his initial commitment is to something less than total cure, the legitimacy of that goal must be respected. One very significant goal at treatment outset for all concerned is to have patient, parents, and professionals eventually come to want the same things and to come ever closer to attaining them.

## How Long Will Recovery Take?

Recovery time is highly variable. Depending on the emotional resiliency and underlying health of the patient's personality, some eating disorders can be licked in a matter of months; others may take years or even decades. A study of hospitalized adolescents found that the average anorexic recovery took from fifty-seven to seventy-nine months.[1] It is reasonable to assume that the vast majority of adolescents who do not require hospitalization recover quicker. In another study, 77 percent of eating disordered individuals reported duration of illness from one to fifteen years. More specifically, 30 percent reported duration from one to five years; 31 percent reported duration from six to ten years; and 16 percent reported duration from eleven to fifteen years.[2] But even short of total recovery, the recovery process can be counted on to improve the patient's quality of life incrementally, with benefits of recovery efforts beginning to appear almost immediately. Don't become discouraged. With perseverance, turnarounds do occur in most instances.

## Is It Ever Too Late to Recover?

It ordinarily takes several months for malnourished organs to regain their healthful function once an eating disordered patient returns to his natural weight. Though gastrointestinal symptoms of an eating disorder may be severe, 100 percent of them can be alleviated through normal eating. Electrolyte imbalances that cause heart arrhythmias can be reversed. Certain kinds of damage however, are irreversible: the heart and brain have been shown to diminish in size as much as 10 to 20 percent when malnourishment is extensive and long-term;[3] bones damaged by osteoporosis never fully restore themselves to predisease health for many former anorexics, leaving the patient with increased long-term risk for fractures.[4] The lower the body weight and the more protracted the illness, the more extensive the damage to bone mineral density. Fertility is usually impaired in individuals with a history of amenorrhea. Excessive vomiting can be highly corrosive to the hard dental tissues, and these dental changes are not reversible. The condition can be remediated only through certain local measures and prosthetic dentistry to prevent further deterioration.[5]

I have, through the years, questioned a number of physicians about the capacity of the human body to subsist in spite of extreme malnutrition and a compromised physical condition. No one knows a definitive answer to this question. What we do know is that the body is a highly resilient organism designed to survive and procreate against all odds and adversity, resourceful in its capacity to sustain itself and compensate for what it lacks. Yet, at some point, even the most finely crafted machine will break down if not maintained; if, when, and under what circumstances this could happen to your eating disordered child simply cannot be predicted. But once again be assured, with early intervention and the right care, recovery odds are strong.

> **Activity Food for Thought** Do you harbor specific fears about your child's health now? What are they? Do you have fears about the effects of disease on your child's future life? What are they? Have you spoken to a physician about them? If not, why not? Some of your fears may be unfounded. Have you spoken with your child about them? If not, why not?

## BEWARE OF RECOVERY PITFALLS

Recovery from eating disorders is a process that can be as elusive of and impenetrable to understanding as the disease itself. However, it is possible to identify various factors that make recovery especially slippery.

### Recovery Deterrents

Becoming aware of the deterrents to recovery may help you to avoid or withstand them.

• Recovery from eating disorders lacks a logical sequence; it is unpredictable and seemingly arbitrary, a particularly difficult notion for patients wanting certainty and control. The only inevitability in this recovery is that when there is extreme weight loss, refeeding and weight restoration are a prerequisite to the capacity to recover.

• From recovery's inception to conclusion, patients resist cure. It is the *disease,* not the recovery from disease, that gives the patient a sense of control and balance. The recovery process is initially perceived by the patient as requiring a retreat from his primary support system, thereby creating discomfort.

- Eating disorders offer solutions of sorts to real-life problems. When distressed about his difficulty establishing successful relationships with members of the opposite sex, an anorexic college student's solution was to try to become more muscular through more ambitious workouts. In recovery, the patient is required to integrate more appropriate and lasting solutions.

- Recovery cannot happen without simultaneous attention to eating behaviors as well as the underlying emotions that drive them. Eating disordered patients commonly complain about therapists who refuse to discuss food, considering it tangential to their work with patients' thoughts and feelings, or too fraught with struggles and hostility. Such compartmentalizing can become an obstacle to recovery. Describing a former therapist, a patient of mine complained, "I was refusing to eat any foods prepared with more than three ingredients, and all she wanted to discuss were my emotions!"

- It is a cruel irony that individuals stricken with eating disorders are generally the *least* prepared emotionally to handle recovery. This is because the emotional tools required for recovery are not yet present within the disordered individual as he approaches the challenge. *Before he can recover from this disease, he must regain or first develop the internal emotional resources and coping skills required to undergo and withstand the process through which he will eventually heal.*

- Ineffective or inconsistent communication between team members can promote *splitting,* in which team members (parents, the child, and professionals) turn against each other through unhealthy alliances and taking sides.

- Early onset of disease and structural personality dysfunctions may extend the recovery process. Also, those eating disordered patients whose symptoms have been of longer duration at the time they enter treatment and who have a history of substance abuse have poorer long-term recovery outcomes.

## Recovery Red Flags

The following are common pitfalls that parents, patients, and professionals encounter throughout the recovery process. Consider whether you might be vulnerable to any of them.

### Being Too Quick to Applaud Recovery Efforts     Don't underestimate the tenacity of a eating disorder, which can hang on despite everyone's efforts. Parents need to respect the enormity of their child's allegiance to disease, even after

years of treatment and when on the verge of full recovery. Threatened with not being allowed to return to college, an anorexic student gained five pounds on the instructions of her physician. Her parents and doctor believed that because she had started to eat and had begun to gain back some weight, she was as good as cured. As soon as she was away, however, she lost this weight and more. They had celebrated too early.

**Equating Weight Gain with Recovery**     Weight gain is significant in that it gives an anorexic person back his body as well as restoring the capacity for clarity of mind, emotion, and perception. Weight restoration is a prerequisite for *but not synonymous with* complete recovery, as temporary or partial weight gain is not a valid measure of true inner changes. Most anorexics are capable of devising routines to gain—and lose—specific amounts of weight at will.

In the case just mentioned of the college student, a two-pound weight gain accomplished through a wholesome eating regime with proper intentions would have been a more optimistic event than her five-pound gain. Because this young woman was never expected by others to regain her preanorexic set-point weight (which might have put her over the top of the recovery hurdle), she has not yet recovered fully. Whether or not to set extraordinary weight goals for a recovering patient at a specific time is a tough call. Asking too much too soon can spur a rebellious response and defeatism. Asking not enough can lead to a prime opportunity lost, as proved to be the case here.

**Assuming Your Child Will Learn How to Eat Properly on His Own**     Habits die hard. Patients may need supervision or an enforced structure for their food intake until they learn to create their own internal structures. After learning the *correct* way to eat, your child will find his *own* way to eat healthfully.

**Believing Common Misconceptions About Food and Eating**     In addition to the myths mentioned in Chapter One, there is a commonly held myth that 1,200 calories is enough food for a healthy woman of average height and weight to consume on a daily basis. In fact, 1,200 calories is the minimum amount required for the average person who is bedridden to maintain his or her weight. If parents are perplexed that their child is not losing weight on so few calories per day, it is a good bet that they are seeing the effects of a considerably lowered metabolic rate or a child who is eating at times and in places that remain undisclosed to them.

**Losing Track of What an Eating Disorder Is and What Recovery Is For**    It is easy to forget that an eating disorder is a disease with distinctive characteristics. According to one young woman, "I think my problem is that I am spoiled. I want what I want, and I get what I want . . . but that's my personality—not my eating disorder." Another patient who remains unable to let go of disease wonders if she has "had it too long for it to be an eating disorder anymore." She assumes that by this time it would have become "an indelible behavior disorder that is an intrinsic part of my personality." Another young woman describing her reluctance to recover said that once she is well she will no longer be able to have things her way: "I would have no guarantees about what life would be like anymore."

**Failing to Deal with Your Own Feelings of Discouragement**    Dealing with your own feelings of discouragement can be challenging. Because of your child's resistance to recovery, the healing process is often slow enough to frustrate your efforts to remain supportive. Ongoing decision making can be exhausting, expenses can be great, and your parental fears can be extensive, diminishing your emotional strength. So as not to lose your perspective, keep your support systems in place and keep on talking, expressing your concerns and feelings, your hopes and satisfactions. If you lose sight of the various facets of your child's resistance to recovery and your own discouragement, you become more at risk and vulnerable to obstacles that you cannot recognize or name. By defining and anticipating resistance and your reaction to it, you make the inevitable faltering less of a threat.

**Failing to Recognize Regression as a Recovery Fact of Life**    If you fail to understand that regressions and backslides are normal and in fact essential during recovery, you may overlook significant opportunities for learning and change. Regression and stagnation can provide necessary time-outs, permitting the patient to regroup and gather forces for the next advance. They reflect an internal wisdom, regulating the amount of change that the patient can safely tolerate at any given time.

**EXERCISE B** **Jumping to Conclusions** Have you found yourself or your child caught up in any of the following misconceptions about recovery? Read each item, and circle Y for yes, N for no.

1. Y/N  Though your child continues to count calories and rigidly control his fat intake, he has been able to gain back some weight, so you feel he must be as good as recovered.

2. Y/N  You feel your child is not making progress. You keep hoping he will make steady, measurable improvements, and instead you find him sporadically falling back into old, destructive eating habits. It feels to you like things are always the same or getting worse.

3. Y/N  When your child made a commitment to therapy, you became hopeful, but the breakthrough you anticipated hasn't materialized, and now you fear he may never be able to fulfill the tasks of recovery.

4. Y/N  Your child refused to eat bread before he began his recovery. Now that he has consented to eat one slice per day you assume he is on his way to recovery. He admits that he still worries when he cannot see his bones sticking out anymore, but he too assumes that he must be over the worst of the disease.

5. Y/N  Your child, having temporarily lost ground in his recovery progress, assumed that all his past efforts had been futile, putting him back to square one in his recovery efforts.

6. Y/N  You've charted your child's recovery course based on his gains in self-esteem. Assuming that he feels better about himself now, it stands to reason in your mind that his disease will soon disappear accordingly.

7. Y/N  While he was involved with his eating disorder, your child assumed that everything he did had to be perfect. Now that he has relaxed his standards for perfection and his expectations for himself have become less stringent, you fear he'll end up losing all control and will get fat again.

8. Y/N  During recovery, your child seems to be feeling worse, not better. He is moodier and more volatile. You are concerned that something has gone awry with his treatment or that somehow his recovery has made him dislike or distrust you now more than ever before.

9. *I have experienced the following specific examples of these misconceptions during my child's recovery:*

_____

_____

_____

**EXERCISE C** Rehearsing Recovery Dialogues   Here are some typical comments that a recovering child makes. Parents need to respond by drawing on their understanding of the recovery process—how it feels, and why it is essential for the child to stick with it. The comments illustrate the confusions your child may have about the recovery in which he is engaged. Read each comment and, in the space provided, outline the response you might offer. (See Appendix A for a discussion of these points.)

1. Why can't I find a girlfriend? My recovery is doing me no good at all.
   *Your response:*

   _____

   _____

   _____

2. You *know* I'm better. I ate out with you at that sushi restaurant, didn't I?
   *Your response:*

   _____

   _____

   _____

3. I ate a cookie last night, so for sure I can't be anorexic.
   *Your response:*

   _____

   _____

   _____

4. I just can't see how what I eat today will effect the quality of my life five years from now.
   *Your response:*

   _____

   _____

   _____

5. How can gaining ten lousy pounds be the thing that stands between me and wellness?

   *Your response:*

   _____

   _____

   _____

6. I decided to not even try to get through Dickens's *Great Expectations* for my English lit. assignment. I'm just using the Cliff Notes.

   *Your response* [you might want to help him see how this behavior reflects an eating disordered approach to life]:

   _____

   _____

   _____

7. How come I have to eat breakfast, and my sister [who is not eating disordered] doesn't?

   *Your response:*

   _____

   _____

   _____

8. Some people get hungry; others don't. I don't. Why do I have to eat dinner?

   *Your response:*

   _____

   _____

   _____

Your child's eating disorder is an important if cryptic means of communication with you about himself, his ideas, and his misconceptions. It is important for you to make the effort to decode the messages and respond to your child's needs.

## RECOVERY HAS MANY FACES

Many parents have spoken of a recurring, overwhelming fear that hits them in waves throughout their child's recovery. In the face of a recovery process that can seem at times interminable, their fear is that their child will never recover.

## Do People Ever Really Recover?

It has been my experience that eating disordered children who have healthy personalities and who come from healthfully functioning families enjoy the greatest chances for complete recovery. What I mean by *healthy* families are those families that know how to face problems together and resolve them through fearless and honest communication and undaunted love. These are the families that tend to be eagerly involved with their child in recovery.

Here are some statistics for you to contemplate.

• Approximately 50 percent of anorexics in eating disorder treatment recover so completely that food ceases to be an issue of any kind.

• Approximately another 30 percent of recovered anorexics, despite cure, may carry into adulthood lingering residual features that wax and wane in severity. These individuals need to remain in treatment on either a regular or an as-needed basis throughout their lives, staying on top of the residual issues and other neurotransmitter disorders that initially led to and drove the disease. These conditions may include anxiety disorder, depression, obsessive-compulsive disorder, and so forth.

• Ten percent of anorexics do not recover, with disease maintaining a chronic and unremitting course.

• From 6 to 10 percent of anorexics will die of the disease.[6] The mortality rate associated with anorexia nervosa is more than twelve times as high as the mortality rate among young women in the general population.[7] Mortality is typically not from starvation directly as much as from the severe medical complications that derive from malnourishment lasting over extended periods of time. For each decade of chronic anorexia, sufferers face a 5 percent risk of dying due to heart problems, infections, or liver or kidney dysfunction.[8] In considering these statistics, keep in mind that eating disorders represent the patient's struggle to stay *alive,* not to take his life. Parents who make it their business to be skilled at early intervention and at mentoring their child's recovery do a good deal to stack the deck in the child's favor.

## Recovery Versus Cure

Recovery is not synonymous with cure. Recovery is the *process* through which various degrees of cure are brought about. The recovery of an individual can be plotted on a continuum of degrees of cure. Patients choose, dependent on their intention, motivation, emotional capacity, and body chemistry, the level of cure to which they will aspire. This level will fluctuate over the course of recovery.

> **Activity** Identifying Your Child's Recovery Level    Using the continuum in Exhibit 6.2, determine the level that matches your child's current degree of cure. If you wish, add a continuum level that more specifically describes where your child is. You may want to return to this activity as your child proceeds with his recovery. Date your notations.

## The Ways People Recover

A failure to recover can be the result of misguided goals or of failed attempts at healthy and legitimate goals. It is important that you fully comprehend your child's goals before you begin to assess whether or not his efforts are fruitful.

**EXERCISE D** Identifying Recovery Goals and Recognizing Outcomes    The following goals and outcomes range from those that are clearly articulated and legitimate in their objectives to those that represent recovery in name only. As you read each recovery scenario, consider whether it applies to your child. (You might mark your child's initials next to the points in each scenario that you feel apply to him.) Then, in the space provided, note your reasons for thinking so.

1. *Full recovery.*    Full recovery entails altering food behaviors, changing attitudes and coping techniques, and restoring the patient's weight to the normal range. With a full recovery, the odds are good that the results will be lasting, because dysfunctional eating behaviors lose their purpose and effectiveness in the face of more effective coping mechanisms and healthier brain function.

   *This applies to my child because:*

   _____

   _____

   _____

   _____

2. *Partial recovery but striving toward total cure.*    When grappling with resistance to treatment and recovery is more difficult than living with disease, patients may be in recovery for years, even decades. They remain in the limbo

**Exhibit 6.2. Continuum of Recovery.**

Illness                                                                                    Cure

```
|------+-------+-------+-------+-------+------|
1      2       3       4       5       6
```

*Levels of Cure*
1. He won't even try to recover.
2. He struggles to recover, but does not approach a cure. It takes great effort for him to eat just enough to stay alive.
3. He feigns what looks like a cure, with the intention to manipulate or deceive observers.
4. He has attained some level of cure, though he hasn't been able to sustain it.
5. He has attained a level of cure that is genuine though incomplete.
6. He has attained a level of cure that is genuine and complete and seems lasting.

of their disorder despite their many emotional and behavioral accomplishments, particularly when they are unable to restore their weight. Chances are that their eating behaviors will improve with the passage of time, maturational life events, and personal readiness if they remain committed to the treatment process.

*This applies to my child because:*

_____

_____

_____

_____

3. *Substantive, but temporary recovery.* Some patients make changes quickly but not permanently. Andy was treated effectively for her bulimia in individual and family treatment and by a nutritionist. Within an eight-week period she had stopped purging completely and had become much more communicative and loving with her family. Still fearful of gaining weight but feeling much improved, Andy left treatment prematurely. Several months later, she was vomiting again and had become withdrawn and noncommunicative with her family. She admitted to her mother that she was not ready to let go of her disease. She had learned a lot from treatment that she could continue to grow with, but she would not return to treatment until she felt ready to recover more lastingly.

*This applies to my child because:*

_____

_____

_____

_____

4. *The eating disorder is "managed."*  Some patients choose not to recover but to develop enough self-control to contain the disease, minimizing its negative effects. I am not convinced that such a balance of power can exist for long; eating disorders either get better or take a greater and greater toll on the individual's physical condition, life function, and interpersonal relationships. The managed eating disorder connotes an enslaved mind, preoccupied with thoughts and fears about eating and weight gain. It represents a type of resistance to full recovery.

*This applies to my child because:*

_____

_____

_____

_____

5. *Just a little bit eating disordered.*  Being a little bit eating disordered is equivalent to being a little bit pregnant. A person may not show severe symptoms, but if there are *any* symptoms of a clinical or subclinical eating disorder, the issues underlying and driving those symptoms remain in place unless they are dealt with and resolved (Chapter Two addresses the various disorders and symptoms). Maintaining a "touch" of disease can ultimately take a significant toll.

*This applies to my child because:*

_____

_____

_____

_____

6. *Fifteen years later: relapse.*  A grown woman who had recovered from bulimia in her youth came back to treatment quite chagrined. In a crisis, her disease had reared its head once again, even after much time had elapsed. This is not uncommon. Talk to smokers who quit twenty-five years ago but

who in the face of tragedy or crisis find themselves unconsciously reaching into their purse or pocket for a cigarette. It took her a few sessions of freshening up her once-retired issues to regain her emotional footing. Don't be surprised or dismayed if you notice your child having a regression at the time of some crisis. It should pass with the appropriate response.

*This applies to my child because:*

_____

_____

_____

_____

7. *Pseudo self-recovery.* A young woman called her mother from college to admit that she was suffering from a "runaway" eating disorder. Mother and daughter believed she had overcome the eating disorder on her own, soon after its inception two years ago. This pseudo-recovery had lasted until she was hired by her college as an aerobics instructor, an event that led her to resume excessive exercise. Though her disordered behaviors had abated in the past, the attitudes and issues underlying them had not gone away. Unresolved, they lay dormant until a relevant behavioral trigger appeared.

*This applies to my child because:*

_____

_____

_____

_____

8. *Ignorance is bliss.* One young woman with anorexia fooled herself into believing that she couldn't "really be sick," as she understood completely what was wrong with her: "I know I have a distorted view of myself and food. I know that the first thing on my mind when I wake up in the morning is what I will eat that day, but I know I can't be eating disordered because I am aware of all these things. Besides, I can eat when I want to—I just don't want to."

*This applies to my child because:*

_____

_____

_____

_____

9. *Nipped in the bud.* Carla was in active treatment twice a week for the month when she came home from college for winter break. In treatment, individually and with her family, she dealt with her attempts to control her life and relationships through extreme and excessive behaviors and food restriction that resulted in unhappiness. By the end of that month's work, Carla was able to return to college with a changed attitude, changed major, changed relationship with her family, and changed eating patterns. By addressing her problems before they became ingrained, she had been spared what might soon have become an eating disorder.

*This applies to my child because:*

_____

_____

_____

_____

10. *Recovery by appeasement.* Penny's eating dysfunctions were considered to be "bad eating habits." Her eating was erratic and quirky; she skipped meals, overate, or underate. She started to become overly anxious, particularly when she spent time away from home, and she frequently missed meals because of her "nervous stomach." Penny's psychotherapist, not wanting to "add to her discomfort," would not discuss food issues nor would she challenge Penny to take behavioral or emotional risks in an effort to overcome her anxiety. When Penny's high school debating team was invited to enter an out-of-state competition, her parents and therapist agreed that there would be "no reason to add to her distress" by asking her to travel, and so she forfeited her spot on the team. The therapy was considered a success because she began an otherwise productive academic year.

*This applies to my child because:*

_____

_____

_____

_____

 **EXERCISE E Facilitating Recovery**   Penny's parents and therapist need to take off their blinders to support her well-being and address her eating dysfunctions more effectively. If you feel that you too might not be seeing the big picture of your child's recovery or the full consequences of your own role in it, this exercise might help you. Determine which of the following steps Penny's parents should pursue. Circle Y for yes, N for no. (See Appendix A for answers and explanations.)

1. Y/N   Penny's parents should create a greater degree of structure for her at home by setting more extensive limits and making more stringent demands.

2. Y/N   Penny's parents need not walk on eggshells in an effort to avoid confronting her with unpleasant realities.

3. Y/N   Penny's parents should avoid discussing food and eating with her.

4. Y/N   Penny's parents should not expect her to eat breakfast, lunch, and dinner every day.

5. Y/N   Penny's parents should avoid addressing her excesses and also her fears in order to protect her from her feelings.

6. Y/N   Penny's parents should take her stomachaches and loss of appetite seriously, having her examined by a gastroenterologist.

7. Y/N   Penny's parents should educate the therapist about what they feel would benefit their daughter.

8. Y/N   If Penny's therapist remains resistant to changing her approach, Penny's parents should consider finding a therapist who is more cognizant of the important role of limit setting and reality testing in the recovery process.

## WHAT RECOVERY IS LIKE

Fear is the single most pervasive feeling that people will face both before and during recovery. In moderation, fear can be a healthy defense mechanism, protecting a person from danger; in excess, fear can demoralize and immobilize its host. People in eating disorder recovery must learn to recognize their fears, then face and overcome them. "If you let the fear inside, if you pull it on like a familiar shirt, then you can say to yourself, 'All right, it's just fear, I don't have to let it control me. I see it for what it is.'"[9]

**EXERCISE F Dealing with Fear** Read each of the following fears that individuals in recovery face. Is your child confronting this fear? Circle Y for yes, N for no.

1. Y/N   Fear of becoming fat.

2. Y/N   Fear of the consequences of becoming too malnourished (for example, fainting in class, having to leave college).

3. Y/N   Fear of their newfound laissez-faire attitudes, the cornerstones of recovery, which they feel border precariously on being out of control.

4. Y/N   Fear of their intermittent drive to be well, recognizing it could put an end to the disorder that has been their primary source of support.

5. Y/N   Fear of others' disapproval—for looking too fat, for not recovering quickly enough, for creating problems for the family, or for incurring high expenses.

6. Y/N   Fear of others' compliments about "looking good," interpreting these as indictments that they look fatter.

7. Y/N   Fear of food and of losing total control over it when they begin to make even a small food-related change: "One bite and I am in a dangerous and scary place."

8. Y/N   Fear of joining the ranks of the ordinary, the non-eating disordered people who have nothing to call attention to themselves.

9. Y/N   Fear of having others expect too much of them if they become well.

10. Y/N   Fear of the inevitable entry into adulthood, along with all that it entails—risk-taking, commitment, intimacy, sexuality, accomplishment, failure, responsibility.

11. Y/N   Fear of having things not go well for them after recovery and having no eating disorder to turn to.

12. Y/N   Fear of coming to grips with their own imperfections and vulnerabilities, which they see as affirmations of worthlessness.

13. *Other fears I believe my child faces are:*

    _____

    _____

    _____

14. *The fears that I continue to face are:*

_____

_____

_____

You may want to remind your child that feeling bigger is synonymous with getting better, that it is not about *being* bigger as much as it is about being afraid. A person may need to forfeit feeling well for a time in order to achieve the longer-term gratification found in recovery. A most significant indicator of recovery nearly achieved is that the fear of having gained weight does not deter your child from *continuing* to eat well and to do what is necessary to sustain his recovery.

## THE FINISH LINE

Your child's recovery from an eating disorder, like life itself, is a process. Attaining recovery can be as complex and in many ways as significant as his first encounter with disease.

### Handling Food Fears Near the End of Recovery

Tess, a young, anorexic woman with whom I've worked for a number of years, finally made her leap into health, and it was sheer pleasure to watch. "I can be normal," she said with surprise in her voice. "I can act and feel and *be* normal with all my friends now." This was clearly a revelation and a relief. But these changes did not happen to her arbitrarily. Tess had changed through hard work; her changes would be lasting and could be counted on to get her through difficult encounters of all types throughout the rest of her life.

As she launched herself into the final stages of recovery, Tess and I had the following conversation about her remaining food fears. It shows how different her thinking is now from that of an untreated eating disordered individual. It suggests how her eating disorder treatment and recovery have been responsible for changing her approach to solving problems and managing her life in general.

TESS:  My fear is that now that I've started to gain weight, I'll never stop.

ABBIE:  Let's think about how you have learned to deal with your *other* fears.

TESS:  I have no others.

ABBIE:  I'm not convinced of that. [*Playing the devils' advocate, I went on to wonder aloud.*] When you graduated college and were about to begin your teaching career and your new life with your boyfriend, are you certain you had no fears then?

TESS: I suppose I did.

ABBIE: So, how did you handle them?

TESS: I guess I turned to friends for support.

ABBIE: And what else?

TESS: I recognized my feelings and accepted them, understanding that my anxious feelings were legitimate.

ABBIE: Keep going.

TESS: I prepared the best lesson plans I could for my students, then made an effort to take risks both with my them and with my peers. I really used myself courageously at school, pushing myself to do things that didn't come naturally to me.

ABBIE: So you called up all the strength and resources you had diligently put into place, and they came through for you. Think about this some more with me.

TESS: Sometimes I would try to anticipate problems before they'd happen, and I'd prepare myself to accommodate difficulties in very concrete ways even before they occurred. When things got really tough, I kept myself busy with things I wanted to accomplish, cleaning closets and whatnot. That calmed me down too.

ABBIE: So what is there to stop you now from using the same techniques that worked so well for you in other contexts in your past? Might there be specific food-related difficulties that you could anticipate and strategize responses to as you did with your job and social life?

**Taking Stock** **Seeing How Other Folks Cope**  A question typically on the minds of many patients on the brink of recovery is: How do non-eating disordered people handle problems? The following lists illustrate typical eating disordered and non-eating disordered responses. They may give you some ideas for guiding your child toward more functional coping. The difference between them lies not so much in the actions themselves but in the way they are accomplished and to what purpose. And consider how encouraging it is that so many *more* options are available to people who have a healthy approach to life! A healthy life is a freeing experience that provides limitless opportunities.

*Eating Disordered Responses*

- Pushing problems under the rug; pretending they don't exist.
- Refusing to let yourself get depressed; thinking about something happy.
- Getting on the treadmill for two hours.
- Eating a lot less, or eating a lot more.
- Discarding your efforts and starting over tomorrow from scratch.

*Non-Eating Disordered Responses*

- Anticipating problems in an effort to be as prepared to deal with them as possible.
- Defining and confronting problems squarely.
- Recognizing and accepting your sadness as well as the unpleasantness causing it.
- Getting on the treadmill.
- Considering your solution options. Taking action.
- Being creative. Letting a problem be a jumping-off point for you to grow and change and to make things better.
- Eating less, or eating more.
- Dialoguing with yourself about what you might do differently next time.
- Trying something else if the first solution doesn't work.
- Reading, relaxing, playing a game of pick-up basketball, listening to opera, doing yoga.
- Turning to others for support and connection.
- Forgiving your imperfections and transgressions that come with your being human. Accepting that living life is a complex and messy process at best!
- Resolving to make something good come out of something bad.
- Using stress management techniques such as deep breathing, visualization, or body movement to promote emotional centeredness in the face of crisis.

## Arriving at Recovery

Here's a conversation I had recently with a highly successful patient whose recovery from anorexia was total and will most probably remain that way.

ABBIE: Can you remember what it was like for you at the point just before your final transition into full recovery?

PATIENT: Once I started to eat freely, I found that I had to let myself swing far to the opposite end of the weight continuum. It was like a free fall as I went from 90 pounds to 150 pounds before my body would finally right itself and find its own comfortable balance at 128 pounds. This stage was so scary for me that one day I found myself running nineteen miles to try to calm myself. But I came through it in one piece and am here to stay.

ABBIE: What do you suppose were the factors that led to this final commitment to healing?

PATIENT: I suppose it was a combination of things. My trust in you and our relationship, which led to my growing trust in myself; all that I had learned in treatment, which helped me make good and competent decisions and to ride life's roller-coaster; and the affirmations of my intrinsic worth that I got through my family, my boyfriend, and the various leadership positions I took on at college. It seems to have all come together at once.

ABBIE: What is the most challenging task you face now, having been recovered for two years? What advice might you give to others following in your footsteps?

PATIENT: The hardest thing for me now is, and has always been, the ignorance and insensitivity of others. My advice? Don't take it in. . . . "Once anorexic, always anorexic" is a statement I hear bantered around a lot, and it still sends me to the ladies room in tears. Words can be so hurtful.

This young woman explained how difficult it is to hear the judgments and criticisms of condescending and self-righteous friends and acquaintances who understand little yet who condemn and mock those whom they perceive as being eating disordered. She went on to say how important she feels it is for people to begin to speak out to educate a misinformed world about these problems: "It's about time that people woke up."

### What Puts Patients Over the Top

I have surveyed several successfully and happily recovered patients about the factors they considered most instrumental in putting them over the top, into recovery. Here are some of their observations:

"Coming to therapy twice a week was important in helping me to maintain my focus on my recovery. Anything less and I would have had too much leeway to lose interest or become distracted."

"Journaling kept me on track. It provided the discipline I needed to stay with myself and my thoughts and feelings about food and eating. It also kept me accountable to myself during my recovery."

"Seeing the nutritionist regularly gave me an additional incentive to master my food and eating habits. The extra support and the accountability to another person who was so interested in my well-being was an incredible boon for me."

"Taking a semester off from college was very helpful. I was hardly able to learn anyway with my mind so taken up with food. Coming home gave me a chance to really be alone with myself, to know more fully than ever that something important was happening to me that took precedence over every other thing in my life."

"My eating disorder gave me an excuse to deal with all the other unknown things that were bothering me. I had been lost to myself, not knowing who I was and what I felt, and I didn't even know it. As a result, I couldn't make decisions or care for myself. Once I recognized this, it gave me a greater incentive to recover."

"What kept me buoyed up even through the worst of it was the incredible realization that the more I matured and recovered, the less chance I had to lose the ground I had gained. The learning that took place during recovery was like learning to swim or ride a bike. Once you've got it, it's yours."

## ENDING THERAPEUTIC ALLIANCES

How a person terminates treatment is a good indication of the quality of the treatment process and what gains have been made. Endings are complex processes that require the courage to face difficult feelings, to let go and say goodbye, to welcome independence and the capacity to determine one's own future and quality of life. How to finish treatment must be thought through as carefully as how to begin it.

People leave treatment for a variety of reasons and at different points in the treatment process, both before and after they have achieved recovery. Termination should be a planned event, discussed and negotiated by therapist and patient over a time span that can vary from a single session to several months worth of sessions. Terminating treatment prior to the successful completion of recovery tasks generally indicates the patient's unresolved resistance to or dissatisfaction with some aspect of treatment.

During the termination process, the patient must learn to deal with the loss of the therapist as well as the therapy process. The healthy termination takes place at a point in the process where the loss is offset by a newly acquired resourcefulness, self-reliance, and capacity to solve problems. Termination becomes a time to look back at what has been accomplished and forward to what remains to be accomplished. When the patient leaves therapy following recovery, he will be leaving as a mature thinker and problem solver and a better-adjusted individual. If he leaves before recovery is complete, there is a good chance that he will experience a recurrence of disease.

 **EXERCISE G  Assessing Termination**   To assess whether your child's termination is premature, ask yourself whether the following statements apply to your child. Circle Y for yes, N for no. If you do not know whether some of these statements apply, you might consider asking your child to complete this exercise himself.

1.  Y/N   My child's leaving was precipitous, impulsive, unplanned.
2.  Y/N   My child left treatment because he was uncomfortable with the therapist (or with the therapy work).
3.  Y/N   My child was never good at good-byes, so he is leaving without saying them.
4.  Y/N   My child thought changes were happening too slowly.
5.  Y/N   My child thought changes were happening too quickly.
6.  Y/N   My child thought the sessions were not productive or enjoyable.
7.  Y/N   My child thought the situation at home was getting more tense since the start of treatment.

8. Y/N My child was responding to my frustration every time I tried to communicate with the therapist. He shared my unmet wish to integrate the family into the recovery process.

9. Y/N My child thought the therapist was too controlling, too nondirective, too eager to please, or not entirely honest with him.

10. Y/N My child started to skip sessions without good reason. He became reluctant to make appointments.

11. Y/N My child became frightened as he started to gain weight.

12. Y/N My child was afraid he would arouse the therapist's wrath or disappointment if he confronted the therapist with his feelings and complaints about their work together.

If any of these statements pertain to your child, there is a good chance that the termination occurred sooner than it should have and as a result of his dissatisfaction with the treatment process or therapist or with the treatment's effects on the family, in combination with his inability to resolve his problems in a mature and open manner together with his therapist.

## Case Study: A Premature Termination

After five years of treatment, Sidley is tired. "Sick of being sick," she says she wants to feel "normal." Normal for her means either letting go of the eating disorder or *pretending* she has by letting go of treatment. Though Sidley feels there are benefits to be had from treatment, she participates because her parents want her to. She describes herself as having become "lazy and wanting to do what I want to do with food." Sidley now has her own apartment, her own car, a good job, a boyfriend, a dog—and her eating disorder. Her boyfriend knows nothing about her anorexia, for if he did, she is certain he would leave her. In her mid-twenties, she describes her life as "ideal. I just will never be able to order a piece of chocolate cake for dessert—that's not so awful."

Sidley has accepted the alternative of being eating disordered throughout her life, of choosing a mate who will accommodate her distorted behaviors and attitudes without question, of raising her children in a home where food will be abused and feared, of not being able to solve problems effectively. She feels she will be able to "carry it off nicely."

"What will you do in the face of conflict or a crisis in your life?" I asked.

"The same thing I always do," was her response. "I'll just make sure nothing bad happens. I will agree with everything my husband wants. Right now I let my boyfriend choose the restaurants we go to, the movies we see. I just don't care, and it works out fine."

"If you were your parents, how would you respond to what you've been telling me?" I asked her.

"Well, I'd probably want to discuss this decision, though I know that discussing it wouldn't help," she explained. "I never tell the truth anyway."

"What would you do if they disapproved of your choice to abandon recovery?" I asked.

"If they disapproved, I guess I couldn't stop coming," she said, "because then they'd stop paying for my car and my apartment."

"And what if they said they *do* support your decision to leave treatment now?" I asked.

"Then, I guess I will have gotten away with something again," she said with a mischievous smile.

After having a culminating family therapy session, Sidley's parents decided that if left to her own devices, perhaps Sidley would come back to treatment of her own accord one day, with a more open mind, more pertinent goals, and renewed energy. In the meantime they would experience deep concern. They had always done what they could for their daughter, offering incentives such as financial and emotional support, TLC, unlimited treatment, and family involvement in the treatment process; by leaving her alone at this juncture, they felt they were doing what was best for her.

 **EXERCISE H** Dealing with Premature Termination   What would you have done if you were a parent of this young woman? How might you have seen through her fabrications? How might you have responded to her decision to discontinue assistance at this time? Outline your thoughts and feelings in the space provided:

_____

_____

_____

_____

_____

## Constructive Termination

When considering treatment termination, your child must understand that the best solution is never walking away from a problem (the eating disordered response) but staying with it, confronting it, and attempting to rectify what has gone wrong. Anything that is worthwhile is worth fighting for; anything one strives for invariably becomes much more worthwhile. Your child should never be a passive player in his treatment.

 **EXERCISE I Acting on Dissatisfaction** If your child is having an unsatisfying treatment experience, you can help him understand his role in that experience and his response to it. Answer the following questions in the space provided.

1. Has my child considered confronting his therapist with his feelings, his opinions, his preferences? If not, why not?

_____

_____

_____

_____

2. If he did, what were the therapist's responses? Did she or he listen well enough?

_____

_____

_____

_____

3. How did my child receive and feel about those responses?

_____

_____

_____

_____

4. Did the interchange resolve the problems at hand? Were changes made? What were they?

_____

_____

_____

_____

Once issues are brought out in the open, adjustments can generally be made to accommodate everyone. If the relationship capacity and potential for improvement have been exhausted, however, and things aren't about to get any better, it may be time for your child to consider making a change in therapist or treatment team. Every therapy relationship is unique. A great therapy relationship can be as hard to find as a great love match. Encourage your child to keep moving forward and to stop at nothing until he has found satisfaction in his treatment and recovery efforts. (The option of changing therapists is discussed further in Chapter Seven.)

### Compensating for Premature Treatment Terminations

Premature terminations from eating disorder recovery, even if in response to financial constraints, can in the long run be a bad investment. In one instance the anorexic mother of two children was forced to withdraw from treatment for herself for financial reasons before she had finished her recovery work. Within seven years her eldest child had become anorexic and her youngest had begun to show signs of disease. Her unresolved attitudes and responses might have been one factor among the undoubtedly multiple factors that stimulated disease predispositions in these youngsters, perhaps functioning as a trigger as described in Chapter One.

When treatment is terminated earlier than is desirable, parents may be able to compensate to some extent. For example, because managed care restricts the amount of time patients can spend in structured hospital settings, you may need to accommodate your child's early hospital discharge in some creative ways. In one instance the family of an anorexic child provided a food structure to replace the one that the hospital would have offered. Parents and child together negotiated a plan in which parents prescribed food for the week, made it available, dished it up in correct portion sizes, made certain they were present during and after the meal, and so forth. If the child followed the plan, she was rewarded with a greater degree of self-determination, becoming entitled to choose her own breakfast foods and to eat alone under certain circumstances. If she found she could not tolerate the increased autonomy, food choices reverted back to parental prescriptions.

Such situations can prove quite sticky; parents run the risk of exerting too much control and getting into power struggles over food. The demands of financial realities, however, may overshadow the loftiest of theoretical guidelines. Parents need to compensate for their increased vulnerability in such situations by being hypervigilant and by gathering the support they need to avoid being seduced into dysfunctional emotional entanglements with their child.

It may be appropriate for your child's therapist to respond to early termination by negotiating a compromise activity, such as having the patient report in to the therapist periodically or fax journal entries. Such activities offer the patient opportunities to recognize and rethink what might have been an impulsive decision.

## BEYOND RECOVERY

Recovery from an eating disorder can be a slippery slope at times. Your child will not realize just *how* slippery until he is experiencing it. It is important that you do your part to keep him self-aware and on track, supporting his recovery goals and helping him cement the gains he has made.

### Retaining and Supporting Recovery Gains

Those who have attained recovery must focus on holding onto their gains; those who have not yet reached the end of the recovery continuum must strive to attain ever deepening levels of cure. Recidivism, or relapse, is the recurrence of disease following recovery or the worsening of symptoms following termination of treatment. Once separate from the rigors and structure of treatment, it is easy to slip back into old familiar habits, especially in the face of emotional distress or newly gained weight. It is the *response* to these regressions, not the regressions themselves, that will determine whether the relapse will be a temporary phenomenon or a backslide into disease. When your child is unaware of the meaning and significance of regressions, he is at risk for greater and more lasting problems.

**Taking Stock** **Reinforcing Recovery Gains to Prevent Relapse**
Children and parents should

- Recognize when they need help and ask for it.
- Continue to communicate their needs to each other, honestly and mutually.
- Face all aspects of life squarely in an effort to address and resolve problems.
- Live healthful and balanced lives in every respect.

- Use their minds creatively and flexibly to resolve problems.
- Recognize their self-worth and their entitlement to the best possible quality of life.
- Remain aware of nuances of mood and feelings in the home, and investigate any issue that appears even remotely problematic.
- Remember that healthy eating is a way of life. You set the standard through your behaviors and expectations as modeled in your home.
- Do not wield disproportionate amounts of power or control over anyone in your household. Everyone's needs are equally legitimate.
- Understand and respect your need to remain parental and authoritative.
- Remain in treatment as long as necessary.
- Return to treatment as needed.

Relapse prevention is *response-ability* through active and purposeful choice making. Your child has learned these positive responses through his eating disorder recovery work. Ideally, you have become equally assertive and sure of yourself, knowing who you are, what you are about, and what you are able to make happen.

### Aftercare

In all instances of recovery, but most specifically in those where recovery gains may be tenuous, the patient's commitment to aftercare protocols is essential to maintaining progress. Successful aftercare, or postrecovery treatment, involves the continued use of resources developed throughout the recovery process—individual, family, or group therapy. Recovery gains are best secured through the patient's commitment to aftercare, with attention to the issues underlying the disease for up to two full years following recovery.

Recovery or halfway houses are alternative transitional living situations that provide a comprehensive aftercare experience. Residents live together with others also in recovery, attending group sessions and recovery meetings on the premises. People in recovery houses go about their independent lives, working or attending school, coming home at night to limited treatment. They must be far enough along in the recovery process to benefit from this amount of independence, even though still requiring regular reinforcement for the progress they have made.

Organizations such as ANAD offer educative support groups free of charge nationwide for sick and recovered individuals, their families, and their friends (see Appendix C). These groups provide an excellent aftercare alternative. Overeaters Anonymous also provides fine opportunities for recovery maintenance free of charge, through interactions with other recovered individuals. Drop-in and ongoing therapy groups offer a place for people to air fears, problems, and concerns while feeling embraced and making friends.

Aftercare presents an opportunity to nip impending problems in the bud, before they have time to materialize and become ingrained, and to reinforce previous and future changes. Spending more time in recovery buys continued hope that recovery will become ever more complete. Your child would do well to participate in some form of aftercare treatment if only to decide if it is necessary and, if so, in what form, and for how long.

### Aftercare Decisions

Having arrived at or being close to recovery, your child will have choices to make. Should continued care be an option for him?

**Activity Discussing Postrecovery Options** Consider the options that your child faces at this time. Your role can include helping him appreciate the consequences of the decisions he makes now concerning his postrecovery period. You may want to discuss the following questions with your child. In any event, they can guide your efforts to help.

- Are there therapeutic issues remaining that need to be addressed?
- Is he in danger of losing some of the ground he has gained if he leaves therapy completely at this point?
- Does he feel confident that he will know how to proceed if he decides to return for help one day?
- Is he confident that he is making his decisions about continued care responsibly? Does he have sufficient access into his own mind and heart to know what he needs and where to find it?
- Does he feel he will remain as internally focused as he needs to be if he withdraws from treatment now? Will he be capable of recognizing and independently resolving personal issues that present themselves?

- Does he understand that if he makes a decision about ending treatment, or about anything else in life, and he finds that it does not work out as he'd hoped, he has the option to simply change his mind? It's never too late.
- Have you and he together redefined what your role might be after his recovery?
- Does he understand and appreciate that he can trust you to remain an important and valued influence the rest of his life?

The following chapter offers some approaches you can try when recovery is not happening as it should, when obstacles must be surmounted to break through to recovery. In these instances, you may need to advocate proactively for recovery, troubleshooting to ensure your child's success.

# Recognizing and Overcoming Recovery Setbacks

Because recovery is frequently marked by a one step forward, one step backward sequence, it is difficult to know if it is progressing as it should. This chapter will help you to know when and how to take appropriate action to revive and infuse life into your child's stalled recovery.

## MEASURING RECOVERY PROGRESS

"I'm a behaviorist," said the father of an anorexic teenager. "I like to see results. In my business, that's how we define success. I want to know that my daughter is not just wasting her time in treatment." As a parent, it is often difficult to know what you are looking at as you observe your child's recovery. It is difficult to remain optimistic and supportive of the work when you do not understand what is happening. It is difficult to know where to look for signs of recovery; these signs are not always easy to see, and they may crop up where you don't expect them. They may be camouflaged, taking on the appearance of failure at first. Consider this example:

> Sue, a college student in recovery for bulimia, returned to school after productive work with me during the summer. A month later she telephoned me to admit that she had "regressed miserably" and felt ashamed and despondent. She had remained weight conscious and vigilant about the food she ate and typically found herself overdoing the partying on weekends, excesses that hurt her studies.
>
> Throughout the course of our conversation, I helped her to assess the *positive* changes she perceived in herself as well. Sue was eating in a more balanced way now, and she had managed to maintain consistency in her efforts to increase her caloric intake. Socially, she had become more honest with others and more expressive of her feelings. She no longer played the role of victim with the young men she dated. In addition, she had learned to face herself, her depression, and the pain of

acknowledging the full impact of what remained of her eating disorder. More significantly, she knew enough to reach out for help when she felt she most needed it.

Sue's situation at this point in her recovery is an example of a glass half full, not half empty. How easy it is for the eating disordered patient (or her parent) to err on the side of self-criticism! And how hard it is for the parent to make a totally accurate assessment of recovery from a distance as the onlooker. In Chapter Three, I discussed listening to what one cannot hear; it is also important to learn to see what is not easily visible in order to appreciate the subtleties of growth within the recovery process.

**EXERCISE A** Watching for Indicators of Change   Even when you are not able to perceive key changes directly, you may see *indicators* of such change. Read each of the following signs of change in such areas as emotional resourcefulness, competence, and values. Are you seeing these signs in your child? Circle Y for yes, N for no.

*Attitudes and Emotional Resourcefulness*

1.  Y/N   She is facing unknowns with excitement, not dread.
2.  Y/N   She can pull herself out of a crisis rather than be defeated by it.
3.  Y/N   She is not so black and white in her thinking; she considers options.
4.  Y/N   She has greater access to her feelings and expresses them more readily.

*Relationships*

5.  Y/N   She is more open and communicative with me, even about her eating disorder.
6.  Y/N   She is less threatened by me and more open to my ideas.
7.  Y/N   She isn't as eager to please or to avoid confrontation; she is acting less like a victim.
8.  Y/N   She is more relaxed with and better liked by her friends.
9.  Y/N   She is more willing to trust others and accept help.

*Thinking and Values*

10.  Y/N   She isn't getting nicer—but she is becoming more *real*.
11.  Y/N   She has found the courage to recognize and face problems honestly and squarely (and can recognize when she is choosing not to do this).
12.  Y/N   She thinks about therapeutic issues outside the therapy session.

*Identity*

13. Y/N    She feels *deserving* of feeling better.

14. Y/N    She is less self-critical and perfectionist.

*Food*

15. Y/N    She is able to separate her food from her feelings.

16. Y/N    She can observe and react to bodily sensations such as satiety and hunger.

17. Y/N    She doesn't conserve calories all day so she can eat freely at night.

18. Y/N    She has stopped relying solely on the kinds of foods often preferred by anorexics.

19. Y/N    The changes she makes are carried over from day to day. If she eats well for three days running, she is able to keep up her momentum for three more days, and three days after that.

20. Y/N    She demonstrates such changes as these in greater number and frequency and with less effort as time goes on.

More and more, you should be seeing these changes taking form in your child. Recovery from an eating disorder requires far more than the capacity to put two slices of cheese between two pieces of bread and eat the resulting sandwich. The kernel of the process lies in the self-awareness, intention, need, choice, and control that it takes to put food to one's lips. Recovery also lies in the individual's ability to change habits and behaviors in response to intention. This is called walking the walk as opposed to talking the talk. At a seminar, Moshe Feldenkrais instructed one very overweight woman always to leave one bite on her plate, one spoonful in her bowl. Because no diet had worked for her, he was instructing her to change her *habits* of eating instead.[1]

> **Troubleshooting Tip** **When You See It, Say It**  Your child may be unaware of changes that are evolving slowly and gradually and therefore may not recognize the extent to which she has progressed. When you observe improved affect, problem solving, and communication capacities in your recovering child, comment on it. A short statement can go a long way toward giving her the staying power she needs to remain committed to the recovery.

## STEPPING IN TO FACILITATE RECOVERY

"It is not so easy to do what you must for your child when your heart is breaking," said the mother of an anorexic teenager actively struggling in recovery. Nevertheless, it remains incumbent on you, as your child's mentor, not to settle for a recovery process that is less than effective. Learning to assess and evaluate recovery advances and derailments accurately is the critical first step in keeping recovery on track. As you assist your child, you may need to consult with her therapist at times. Parents sometimes think that because the therapist is "taking care of my child, not me," it is the therapist's prerogative to ignore parental needs. This is never true, and it represents a contradiction in terms; as I have emphasized earlier, there is no such thing as taking care of a child to the exclusion and detriment of that child's concerned parents.

Problems might represent a temporary stall or a pervasive recovery derailment. The father of an anorexic youngster described his daughter's progress after a year of her treatment: "She can vary her diet somewhat now, and she eats three meals a day. How can I complain? This represents progress." Yet as an aside, he expressed his deep-seated fears about her continued refusal to put on weight and to reduce her excessive exercise routine. His fears were well-founded; despite her efforts and her progress, this child remained firmly entrenched in disease. Is it safe to assume that her progress will continue at a pace sufficient to overcome the ever intensifying forces of disease? Will the passage of time and her maturity suffice to remedy what remains wrong? Should the treatment be augmented in any way? If changes are in order, what should they be?

It may be up to you to distinguish the fine line between a temporary recovery stall and a not so temporary, heels-dug-in derailment. You will find the distinction in your child's intentions and goals, in her response to her regression, and in the therapist's ability to frame the event as an opportunity for learning and personal growth.

## WHY TREATMENT DERAILS

Therapeutic derailments may be brought on through problems occurring in your child, yourself or your partner, your family, the professionals treating your child, the therapy process, or any combination of these. The following sections look in depth at a few of these factors.

## Your Child's Resistance to Recovery

Your child's acceptance of treatment does not necessarily imply her acceptance of recovery. Nor does resistance to recovery imply a breakdown in the healing process. In fact, the drive to recover waxes and wanes, and unless you and your child remain vigilant, this phenomenon can sap your child's motivation to heal and your efforts to support her healing. Is resistance still a major force in your child? Are recovery efforts too painful a reminder to her that she is not normal? Squarely confronting resistance can reveal and overcome significant obstacles to recovery.

**Troubleshooting Tip** Recognize How Cognitive Distortions Feed into Resistance  What your child doesn't know *can* hurt her. Children who delude themselves with false beliefs and information cannot recover. The following activity will help you address this problem.

**Activity** Teaching Your Child the Body's Wisdom  Is your child aware of the following basic truths about the human body and how it works? If not, this lack of knowledge could be the cause of a recovery derailment. Talk to your child to see if she knows these truths.

- Food restriction and hunger lead to gorging.
- A person must eat well and eat often to maintain a healthful metabolism. Naturally thin people do not get that way from dieting.
- The body does whatever it needs to do to survive. If it does not have enough food or stored fat to burn, it will sustain itself by feeding off its own muscle. If it is not fed regularly, it will conserve energy by slowing down functions, decreasing its metabolism somewhat as a hibernating bear does. If it does not receive enough water, it will retain whatever water it has, as does the cactus in the desert, resulting in swelling and bloating.
- Laxative abuse results in loss of body *fluids*, not weight in the form of body tissue. Though this may reduce the numbers on the scale for the moment, if the body cannot count on consistent access to water, it will survive as the above mentioned cactus does, retaining water in response to a regularly imposed drought. In addition, abuse of laxatives can irreparably damage the colon's capacity to expel waste naturally through peristalsis.

- A menstrual period amounts to more than an inconvenience in your daughter's life. It is an indication that her hormonal and reproductive systems are healthy and functional, capable of maintaining healthy bones and of fulfilling their design to create and sustain new life. Her eating disorder may have caused her to lose sight of the fact that there are things that matter beyond her own narrow preferences.

- Vegetarianism should not be used as an excuse for refusing to eat protein. Your child's body needs protein. Conscientious vegans eat sufficient amounts of vegetarian proteins from such sources as soy, tofu, and combinations of foods such as beans and rice to ensure proper nutrition through an adequate intake of amino acids.

- Dieting is the worst way to lose weight. The more a person diets, the higher her percentage of body fat when the weight is restored (which generally happens). Diets are short-term efforts with short-term results; a healthy and moderated eating lifestyle is forever. Healthy, balanced eating, not dieting, is the best way to lose weight and *keep it off*. A diet is just another form of self-deprivation; it is not synonymous with a recovery food plan.

- Except for certain very specific medical conditions, fat-free eating is not healthy eating. The body needs some fat in order to carry on its daily functions and sustain the hormone estrogen.

- Certain vitamins are fat soluble. Without enough body fat, a person cannot absorb them or benefit from vitamin supplements containing them.

- Ingesting approximately 40 percent of one's calories during the early part of the day cuts down on the tendency to overeat in the latter part of the day.

- A malnourished brain cannot think, learn, or recover effectively.

- People don't need to *control* their eating. When they trust the wisdom of their bodies, eating becomes a function as naturally regulated as breathing or sleeping.

- By taking in the right foods, with the right frequency, in the right amounts, the body will attain and maintain a stable set-point weight.

## Revisiting Your Own Resistance to Recovery

In Chapter One you identified your attitudes, beliefs, and behaviors that might be contributing to your child's eating disorder. Similar thoughts and actions may be impeding your child's recovery, as the following exercise will help you determine.

 **EXERCISE B** **Avoiding Inadvertent Sabotage** Read each of the following descriptions of attitudes and behaviors. Might the description pertain to you? Circle Y for yes, N for no.

1. Y/N   I prefer the way my child looks when she is thinner. I may feel like asking her, "Aren't you overdoing it a little? You really don't need to eat *that* much so soon, do you?" I may want to confide in her nutritionist that I am worried she is "putting on pounds."

2. Y/N   I have a hard time dealing with my child's anger which feels hurtful and intimidating to me.

3. Y/N   I still look to treatment and the therapist to *fix* my child. I can see myself losing interest in my child's treatment because the therapist can't get her to lose weight.

4. Y/N   I sometimes let my overly powerful child push me around. I believe that if she gets her way, it will make her happier. I frequently do not speak candidly with her. I feel that her decision to become a vegetarian has been made for the wrong reasons, but I dare not suggest this.

5. Y/N   I don't know if I'm capable of making the changes required to enhance my child's recovery, and therefore I don't even try. I like my life the way it is, and I'd prefer that my child make the changes.

6. Y/N   My partner and I do not see eye to eye on child rearing, and so we send our child mixed messages.

7. Y/N   Determining how to handle our child and engage in her recovery process together is creating a growing rift between my partner and me.

8. Y/N   Though on some level I know my recovering child is still sick and struggling with her eating disorder, it is easy to become complacent and just forget she is sick when she goes to school every day and acts completely normal in so many ways.

9. Y/N  It is hard to live with the constant, nagging fear that my child may not get better; I try to put the reality of her illness aside much of the time, pretending that things are normal and that she is just misbehaving.

10. Y/N  I still have a hard time letting go of my own eating quirks and exercise excesses.

**From Generation to Generation**     In addition, you may find yourself losing objectivity or tolerance for the recovery process when issues strike too close to home, reflecting upon you personally. Consider the following case study.

> A seven-year-old girl became phobic about leaving her mother to go to school, ballet class, and friends' houses. Her overly protective mother would not allow her the freedom to walk into school and ballet class by herself for fear that harm might befall her. At the same time, fearful of arousing her child's anger, this mother failed to provide adequate controls in appropriate contexts. This little girl had no set mealtimes, no set bedtimes, no guidelines about behaviors that were appropriate and inappropriate in playing with others. She started coming into her parents' bed regularly in the middle of the night, which her mother claimed was "not a problem for us." This mother, who disliked structure in her own life, never ate breakfast. She also claimed that her daughter was "never hungry in the morning" and that she didn't need to provide breakfast for her before school. She stated that "eating is not an issue here either. What *is* a problem is that she cries in school, and I'm afraid the kids are going to start making fun of her." When I pointed out that a child who goes without breakfast and has a malnourished brain cannot learn effectively, she responded, "But you can't force another person to eat."

**EXERCISE C Understanding Parental Influence on Disease and Recovery Processes**     The parent described here was unable to see just how significant the considerations she and I discussed were, how each had a bearing upon the other, and how they all foretold the possibility of an eating disorder in her child. Most important, such attitudes and behaviors are also counterproductive to a child in recovery. This mother would do well to get help for herself now rather than hand down a legacy of excess, misunderstanding, and lack of judgment to the next generation. Consider the relationship between parenting and eating disorders by answering the following questions about the case study in the spaces provided.

1. What issues or circumstances could lead to the onset of an eating disorder in this child and make recovery particularly difficult?

_____

_____

_____

2. How might the addition of more structure in this child's life lead her to a greater sense of security and safety?

_____

_____

_____

3. Where do you see this mother's personal issues interfering with her parental responsibilities to her child?

_____

_____

_____

4. What relationship exists between the handling of food in this or any household and the development of a child's values, priorities, and problems?

_____

_____

_____

This parent's messages are apparently *not* lost on her daughter, who at age seven is already paralyzed by her fears of being without the parameters she needs to exist confidently in a highly unpredictable world. A child who remains without limits and boundaries, without set bedtimes and meals, without a sense of what is supposed to happen in the world and how she is supposed to function within it, will feel out of control and frightened, becoming a likely candidate for developing an eating disorder and for having a hard time recovering from it. It is a good guess that this mother has some control and food-related issues of her own. I am hard-pressed to believe that if a good breakfast is put in front of a first-grader in the morning before school, with enough time and the expectation that she will eat it, her mother would have to "force" her to eat it.

**Parental Food Shtick**     Our society is full of children who are growing up in cooking-free kitchens and in dinnerless homes. As parenting becomes increasingly a nonmarket commodity in a market-driven society, parents are busy with other things. Eating out and ordering in have become ways of life. I am not suggesting that parents give up their livelihoods and interests to stand over a hot stove, but I ask that you revisit the notion that eating disorders are about *extremes* in living—all kinds of extremes. When children grow up in homes with food- and cooking-phobic parents, how are they to learn to enjoy a healthy relationship with healthy foods? And what message do parents convey when they do cook? A non–eating disordered young mother of toddlers described this meal she had prepared for her family: "I made a lean turkey breast with low-fat seasoning, low-fat soup, and lite yogurt, and so I got away without having to use oil."

In another instance, the recovered mother of a non–eating disordered teenage girl still struggles with her own relationship to food. She admits to feeling bad when her daughter eats "better" (less) than she does, and she wishes she could be "like my daughter in not eating dinner at all when she isn't hungry." She does not understand that it is *not* all right for her daughter, or for anyone, to skip dinner. *Dinner belongs at the end of every person's day, not simply as necessary sustenance but also as a guaranteed daily comfort, reward, and chance to interact with those you love.*

> **Activity** Monitoring Your Own Changes   Have your attitudes about food and how you handle it changed since the start of your child's recovery? Are these changes as apparent to her as they are to you? How do these changes affect your child's situation? Do you feel there are additional changes you should try to accomplish? What are they? Note your thoughts in your journal.

> **Troubleshooting Tip** Don't Worry About Being Perfect   Parents need not be perfect in their role as parents, or for that matter, in anything they do. This is an invaluable notion to model for your perfectionist child. There is a sublime sense of freedom and relief in not having to meet impossible and unrealistic standards. The woolen afghan in my office is one of my most valued objects, toasty warm, though riddled with holes from old age and loving use. Intrinsic worth arises not out of perfection, but rather from a core of meaning and values.

## Resistance or Problems Within the Family

If your child has been unable to bring about either behavioral or emotional changes, you might consider infusing the therapy process with new life by involving the entire family in family treatment now, if you haven't already done so. Family participation can bring to light information that is both diagnostic and healing. If therapeutic attention is not being given to the family, you may be missing a prime opportunity to enhance recovery and, even more significantly, to reinvigorate a stuck process.

One family problem that can stall recovery is the failure to include the eating disordered child's siblings in the recovery process. When siblings are ignored, not only can healing digress but you as a parent will be giving up a prime and potent opportunity for teaching all of your children to face and resolve problems, to care about and for their loved ones, and to become kind and supportive *persons,* in the best sense of that word. According to the concepts, theory, and practice of the family systems approach, all your children are affected by one child's eating disorder. Everyone needs to be confided in and educated about the disease and its meaning to the individual and to the family. A change in *any* family member can have a positive or negative effect on the recovery process for everyone. Why not ensure that the change is a positive one?

 **EXERCISE D  Looking at Your Family**   Read each of the following scenarios and think of what you might say in each instance to make the sibling described part of the solution rather than the problem. Outline your thoughts in the space provided.

1. The little sister of an eating disordered child is so anxious about getting through the tensions of mealtime that she can't sit still through a family dinner but jumps up to leave the table numerous times.

   _____

   _____

   _____

2. A sibling develops tremendous rage at the attention given to the sick child, at the worry and strife it creates in the home, and at the tightness it creates in the family budget.

   _____

   _____

   _____

3. Siblings express their impatience or anger at the sick child's rudeness and irritability; as a parent you want to protect the fragile patient, and so you silence the others.

   _____

   _____

   _____

4. The brothers of a bulimic teenager pretend to stick their fingers down their throats in a taunting imitation of what their sister does.

   _____

   _____

   _____

5. A sibling talks disparagingly about how much he dislikes the overweight kids at school.

   _____

   _____

   _____

6. "I'm so concerned about you," a sibling says in a self-righteous and condescending way to her eating disordered sister. The speaker has almost as many issues and quirky behaviors around food as does the patient.

   _____

   _____

   _____

**Activity** Altering Sibling Dynamics   Think about the sibling dynamics in your home. How does your eating disordered child affect the other children in your home, and vice versa? How have you responded? What might you do to make your response more effective and have it address everyone's needs? Siblings have the potential to comfort and support the disordered child once they are included in the process and become knowledgeable about what to do. If your child's siblings are not emotionally supportive, what might you do about it?

**Troubleshooting Tip** **Be Open and Honest** When an eating disorder reinforces the keeping of secrets, depth and intimacy in family relationships are forfeited. The various communication techniques I have discussed for making effective and supportive connections with your eating-disordered child apply to your other children as well. "Tell me about it" is a simple remark that carries great potential for getting the family through both the best and the worst of times. Remember that by *discussing* a situation you are not *creating* it; you are simply acknowledging and defining more clearly an issue that already exists. Discussion ultimately makes a problem *less* intimidating and insurmountable—not more so.

**Troubleshooting Tip** **Describe What's Happening Now** Use this technique to improve family communication:

- Identify what you see happening.
- State what you think and feel about it.
- Describe how you will choose to react.
- Anticipate responses; address defensive responses before they emerge.

For example, a parent might say to a child: "There is something I really need to discuss with you. I am reluctant to do so, knowing that what I am about to say could make Beth feel uncomfortable and you feel angry and defensive. Despite this, in my opinion, this topic needs to be shared, so here goes. I'm open to hearing complaints after I have finished."

## Resistance or Other Problems with Professionals

Your efforts to facilitate your child's recovery may require assessing the attitudes and techniques of the professionals on the case.

**When the Team Doesn't Function Collaboratively** When the professionals on the treatment team do not work collaboratively, their input can begin to sound like a melee of many discordant voices to the patient. She may be confused by differing messages from different professionals who strive to attain different goals at different paces. An internist, in an effort to placate her teenage anorexic patient, encouraged her to ignore her psychotherapist's request that she discontinue her eighteen hours of dance practice at school each week in preparation for an annual performance. The therapist's request was not meant to be punitive but to limit the excess that was so central a part of the patient's illness. Rather than discussing the situation with the therapist, however, the girl and her parents chose to follow the much preferred suggestion of the physician and also chose to leave the therapist precipitously, seeking a different therapist with a less purposeful approach. A professional united front is as important as a parental united front to a successful recovery.

**Miscommunications**    Miscommunications are inevitable, varying in direct proportion to the number of people involved in your child's team: the more people, the more miscommunications. Messages, no matter how stringently synchronized, vary from person to person in how they are sent and how they are interpreted. It is therefore critical that both you and your child speak directly to the individuals with whom you have problems or from whom you need answers. In addition, at the start of treatment, the professionals should have asked for your written permission to speak freely and directly with other professionals on the team, sharing any information that might benefit them in attending to the needs of your child. If you were not asked to sign release forms, *offer* to do so, thus encouraging team members to consult with one another in the interest of providing the best possible care for your child.

**EXERCISE E Correcting Miscommunications**    Have you or your child experienced any miscommunications with members of the treatment team? If so, consider for a moment how you might have rectified those problems. Then ask yourself how miscommunications might be getting in the way of your child's recovery *now*. In the space provided, write down what you might do about these current miscommunications.

_____

_____

_____

## TAKING ACTION

Should you intervene when recovery stalls? If so, how, and when? What if you do not see eye to eye with the professionals on the specific actions to take? Here are some suggestions.

## Making Difficult Decisions

Treatment team members may legitimately differ about how to proceed. A disparity in approaches is not problematic as long as people debate their points of view in order to bridge differences and negotiate decisions, ultimately arriving at a creative integration of ideas. Reality factors as arbitrary as school semesters, vacation schedules, insurance coverage, treatment program availability, and the like will also affect treatment decisions. Moreover, there is typically more than one appropriate solution to any treatment issue.

As you read the following case study and the treatment team meeting it describes, ask yourself how many of the various solutions proposed make sense to you.

> Julius, a young anorexic man, had been in and out of hospitals throughout his eating disorder recovery over the period of a year. As his weight began to slip once more and he was faced again with the threat of hospitalization, the members of his treatment team discussed their various viewpoints on the best action to take:
>
> - Julius's father sensed that his son had finally been inspired to "turn the corner" when confronted with the possibility of yet another hospitalization. Because of Julius's apparently renewed motivation to recover, his father advocated that he remain in outpatient care for a time to test his newly determined capacities to change.
> - The psychiatrist felt he should be hospitalized. If Julius's motivation hadn't been adequate to propel him into recovery by this time, she said, the outpatient team could not bank on its working for him now. She cited "games" he had played with recovery, such as water loading (to increase his weight before stepping on a scale), skipping lunches at school, and so forth, and encouraged the father to remember what a deceptive disease this is. She also felt that Julius's father, in advocating for his son, might inadvertently have fallen into the seductive trap of "buying into" the disease.
> - The internist wanted Julius to be hospitalized immediately to gain a minimum of seven pounds, which would have only gotten him up to 102 pounds, a fraction of the total amount he needed to gain.
> - Julius's mother was concerned that if he was tube-fed as was recommended and forced to gain so much weight so quickly, he would begin purging following discharge in order to lose the weight he'd been required to gain.
> - The consultant on the case (an outside professional brought in to offer an additional opinion) felt that if (Julius) were to reenter an inpatient milieu, the goals

for the hospitalization should be changed; she felt that Julius should not be discharged until he had gained back enough weight to positively affect brain function and his capacity to make a recovery. She thought he should be expected to gain nothing short of twelve to eighteen pounds, putting him back in a normal weight range.

- The consultant also felt that refeeding should be done by requiring the patient to eat 3,500 calories a day, rather than feeding him through a tube (the tube is inserted into the nose and down the throat). This would more closely simulate the eating lifestyle required to maintain the weight gain.

- The insurance company was reluctant to consider paying for more than one week of treatment and therefore favored the tube-feeding approach.

If you felt that every single approach made sense, your answers would all be valid. This is what makes eating disorder treatment and recovery such a challenge. There is no one *right* solution. No matter what tack is taken, another might be as good or even better.

> **Troubleshooting Tip** Recognize the Value of Your Own Contributions
> Beware of feeling that your ideas are less valid than everyone else's or that you are a burden to the team. Neither of these self-effacing notions is true. No one knows your child as well as you do, and your observations are valuable. The best professionals will welcome your input, freely admitting that nobody has all the answers.

## Considering a Milieu Change

In the face of a seriously stalled recovery process, your options include:

1. Doing nothing, in the hope that things will get better on their own.
2. Expanding (adding different disciplines to) the treatment team.
3. Changing team members.
4. Deciding if a milieu change is appropriate.

> **Taking Stock** Changing the Treatment Setting   If you decide a milieu change is appropriate, you will need to evaluate the following:
>
> - Why is a milieu change necessary? What might be the consequences of *not* making the change?

- When should this change take place?
- What will the new milieu be: hospital inpatient, hospital day program, or residential treatment?
- How long should it last?
- What is the specific goal?
- If inpatient placement is chosen, should it be followed by an eating disorder day program or outpatient therapy?

## A Process Catalyst: Going into Treatment Yourself

Parents may enhance their child's recovery efforts by attending treatment themselves in lieu of or at the same time as their eating disordered child. Carole, an overly powerful and headstrong youngster who was verbally and physically abusive to her parents, refused treatment for her anorexia. Her parents entered treatment instead, where they came to understand their role in enabling their daughter's out-of-control behaviors and thus her disease. Carole's symptoms subsided in response to her parents' asserting more appropriate limits for her.

Parents should consider therapy for themselves when:

- The child cannot or will not engage in treatment.
- The child's symptoms are specific reactions to issues of parenting and the family.
- The issues are developmental; this may be the case particularly with early onset disease in young children.
- The parents need support to remain strong for their child. (Strength in this case is measured by parents' capacity to *understand* what the child needs and to *respond* to those needs.)

In the following case study, consider how the parents' emotional issues directly affected their son's development and how help for themselves could have been helpful to him.

## Case Study

Seth is a young adult with anorexia. While he was dating a young woman who emotionally abused him, his parents were loath to express their displeasure with her because they didn't want to "upset" him. When the girl ultimately left him, they were also silent about their relief, because their son was "too hurt to hear such an unsympathetic response."

Seth's mother removed the nutritional labels from foods so knowledge of their contents would not deter him from eating. His physician prescribed a serotonin medication to correct what she felt was a chemical imbalance, but his parents would not hear of his taking it for fear that it would make him feel "abnormal." When the doctor asked if Seth was eating meals, his mother replied, "Well, he's trying, and that's good enough for us."

For fear of creating additional anxiety in their son, they chose not to invite him to join the family in viewing the movie *Saving Private Ryan*. The movie, historical fiction about the Second World War and the courage of the soldiers who fought to leave a legacy of democracy for the free world, was disturbing but very much based in reality. Seth's own father had fought in the front lines in Vietnam. "Why subject him to unnecessary unpleasantness? Life is unpleasant enough as it is!" his mother commented, despite the fact that the young man had no problem watching movies portraying less meaningful violence.

These parents' best attempts to protect their son from reality's barbs are fruitless. We are all at the mercy of the unknown, and subject to the tough realities of life, but Seth's struggle is compounded by his internal demons. It is the children who are *not* overprotected in life who learn to face reality with the knowledge and confidence that they can survive it; those who are overly sheltered, learn to respond to it with dread and foreboding, never coming to know or trust their internal strength because they have never been tested by exercising it. A child cannot know her coping capacities and internal resources until she has come face to face with adversity, unabridged and uncensored, and has come out the other side.

"How can seeing a movie have anything to do with recovery from an eating disorder anyway?" Seth's mother wanted to know. For Seth, seeing this movie would have been about challenging himself to change behaviors and lifestyle patterns, about coming to grips with his capacity to take risks and survive them. (Similarly, learning to eat normally is about learning to take risks for another kind of survival.) In addition, seeing the film and discussing it afterwards with his family would have been invaluable reassurance that his family anticipates and trusts his capacity to deal with unpleasantness and manage his life. Such reassurance is what creates positive self-esteem. If these parents were to get help for themselves, their personal changes would probably not need to be particularly deep or esoteric; what they would need to learn might be as simple as what I have stated here.

> **Troubleshooting Tip** Practice Self-Help   If you and your child have not yet discovered the benefits of food plans and journals and if you have not kept a journal of your own thoughts and feelings so far throughout your child's recovery, this may be a good time to start. Journaling allows you to identify changes, triggers, preferences, moods, behavioral patterns, and motivators; a journal is like a camera, stopping time by capturing how you think and who you are at a given time. Heightening your awareness, journals are diagnostic tools and recovery enhancers as well as vehicles for creativity. As reassuring indicators of just how far you have come, they sustain your forward momentum and limit your backward slides.

## Joining with the Therapist

If you believe that your child's recovery has begun to derail, you may consider intervening with members of her treatment team. If you choose to consult with your child's therapist about your observations and concerns, you will need to make your child aware of your intentions and purpose. Be careful to tread lightly when judging someone else's treatment; your vision is surely obscured by your being once removed from the experience for which you are advocating.

Once in contact with your child's therapist, you might consider playing the role of devil's advocate, offering up your concerns, then asking the therapist to prove them unfounded. When you and the therapist want the same things for your child, the therapist will welcome your input. Your observations and insights may be instrumental in redefining the goals of treatment and facilitating recovery progress.

Exercise F in Chapter Five suggested appropriate and inappropriate ways to intervene in your child's treatment when it seemed to be going off course. Here are some additional interventions you might use with specific team members:

- To the therapist: "I have some questions and concerns. What might be an appropriate way and time for me to air some of these with you?"
- To any team member: "I don't understand the team's decision to require this of my child. Can you explain?"

- To the therapist: "Something has started to happen at home that has me worried."
- To the pediatrician's secretary: "I will accompany my child to her next office visit and would like permission to come in to talk with them both after the doctor has had an opportunity to spend time with her alone."

It is inappropriate, however, to try to use these interventions:

- To the therapist: "I have things to discuss with you, and I plan to come to my child's next therapy session."
- To the nutritionist: "What can I do to stop my daughter from gaining too much weight now that she has started eating?"
- To the therapist: "Is my child still purging?"
- To the internist: "How are the weigh-ins going?"

> **Troubleshooting Tip Don't Be Afraid to Contribute to the Process**    It is your job as the wheel to squeak. You should probe, require explanations, and evoke discourse and reassurance where appropriate. There are no rules determining the frequency of your interventions or of other contacts among team members. Appropriateness depends on circumstances and needs and may range from several times a week, to occasionally, or not at all. If you find yourself attempting to micromanage your child's case, step back and observe these reactions; there may be something important to be learned about yourself here.

 **EXERCISE F Assessing the Therapist's Response**    Your intervention may stimulate various reactions from the therapist. Read each of the following responses. Does the response match what your child's therapist has done or what you believe she or he might do? Circle Y for yes, N for no.

1. Y/N   The therapist wants to bring you in for a conjoint family session (assuming you are not already having such sessions). You may also be invited to a session as a one-time or occasional guest participant.
2. Y/N   The therapist invites you to participate in a series of family sessions.
3. Y/N   Your child and her therapist decide to hear you out and then determine the validity of your observations between themselves. They

decide to consider some changes as a result of your observations or participation.

4. Y/N  The therapist feels threatened by you. She or he reacts defensively.

5. Y/N  The therapist aligns with your child against you, inciting her to see you as intrusive and inappropriate.

6. Y/N  The therapist and your child solicit additional suggestions from you.

7. Y/N  The therapist alienates you from the process, in an effort to become closer to your child.

8. Y/N  The therapist charges you for each contact made by phone, even when it is for a brief question or statement of concern.

This exercise will tell you a lot about the therapist and her or his attitude. If you notice closed-mindedness or resistance on the part of the therapist, it may give you some insight into the dynamics of your child's treatment and her responsiveness, or lack thereof, to you. It is time to think deeply about her current treatment. Are you comfortable with the way things are? Is your child?

## Contacting Other Team Members

Now may be as good a time as any to assess the quality of team members' communication about your child's case. Have team members kept up with each other about your child, her progress, and her changing needs? If not, it is time that they did.

As a member of the treatment team, you need to understand how assessments and professional decisions get made and shared. Such communication can happen by mail, e-mail, or fax, on the phone or face to face; if it does not happen, your child stands to lose. If communication isn't happening, why not call a meeting of the team and make it happen? The parental involvement that I describe here is not meant to be adversarial; it is simply a reality check, and you are simply asking for what is due you and your child.

> **Taking Stock** Using the Professional Grapevine    Here is a sample of a helpful communication. It was sent by a psychotherapist to the internist who referred the patient in question to her.

Re: Jane Doe
Dear Dr. X:

Thank you so much for the referral of Jane Doe. She is a lovely and emotionally healthy young woman who has already made significant changes in her perspectives and actions in the short time that we have worked together. Her weight loss is one piece of a larger emotional and behavioral picture which we have begun to address.

Because work on emotions alone is not sufficient to manage and eradicate the beginnings of what I feel could become a genuine eating disorder, I am sending her to the nutritionist I work with for a greater focus now on food and eating. This will give her the opportunity to try her hand at more balanced eating, challenging her to make changes in this sphere which will generalize to other spheres. I have also brought her parents in for a family session which I feel was helpful for them all.

I do not see her as being depressed, but she does speak of fears about returning to college and of behaving in compulsive, rigid, and extreme ways with regard to her studying and exercise. She describes feeling agitated, "empty," and irritable. Though her symptoms are mild, I am seeing a slightly depressed, slightly anxious, slightly compulsive and slightly out-of-control young woman whom I think would benefit from three to six months prescription of a serotonin medication.

When I mentioned it to her and described how such a medication might help her, she felt eager to try it. She was going to communicate with her parents about it, and I suggested that they call either me or you to speak more about this alternative. I think it will give her "a leg up" in returning to school, as she has become quite unhappy there, and she goes back facing major decisions now about transferring to a new school, changing her major, etc. Would you feel comfortable prescribing such a medication if she decided to try it, or would you prefer that she be referred to a psychiatrist? Please let me know. Thank you.

## Listening to Your Child's Feedback: Fielding Complaints

By now, your responses to your child are probably vastly more effective than they were earlier in treatment. If she comes to you to ask your opinion about something that happened in treatment or about her relationship with her therapist, you are now better able than ever to facilitate her recovery by

• Remaining nonjudgmental and being supportive of the therapy process.

- Turning the question around to ask her what *she* thinks. This display of confidence in her judgment and ability to solve problems encourages her to learn to make such assessments independently.
- Checking out whether she has spoken to her therapist about her concerns and feelings. If she hasn't, can she tell you why?
- Helping her evaluate the therapist's response.
- Not doing for her what she is capable of doing for herself.

**Activity** **Responding to Treatment Complaints** Imagine that your child comes to you complaining about her therapist: "Can you believe what she said!?" Perhaps she is annoyed at the therapist for wanting to discuss food issues, or she feels the therapist is being too intrusive. She may feel outraged that the therapist tends to be inactive (one of my patients described her psychotherapist at college as being so indirect and nonparticipatory that "sitting with her is equivalent to writing in a journal"). Or perhaps she is upset that the therapist isn't as sympathetic about something as she would have liked, or she feels the therapist is being judgmental. What would you say? Now think of an actual complaint that you have heard from your child about her therapist. How did you reply then? How might you reply now? Record your ideas in your journal.

### Being an Advocate to the Team

As a member of your child's treatment team, you have considerable capacity to throw your influence behind the professionals, thereby bolstering the recovery effort. Here's how. When a child complained that her therapist was "so prying," her mother explained the therapist's purpose: to teach a process of self-questioning key to the child's knowing herself and resolving her own problems one day. She explained that the questions asked in therapy don't require specific answers at the moment and are not tests. Questions can be instructive simply in the asking; they are the planting of therapeutic seeds (thoughts and ideas) that may or may not sprout into self-knowledge.

In another situation, a teenager complained to her mother about a statement made by her therapist, but it sounded to the mother as though her child might have distorted the true meaning of the therapist's words. Having trust in the quality of the therapist's work and her good intentions, the parent responded by suggesting that her daughter might have misconstrued the therapist's message here, and she encouraged her daughter to follow up with a direct discussion with the therapist.

Both these parents were in a position to foster the trust and communication that are essential components of the patient-professional relationship, and they took that responsibility seriously. Likewise, the therapist should interpret to the child the efforts, role, and intentions of the well-meaning parent.

Under certain circumstances, parents may need to intervene quite actively to facilitate the recovery process. In one instance a teenager who had made great headway in recovery stopped attending therapy sessions and began to engage in purging behaviors again. After observing her sullen and angry response to her parents' encouragement to return to treatment, her mother called the therapist to inform her what was happening, asking if she and her husband could bring their daughter in for a conjoint intervention. "She may not speak to us after this," declared the mother, "but we feel we have no choice." They didn't. Not when what was at stake was their child's health and happiness.

## Functioning as an Empowered Parent

When a child is unable to regulate herself, the enlightened parent sets *consistent limits, based on a clear and constant value system,* well into the youngster's adolescence and young adult years. Appropriate limit setting charts a secure and directed journey for the lost or floundering child. Through setting limits, the parent teaches and empowers the child to eventually take over the task of regulating herself. The time for a parent to impose limits is when a child demonstrates a lack of internal wisdom and a clear need for corrective input.

*Limits are not the same as rules.* They are to some degree and in certain situations flexible, responsive to the requirements of the moment and the child's self-monitoring capacity. Rules are carved in rock, rigidities that create power struggles as they encourage and strengthen the eating disordered child's own rigidity. The limits essential to your child's security can become a crippling force when imposed as rules, gratuitously and unnecessarily. A mother, in an effort to teach her child to eat properly, required that she eat "at least a nibble" of everything served to her. This was counterproductive for several reasons: this child was never given the option to learn to regulate her own eating, she learned to rely on others for decisions that should have been based on her own responsiveness to internal cues; and finally, learning to nibble at portions is hardly a lesson in healthy eating.

**Taking Stock** **Teaching Good Judgment**   A parent teaches good judgment through his or her power to *reason* with the child, not through nagging, violence, or emotional blackmail. Compare the following examples to understand the difference between effective and ineffective parenting, between rules and limits, between becoming involved in power struggles and asserting healthy values.

*What empowered parenting is not.*   A father felt exasperated after attempting unsuccessfully to set a firm limit for his anorexic daughter. In an effort to limit her excessive use of a video game, and to show her "who's boss," he proclaimed, "Do what I say because I am your father!" Ripping the game out of its player, he destroyed it.

*What empowered parenting is.*   A father who wanted his high school senior to stop spending protracted hours playing a video game approached her with the specific reasons why he felt she needed to stop the excessive activity and do something else. He explained that occupying herself in this way precluded her spending time actively reading, studying, involving herself with others, playing sports, or enjoying hobbies. He gave her the option of finishing her game and an opportunity for rebuttal, but the die was cast for ending the game playing.

*What empowered parenting is not.*   When an anorexic teenager made her family late for work and school every morning by refusing to let them into the bathroom where she spent protracted time in front of the mirror measuring fat deposits on her body, they chose to defer to her wishes, thereby feeding her tyrannical "monster within." Their likelihood of getting such a willful and out-of-control child to cooperate in eating disorder treatment and recovery is slim if they can't even dislodge her from the family bathroom in the morning.

*What empowered parenting is.*   In an identical situation, the parents, united in their values and their determination to instruct their daughter to be a considerate and civil family member, forcibly removed her from the bathroom, with a stern and clear statement about the requirements of living within the community of a household. They clearly outlined her need to respect the rights of others, and which behaviors were and were not acceptable in the home. The issue ceased to be an issue with this action.

Don't be put off by a child's resistance to controls. Your limit setting is perfectly acceptable and in fact required. What *is not* acceptable is parental resistance to exerting appropriate controls and to committing to these actions. Remember that as a parent you can never be blamed for intrusiveness or boundary crossing (infringing on your child's personal space) when what concerns you is

- Being true to your needs and obligations as a parent.
- Expressing what you notice, feel, and require.
- Making certain that your child is learning what she needs to know.
- Setting limits based on meaningful values.

These are your rights. Do not be afraid to exercise them. The tyrannical and tantrumming child *of any age* is begging to be contained. Whether the child is merely spoiled or truly eating disordered, the solution needs to be the same. Hear her cry and respond with meaningful limits and consequences. At the same time you are attempting to extinguish her dysfunctional *behaviors,* be sure to hear and respond to your child's *feelings.* Make your response through a united parental partnership that is persistent, consistent, assured, and loving.

## Dealing with the Insurance Company

In Chapter Five, I discussed the parents' role in advocating for their child's benefits with insurance companies. It may be time to take further action now with your insurance company. The insurer may need to be apprised of your child's current status. If she is improved or stable, the need for care may be ongoing. If she is starting to slide backward, the company needs to be made aware that her needs are pressing and the treatment needs to be continued, changed, or expanded—and the sooner the better, for the longer one waits, the more ingrained the negative forces can become and the more extensive the recovery work will be.

As in your earlier dealings with your insurance company, get the name of the person to whom you are talking and be sure to get your commitments from the insurance company in writing. Do not hesitate to go directly to the top of the hierarchical heap, requesting to speak with your liaison's supervisor or that supervisor's supervisor, should you not be satisfied with the services offered.

> **Troubleshooting Tip** Make Buy-In a Reality  If your child appears to be marking time in treatment, you might ask her to contribute to financing her recovery by making small payments with the money she makes from an after-school job or an allowance. You are providing an incentive by asking her to buy in to the process and to own part of it, encouraging her to assume responsibility for what she values in her life.

## Creating an Intervention

An intervention is a meeting of caring, loving others who come together to make a collective appeal to the eating disordered individual for her recovery. This technique is dramatic proof of the axiom that the whole can be greater than the sum of its parts. Interventions can be instrumental in first bringing your resistant child to treatment; they can also be powerful devices for inspiring your child to make a more substantive commitment to recovery after she has been involved in a treatment process that has been going nowhere. The device is particularly helpful when the setbacks in treatment are due to her own resistance to change. Participants are generally not part of the professional team but are members of the immediate and extended family, coaches, teachers, and concerned friends.

The experience is an affirmation to the patient that she is loved and that her health and well-being are highly significant to others, if not to herself at the moment. In some instances interventions create an emotional experience powerful enough to motivate the patient to open her mind to some new ideas or at least to make some movement off dead center.

> **Taking Stock**  Organizing an Intervention  Here are some steps to take as you prepare for an intervention.
>
> - Consider your goals in holding the intervention.
> - Research with, and about, the people who interact significantly with your child. Invite those who might have clout with your child.

- Decide who will run the meeting. Who will speak first? What will be said?
- Determine whether you should hire a professional facilitator to conduct the process.
- Decide where the meeting will be held.
- Decide how formal or informal you would like it to be.
- Prepare a statement you will make about your child's current situation, her progress to date, what has worked so far, and what has not.
- Prepare yourself to hear your child out, to understand her fears.
- Decide whether you will prepare a contract for your child to sign during the intervention. If you do, it should include spaces where she can write in the goals she feels she can realistically attempt to achieve and the time she thinks it may take her.
- Make the goals you encourage specific, realistic, and short term; break tasks into their smallest components.
- Request each participant to prepare to speak, presenting specific problems and discussing consequences for his or her own relationship with your child if she chooses not to recover. (These are reality checks, not emotional threats.)
- Anticipate your child's anger. It will not be easy for her to be taken by surprise and confronted in this way. It may take some time before you know the full extent of what the intervention has meant to her.
- Do your homework; line up professionals who can step in and take over the treatment and recovery process from here.
- Consider whether you will feel secure that you have done the right thing.

## Using a Consultant

When recovery seems to be no longer progressing, it is sometimes valuable to seek out another professional to serve as a consultant. A fresh ear and eye can provide an invaluable perspective.

## Case Study

Gloria, the mother of an anorexic teenager, came to me in search of a second opinion. Her daughter, who was verbally abusive and difficult to live with, had been in protracted treatment with a therapist but showed no signs of change. Issues concerning food and the troubled family relationships were being systematically avoided in treatment, though the therapist had been successful in making a long-term emotional alliance with the child.

At first, I encouraged Gloria to approach her daughter's therapist in an effort to learn how to become more a part of her daughter's recovery. She requested a few family treatment sessions. The therapist implied that it was the mother's "intrusive quality," as seen in this request, that had caused her daughter's illness in the first place. The therapist expressed fear that bringing the family into treatment would alienate her patient from the therapeutic alliance they shared. She mistakenly believed that by speaking with the child's mother she was *already* in violation of the patient's privacy and confidences.

As her daughter continued to lose weight, I advised Gloria to have her daughter seen by a physician who could monitor her physical condition. Again, she pleaded her case to the therapist, who claimed this time that the patient might "bolt" from treatment if the therapist were to introduce this option, which would "cause such discomfort." Apparently caught up in her own issues and need for approval, this therapist had failed to recognize that by placating the patient and giving her too much responsibility for self-care too early in her recovery, she was *enabling* the patient's inappropriate power and thus her illness—not her recovery.

I then encouraged Gloria to take responsibility for finding a doctor for her daughter on her own. Ironically, the person she found told her that her worries were "unfounded" because her daughter was "not significantly underweight."

Over the next several months and through several more conversations, I educated Gloria about eating disorders and about her role as advocate for her child's wellness. Together we looked at her options and the consequences of various courses of action.

Through our work together, Gloria ultimately found the internal strength to offer her daughter and the therapist a respectful but reality-based ultimatum: if there were no observable strides behaviorally or emotionally within the six-month period before her daughter left for college, her daughter would either have to submit to a change in therapist or forfeit her opportunity to go away to college.

Gloria constructively exercised her role as parent, modeling sound judgment and proactive problem solving by refusing to back down in the face of confrontation yet remaining sensitive to her daughter's needs.

**Activity** Preparing to Meet with the Consultant   In preparing to meet a consultant outside the treatment team, it is important that you gather certain useful information. The consultant will need to know

- The history of the problem: what has worked well to date, and what hasn't worked.
- Where you have seen indicators of progress and lack of progress.
- What goals have been tried and attained, and what goals remain untried.
- Where you continue to see elements of the disorder outside of your child's eating problems.
- What your role has been to date.
- What you would like your role to become.
- How you see yourself acting to move the treatment along in the right direction.
- Your description of the input of various members of the treatment team. Are all the necessary experts in place?
- What you like and do not like about the professionals your child is working with.
- How happy your child is with the treatment efforts so far.
- Whether your child knows you are seeking outside help. If she does, how does she feel about it?
- What your child's medical and psychological records contain. (You have the right to access your child's records if she is under the age of eighteen. If she is over eighteen, she needs to sign a release of information permission form for you, or anyone, to have access to these materials.)

**Troubleshooting Tip** Feed Your Child   When your child was a baby, you had no trouble knowing how to feed her. Do now what you did then. Yogurt and salad, or no meals at all, will not nourish her as will meat and potatoes, fish and pasta, bread and butter, rice and dressing. You know what to do. Trust yourself and expect that your child will do the same.

**Troubleshooting Tip** **Turn off the Television Set** Your child's job in life is to become an educated, socially involved, and functional human being. Television watching promotes passivity and the loss of a sense of purpose, initiative, and self-control. It fosters erroneous ideas about what life is like, encouraging children to live through the lives of others rather than actively creating and living out their own. If your child needs television to "relax," as so many children assert, it may be time to investigate what is causing your child so much stress.

## When Fine-Tuning Isn't Enough: Changing Therapists

When your child's attempts to cope with recovery have been unproductive, she may need to consider the option of changing therapists or her team. This is not a suggestion I make lightly. Having a leaky roof does not mean you have to move to another house. The choice to make such a change must be purposeful and based on a clear understanding of what went wrong and on a healthy drive toward attaining goals yet unfulfilled. Arbitrary, impulsive, or mindless change without understanding leaves your child vulnerable to repeating old mistakes; furthermore, it can be decidedly countertherapeutic, enabling your recovering child to once again escape from problems rather than confront them head on.

Before making such a decision, all involved parties need to hold a substantive discussion in an effort to repair what has broken down. Will your child's therapist listen? Does she or he have the capacity to make things better? If not, a purposeful change in therapists might allow your child to find a therapist who better speaks her language. All individuals learn differently. Through their particular, diverse use of language, images, and self, different therapists enjoy varying degrees of potency with patients. By being more discriminating the next time around, you will also increase your chances of finding someone who is more in tune with parental roles, family systems theory, and a coordinated team effort, all requirements of successful eating disorder treatment and recovery.

Because of the difficulties of eating disorder recovery, some treatment teams require that patients commit to treatment for at least one year, to allow for the frustrations of an arduous process. Your child needn't be in treatment nearly that long to know whether the process she is engaged in will be a dynamic and productive one. Whether she remains involved when the going gets rough depends on much more than a commitment made outside of and prior to the treatment process. You can be a significant force in supporting her decision to stick with treatment and weather the tough times, no matter what therapist she chooses to work with.

> **Troubleshooting Tip Be Open to Alternative Treatments** Your child may wish to try nonmainstream techniques to augment healing. Hypnosis, imagery work, art, or dance therapy, biofeedback, the Feldenkrais Method,[2] acupuncture—each may possibly represent a different way *in*, an alternate route to making a connection with the patient's needs and inner strengths. What is most helpful to any individual patient is whatever *speaks* most poignantly to her, whatever allows her the greatest opportunity to experience herself in a changed way.

## THE CHOICE TO REMAIN ILL

If you have done everything in your power to bring about positive change and your child still refuses treatment or the option to recover, if she remains beyond your reach as well as beyond the reach of her professionals, you may have no alternative but to let go of the process for a time, allowing life experience to take its course (such a scenario is described in Chapter Six).

### You Can Lead a Horse to Water—Then Take Care of Yourself

I recently bumped into the mother of a now recovered patient whom I had treated ten years previously. At my mention of writing this book and her recollection of those "tormented years," tears filled her eyes. There is nothing as painful, she explained, "as when it happens to your child, the one you were up with at night, stayed home for, loved, and feel privileged to have raised."

She went on to say: "You never think you'll be able to muster the strength that you do. The most important thing I could do for us all at the time was whatever it took to take care of *me*. In my efforts to maintain my sanity, I volunteered to man the eating disorder telephone hot line at ANAD, helping other victims of eating disorders, even while my own daughter was having problems accepting help. It was also my chance to get away from my own phone, where my daughter would ensnare me with unproductive calls from school a dozen times a day."

## Achieving Internal Peace: Knowing You've Done Right by Your Child

Sharon, at age twenty-five, had been in and out of hospitals and residential care for the treatment of her anorexia for seven years. Her highly supportive parents were in a quandary, not knowing how to respond to their daughter in her still tenuous state. Sharon's mother described how she and her husband were faced with significant differences of opinion as they continued to grapple with the disease, their daughter, and their mutual fear that Sharon would never recover, or worse, that she might die. "This may sound petty," she began, then proceeded to discuss issues at the very heart of relationships between parents and their eating disordered children. "Bringing our daughter home from the hospital, we promptly kicked off our dirty shoes so as not to soil the newly laid white carpeting; Sharon, however, paid no heed to her surroundings, unabashedly tracking mud across the floor. 'Sharon, please take off your shoes!' I said. My husband promptly scolded me for 'telling her what to do and treating her like a baby;' I was certain I'd undone whatever progress she had made at the hospital."

"Her living situation really has us concerned, too," this mother continued. "Sharon is frightened to live on her own unless in the poshest (safest) section of town in a fancy high-rise with a doorman, yet she refuses to go back to school to get the education she needs to support a job that will support this lifestyle. My husband and I are left to support her. Knowing that we are probably enabling her so that she will never become self-reliant, I fear that we will have to financially support her for the rest of our lives. And what if something happens to us? But then I think, 'How can I be so callous as to think about money when my child's safety is at stake?!'"

Sharon's disorder had handcuffed her parents, leaving them emotionally paralyzed. In fact, the less Sharon is expected to behave like everyone else, the more overly powerful and further entrenched she becomes in disease, unreality, and poor judgment. Her shoes needed to come off, and she needs to live within her means. Financial support can facilitate emotional maturity, or a child's undoing. Unless Sharon's parents stipulate that their financial support would be time-limited and based on the requirement that Sharon prepares to eventually support herself or move in with others, the arrangement is certainly self-defeating. This message is not about deprivation or punishment. It is about reality testing.

"But what if the worst happens? I would never forgive myself," this mother continued, assuming responsibility for her daughter's life or death.

"In the face of an unsuccessful outcome, you must know now, as in the future looking back to this time, that you have made purposeful decisions true to your values and based on sound judgment in consensus with your partner, leaving no opportunity for self-recrimination. Can you think of careless decisions or any omissions that might one day come back to haunt you?" I asked.

"There is only one thing we have not yet done," she replied. "That is for my husband and I to step out of her life. That won't be easy, though, as she is so childlike and vulnerable, we just melt every time we look at her. So when do we hit her with the fact that we will take the hard line on financial independence? When are we asking too much, too soon, and when might too soon be too late?"

"These answers lie in the timing of these decisions as they appear in your thoughts and in your heart," I responded. "As they arise, these thoughts and decisions belong on your tongue, shared and available for mutual discussion, understanding, negotiation, and consensus, both with your partner and your child."

"A parent can only be as happy as her least happy child," she stated. "I know my life won't get better until she gets better." However, she promptly contradicted her theory as she proceeded to describe her decision to get back into her own life; after dropping out of her bridge club because "it was too painful to answer the continual question, 'How is Sharon doing?'" she had made the choice to rejoin. "I'm back," she said, "though I know that playing bridge or golf and lunching with my friends is only a Band-Aid." These responses are hardly Band-Aids; instead, they are honest and effective means to repair a saddened heart. *There is life and fulfillment for you beyond your child's eating disorder, even in those rare instances when the eating disorder does not go away or your child succumbs to disease.*

Parents are not responsible for saving their child's life, as long as they have done everything in their power to try. Your child is ultimately responsible to no one but herself in choosing her destiny. When you have left no option untried, acting knowledgeably and with generosity of spirit, you have done all you can do. The *best* you can do is *all* you can do. Although your child's failed recovery outcome will not have been because of you and what you did, if your child *does* recover, it may very well be in response to efforts you have continued to make throughout her recovery. It is important that you grasp this distinction.

## YOU ARE ON THE RIGHT TRACK

Shortly before this book was about to go to press, an article appeared in the *Wall Street Journal* describing the results of a scientific research study on a new and highly effective technique for treating anorexics.[3] The Maudsley model, developed by Ivan Eisler and Christopher Dare at the Institute of Psychiatry and Maudsley Hospital in London, England, is a treatment technique that enlists parents as active participants in their child's recovery, coaching them to discover their own strengths and resources so as to exercise a proactive and positive influence over their child in eating disorder recovery. Their research suggests that

"Early aggressive interventions that engage the whole family offer the best chance of saving the lives of anorexics."[4]

The Maudsley model recognizes that parents are not to blame for their child's disorder, but they are in a prime position to help effect cure. Highly specific in its techniques, the method offers a protocol for parents who are coached by specially trained professionals as they respond to their child's dysfunctional eating behaviors. The Maudsley approach advocates proactive interventions modeled after the role of inpatient nurses in monitoring the child's eating behaviors.[5] Some scholars have questioned whether techniques that may be successful abroad will enjoy the same impact in the United States, particularly where parents are not models of healthy eating themselves, where they exercise compulsively, won't sit down to eat with their children, or are not willing to make personal sacrifices.[6] It will be important to watch for results as work continues with this project.

Scholarly research based on the Maudsley method confirms conclusions similar to those arrived at through my own clinical observations as presented in this book. You are no stranger to these results. The researchers concur that

- Parents need not feel defeated by this illness.
- Parents need to learn to tap into their own internal strengths and to use the resources implicit in their role as parents.
- Parents who learn to become child advocates will be most readily able to promote recovery, prevent relapse, and enhance a healthy relationship with their child, and to do so while relying less on professional assistance.
- Parents who have confidence in themselves and in their parenting role, and who can exercise their parental authority appropriately with consistency and consensus, are in the best position to facilitate their child's eating disorder recovery.

As you begin to uncover and utilize the full range of your internal and external resources to help your child, you will find that there is no more potent way to demonstrate effective functioning to your child. You will probably also find that the only pleasure greater than experiencing the sense of personal empowerment that comes from a proactive and positive use of yourself is watching your child learn to do the same from modeling herself after you.

# Appendix A:
# Answers to Exercises

## CHAPTER ONE

### Answers to Exercise A

1. Control, relationships, behavior
2. Thinking
3. Identity, relationships
4. Coping, relationships, feelings, behavior, values
5. Thinking
6. Control, coping, relationships, behavior
7. Relationships, thinking
8. Thinking, feelings, values
9. Control, coping, relationships, behavior
10. Relationships, behavior, lifestyle, values
11. Control, coping, behavior
12. Thinking, coping, relationships
13. Control, coping, relationships
14. Identity, values

### Answers to Exercise F

1. a
2. b, c
3. b
4. b

5. a, c

6. b

7. b

8. a

9. b

10. c

11. a, c

12. a, b, c

# CHAPTER THREE

## Sample Answers to Exercise G

1. *Heard:* You are skinny, and I like the way you look. I wish I could look that thin. *Meant:* Stop worrying about your weight. You look fine. You don't look fat or ugly.

2. *Heard:* You are no longer of concern for me. I will forget about you now. *Meant:* I am relieved that you have begun to get things under control.

3. *Heard:* You look like you've put on weight. You are getting fat. *Meant:* The treatment seems to be working. You seem to be recovering.

4. *Heard:* You have nothing to say about how I live my life. *Meant:* Can you do something to help me sit down here and eat with you?

5. *Heard:* Cake is the reward for eating something as unpleasant as beans. *Meant:* If you eat dessert first, you may not have an appetite for your meal.

6. *Heard:* You shouldn't eat that. It will make you fat. *Meant:* Are you being true to your own needs?

7. *Heard:* I am trying to interfere in your work with my child, to tell you what to do and how to do it. *Meant:* Is there something more I can do to help? I would so like to become a part of my child's recovery and life.

8. *Heard:* I want to control my child's life—to tell her what to do and to tell you what to do and how to run your practice. *Meant:* I want to contribute to my child's recovery, learn about eating disorders, and make personal changes that will enhance my child's recovery.

## CHAPTER FOUR

### Answers to Exercise F

1. a, c
2. a
3. d, a
4. b or c
5. a
6. b or c
7. b
8. c, a, d
9. a, b, or c
10. a, b, or c

## CHAPTER FIVE

### Sample Answers to Exercise D

1. *Heard:* Under no circumstances should a parent mention food to a child, even if she is in severe trouble with it. Parents should avoid pressuring their child to attend family meals and instructing her about healthy food attitudes and lifestyles. *Meant:* Under normal circumstances, parents needn't be intrusive or controlling about what their child eats. This is something the child should self-regulate. Let her take as much initiative as she can first. If the child is *incapable* of self-regulation, then parents are remiss if they do not respond.

2. *Heard:* You are getting fat. Your punishment is to see a nutritionist. *Meant:* If there is something awry in your eating lifestyle, you may do well to talk to a nutritionist about correcting it.

3. *Heard:* It is critical not to be fat, even if you have to take extreme measures to take off the pounds. *Meant:* If you want to make changes in your life, I am here to help you in every way I can.

4. *Heard:* There is some magic in the number five. If you gain five pounds you are recovered enough to function healthfully in school. *Meant:* If you are still

so incapable of eating healthfully, it would be irresponsible of me to allow you to go away to school, where you would surely become more ill.

5. *Heard:* You are being punished for behaving badly. Punishment will be your incentive to change. *Meant:* If you won't assume responsibility for nourishing your body adequately, it is unsafe and unwise for you to tax it further through excessive exercise.

6. *Heard:* No need to respond to an eating disorder that is not in full flower. Once it gets bad enough, hospitalization can cure it. *Meant:* Let's hold off a bit to see how things evolve.

7. *Heard:* Don't intervene in your child's life regarding food under any circumstances. *Meant:* It is important to be respectful of an adolescent's growing need for independence.

8. *Heard:* Weight is the ultimate criterion for assessing recovery. If you haven't lost weight, you must be doing well in your recovery. Whatever you're doing is good enough for me. *Meant:* I am pleased with your progress in recovery.

9. *Heard:* Appearance is what counts in eating disorder recovery. How you manipulate your weight determines how your treatment team will respond to you. You are looking fat. You don't need to recover any more than you already have. *Meant:* Your recovery is secure enough that you are out of physiological danger.

10. *Heard:* Unless a person is in physical danger, medical intervention is unnecessary. *Meant:* Try not to get hysterical and catastrophize things.

11. *Heard:* If your child is uncomfortable facing food issues, it is okay not to address them. There are other ways to bring about healing. *Meant:* You can't fix an eating problem without first addressing the issues that drive the problem.

12. *Heard:* I am issuing you an ultimatum. Cross me and you are in trouble. *Meant:* If my treatment is not sufficient to help you gain control of your disease, perhaps outpatient treatment may not be the treatment of choice.

13. *Heard:* Don't initiate discussion with your child, even if you see that she is in trouble and does not know how to reach out and ask for assistance. *Meant:* Timing is everything in life. You can only lead a horse to water.

14. *Heard:* Whatever you eat, no matter when and how or in what quantity, it's good enough as long as you are eating something. *Meant:* If you need to start out slowly in your efforts to begin eating at all, go ahead and pace yourself comfortably. But remember that recovery is about the capacity to nourish yourself completely, positively, and normally. Eventually you will need to be able to eat almost everything.

**Answers to Exercise F**

1. N
2. Y
3. Y
4. N
5. N
6. Y
7. Y
8. Y
9. Y
10. N

# CHAPTER SIX

## Sample Answers to Exercise C

1. Not finding a girlfriend has less to do with appearance and more to do with the issues that underlie and drive the eating disorder. It is your *disorder*, not your looks, your problem with establishing lasting intimacies and being a whole person that interferes with your making a sound connection with another person. With recovery will come better people skills.

2. Your ability to eat now and then is not an indicator that you have grown more comfortable with food and with yourself. Besides, I am aware that sushi is a low-fat meal. My guess is that you are aware of the same thing. Would you be as free to join us at an Italian or Greek restaurant? And would you feel free to order something other than salad at those places? I

think it is important to be honest with yourself as well as with us about your ability to eat.

3. It is so easy to get sidetracked every now and then, thinking eating disorders are about food. They are not.

4. Recovery will return you to a sense of balance and normalcy in *all* of your lifestyle habits. What you do today with your eating disorder is an investment in the rest of your life.

5. The ten pounds by themselves do not represent cure. They help to restore your weight sufficiently so that your brain will be more capable of grasping the tasks and requirements of recovery. It is what you have to *do* and to *become* in order to recover—not the weight itself—that brings about healing.

6. The eating disordered existence lacks authenticity. It is truncated and minimal, causing you to miss the joy and the very point of living life, of learning and studying. How sad it is that the disorder has robbed you of the intellectual curiosity and imagination you need to derive pleasure from this book.

7. A nondisordered person's missing a meal is an insignificant event. It might indicate lateness, lack of hunger, or preoccupation, and the calories will be made up. With eating disorders, it is the *purpose* behind missing a meal that becomes significant; in addition, your anxious response to your *failed* intention to miss a meal sets you apart from your sister.

8. People need to eat three meals a day for the same reason that they need a good night's sleep and need to brush their teeth in the morning. Your body needs and deserves this fuel in order to function optimally. It is that simple.

## Answers to Exercise E

1. Y. By creating an external structure of limits and boundaries for Penny, her parents would establish a sense of security for her that would increase her confidence and diminish her fears.

2. Y. Instead, Penny's parents should readily confront Penny with difficult realities and encourage her to deal with them.

3. N. If they do not discuss food with her, they are encouraging her to do as they do, which is to opt for the path of least resistance. Because Penny has made food and eating an issue, her parents must respond to the issue and

then extrapolate to the excessiveness and imbalance in areas of her life beyond food. They should also take her to see a gastroenterologist.

4. N. Every person should eat three meals a day. We all live inside our bodies, which are machines that must be perpetually fueled. Along with sleeping and cleanliness, eating is one of the most basic ways a person can take care of himself.

5. N. Please see the explanation for item 2.

6. Y. Please see the explanation for item 2.

7. Y. Perhaps this therapist has not met with the family and does not know its dynamics. She may not have a clear and unbiased picture of what goes on at home and may need to be informed.

8. Y. Try to make the treatment with this therapist work first. But at some point things will need to change so the family is not wasting precious time and money.

# Appendix B: Taking an Eating Disorder to College

The college environment is particularly conducive to the development of eating disorders because of the stress of leaving home; the unlimited freedoms afforded to students, many of whom are away from home for the first time; academic pressures; and social pressures to find friends and be accepted. Of great significance is the tendency for excess that is everywhere a part of college life for so many students. Weekends (considered times to unwind from the rigors of the week and drink with friends) too frequently begin on Thursday night and extend through Sunday. The primary form of recreation on college campuses today typically involves free-flowing alcohol, drugs, and television watching.

Increased opportunities for indulging in fast foods, take-out, and alcohol cause students to put on weight (the notorious *freshman fifteen*) just as they most yearn to be attractive to others. Describing sorority life, a patient explained: "Nobody eats. Everyone is hypervigilant of everybody else, watching what they eat so as not to eat more." Sorority war stories include plugged-up sinks and toilets, scarf and barf parties, and girls standing around naked, comparing and measuring the fat on fleshy parts of their bodies.

## Dealing with the Phone Call in the Night

Your child calls home in a frenzy, realizing that her eating disorder has become out of control. You will need to *listen* to hear every detail about her experience; *encourage* her to get psychotherapeutic help at school (the nonspecialist can successfully begin to treat the emotional underpinnings of the disease if not the complete disorder); and *make contact* with local hospitals near the school for referrals to specialists. You may need to *set limits* for her if she remains ill (study abroad may be unrealistic, for instance); *suggest* that she stop weighing herself or consider setting minimal food goals each day; *educate* her (or remind her) about what an eating disorder implies about her life; *help* her see how the disease entails more than what she is or is not putting in her mouth; *reassure* her that she can recover if she chooses and that you will be behind her efforts in every way possible; *offer* her the option of coming home and forfeiting a semester; *anticipate* the problems she faces daily and *rehearse* some more effective coping methods with her; if she does not have a therapist at home, *put out feelers* in your home community to find good professional resources for her when she returns home on vacations (sometimes an adept therapist can accomplish more in several sessions than a less competent one over a period of months); *arrange* how and when the next communication about this problem will take place between the two of you.

## Leaving an Unfinished Treatment to Begin College

It is often frightening for both child and parent when the child must leave an unfinished treatment process to go away to school. Formative changes are still in the works. They remain tentative and the patient feels untried. Furthermore, she is about to experience an acid test, immersion in an environment of thinness awareness. I have found that for those patients going off to school who choose not to find a new therapist, weekly telephone sessions with the home-based therapist can be a constructive alternative to no therapy at all. The continued therapeutic contact serves many purposes for the patient, not the least of which is knowing that she will be accountable for reporting to someone and to herself, that she must exercise vigilant self-awareness to be emotionally and mentally prepared for her long-distance therapy sessions.

## Deciding If Your Child Is Ready to Leave Home

In determining whether or not your child is ready to return to college: discuss the implications of leaving treatment now; does she feel ready to undertake the challenges of school and of being away from treatment and from home? Can she continue the work of therapy while she is away? Does she have adequate internal resources now to keep her afloat? Can she tap external resources available on campus? What are her greatest fears?

How might she handle troublesome situations when they arise? Does she know that if returning to school has been premature, she and you together will act to resolve that situation and that you will take her home again if need be? Prepare to speak to the school administration, if necessary, in order to apprise them of her situation and line up the best help available. Consider allowing fewer courses this semester so as to give her more time for self-care. Can she go to school prepared to keep her expectations realistic and to institute structure in her life in *all* areas, not just around meals?

### Anticipating Problems and Rehearsing Solutions

A big help for your child when she is returning to school is anticipating hard times and vulnerable moments and preparing for them in advance; this is an example of attempting to take control of aspects of life that realistically could be within her control. Are there particular fellow students who trigger an anxious or disordered response in her? What can she do to prepare for and survive interaction with them?

### Keeping Expectations Realistic

Losing some ground, especially at times of transition, is normal, not an indication of failure. Interruptions in treatment, setbacks, and your child's responses to them will provide constructive grist for the therapy learning mill.

If your child goes away to school determined to be happy, she is setting herself up for disappointment. Advise her not to expend fruitless energy hoping for happiness, a goal that is unrealistic and arbitrary. Setting her sights on goals that are concrete and within her grasp and keeping them small and doable will amount to creating a realistic plan of action. This is the best insurance for finding happiness.

### Coping with an Eating Disordered Roommate

Your child may find it debilitating to be living side by side with the perfectionism, judgmentalism, intolerance, rigidity, ritualistic behaviors, and often condescending attitudes that typically describe an eating disordered roommate. In this too-close-for-comfort situation, she will find that maintaining her personal boundaries is vital. Encourage her to attempt to resolve differences through discussion and compromise; short of that, the alternative is to establish distance. She may do well to investigate the option of changing rooms. In most instances, though this can be disruptive and not easy to maneuver, it can be arranged either after the first month of classes or after the first semester. Your child is in school to learn, and the college should be similarly invested in removing any impediment to her academic success. Ultimately, the roommate situation will be hers to resolve, and she will have to endure the consequences of her choices.

## Responding to College Jitters and Blues

The following are some specific concerns of students returning to school with eating disorders, and some parental responses that may be helpful:

CHILD: If I try to work on my eating disorder recovery in school, will it consume all my thoughts and energies, leaving no time for anything else? And will I be consumed by disease if I do *not*?

PARENT: It sounds like some of these worries could be remnants of the black-and-white, distorted thinking that you have come to know as part of the disease.

CHILD: I am eating better, but I feel that I am eating more than everybody else. I feel as though people see me as being a pig.

PARENT: If you lose track of what is appropriate to eat and what is not, it may be helpful to consult your old food plans that you once used with your nutritionist. If the kids you eat with are food restricters, find other eating buddies.

CHILD: I am eating better, but I am still so fearful of putting on an ounce.

PARENT: This eating disorder took a long time in coming; don't expect it to disappear overnight.

CHILD: I am feeling ravenous here all the time.

PARENT: If you feel hungry, eat. Just be sure that what you are eating is good, nutritious food. Stay away from the junk and fast foods if you feel a need to eat more. One more thought; if you exercise, you are free to eat more, but remember not to be excessive about this exercise or any other aspect of your life now.

CHILD: I know I am going to lose it when I see all those skinny girls eating a few leaves of lettuce for dinner.

PARENT: Why not decide before you go to the dining hall just what you will have for your meal? Would it be helpful to eat with different kids?

## Mentoring from a Distance

Now that your child is away from home, be as clear with her as you are with yourself that even if you stop *asking*, it does not mean you have stopped *caring*. She will now be accountable to *herself* through her actions, and you will be taking your cues from her about if, how, when, and to what extent you will be involved.

> **Troubleshooting Tip** **Listen for Code Words**  Beware of euphemisms that are accepted lingo on college campuses today. They can spell trouble. *Partying* defines a recreational lifestyle of excess that typically includes binge drinking and drug abuse. The *healthy food choice* may describe a lettuce salad or fat-free pretzel for dinner, not a tuna fish sandwich on a roll with mayonnaise. "We were in a *pregame mode*," means, "We were taking drugs and drinking alcohol in preparation for watching the game." "We were in a *drinking mode* by six o'clock," means, "We never bothered to eat dinner."

# Appendix C: Resources

The following organizations and institutions enjoy very fine reputations. (However, this list should not be considered my personal endorsement of any particular organization, form of therapy, or therapist.)

> National Association for Anorexia Nervosa and Associated Disorders (ANAD) Eating Disorder Crisis Hot Line
> 847-831-3438
> 9:00 A.M. to 5:00 P.M. CST Monday–Friday

## INPATIENT PROGRAMS

The following are nationally reputed inpatient units for patients with eating disorders. When choosing a hospital for your child, select an inpatient unit that deals specifically with eating disorders if you can, rather than a general psychiatric unit.

The Center for Eating Disorders
7601 Osler Dr.
Towson, MD 21204
Tel.: 410-427-2100

The center provides inpatient care, day treatment, and intensive outpatient programs through the St. Joseph Medical Center. The program has a behavior modification focus, extinguishing the triggers of dysfunctional behaviors.

Laureate
6655 S. Yale
Tulsa, OK 74136
Tel.: 800-322-5173, 918-491-8106, or 918-298-7804

Laureate's program incorporates the twelve step philosophy with other treatment modalities.

Linden Oaks Hospital
852 West Street
Naperville, IL 60540-6400
Tel.: 800-955-OAKS or 630-305-5500

Linden Oaks is a full-service psychiatric hospital, using a multidisciplinary treatment team approach.

The Meadows
1655 North Tegner Street
Wickenburg, AZ 85390
Tel.: 800-MEADOWS or 520-684-3926; fax: 520-684-3935

The primarily group-based program at the Meadows offers a twelve step orientation. Eating disordered patients are in a unit with patients who have other diagnoses, but the facility specializes in eating disorders.

Menninger Clinic
P.O. Box 829
Topeka, KS 66601-0829
Tel.: 800-351-9058 or 913-273-7500, ext. 5311

The Menninger Clinic offers a structured, four-week, comprehensive program.

Rader Institute
1663 Sawtelle Boulevard
Los Angeles, CA 90025
Tel.: 800-255-1818

Rader has several locations across the nation; this is the address of the central office. The institute incorporates cognitive-behavioral and psychodynamic treatment into the twelve step approach.

Ridgeview Institute
3995 South Cobb Drive
Smyra, GA 30080
Tel.: 800-329-9775, ext. 4114

The program at Ridgeview takes five to ten eating disordered patients at a time in a women's unit.

River Oaks
1525 River Oaks Road West
New Orleans, LA 70123
Tel.: 800-366-1740; fax: 504-733-7020

River Oaks provides treatment for eating disorders in its trauma, dissociative disorders, and sexual compulsivity programs.

The Willough at Naples
9001 Tamiami Trail East
Naples, FL 33962
Tel.: 800-722-0100 or 813-775-4500

The program at The Willough at Naples blends psychodynamic, medical, and behavioral approaches with the twelve step and family system models.


## Programs Associated with Universities

Center for Overcoming Problem Eating (COPE)
Western Psychiatric Institute and Clinic
University of Pittsburgh Medical Center
3811 O'Hara Street
Pittsburgh, PA 15213
Tel.: 412-624-0012 (inpatient unit)

The COPE program provides comprehensive assessments for individuals and treatment designed to address the specific needs of patients requiring different levels of care.

Institute of Psychiatry
Medical University of South Carolina
171 Ashley Ave.
Charleston, SC 29425-0742
Tel.: 843-792-0092

The institute's program, based on a biopsychosocial model, provides an interdisciplinary treatment team approach.

Neuro Psychiatric Institute and Hospital
University of California, Los Angeles
760 Westwood Plaza, Suite B8-213
Los Angeles, CA 90024
Tel.: 310-794-1022

Principles of treatment at the institute rest on an integration of dynamic, expressive, and cognitive behavioral therapies. It is principally an inpatient program, but program graduates can receive outpatient treatment.

University of Iowa Hospitals and Clinics (UIHC)
200 Hawkins Drive 2887 JPP
Iowa City, IA 52242
Tel.: 319-356-1354 (inpatient); 319-353-6149 (partial or day hospital); 319-353-6314 (outpatient unit)

Individualized care at UIHC centers around a process-oriented therapeutic milieu in which the interactional issues between patients are used to facilitate growth and recovery. The general range of stay is five to ten weeks for anorexia patients and two to six weeks for bulimia patients.

University of Minnesota Eating Disorder Program
Dr. Elke Eckert
Department of Psychiatry
Box 393 Mayo Building
Minneapolis, MN 55455
Tel.: 612-626-6871 (doctor's office); 612-626-6188 (outpatient clinic); 612-993-6200 (partial hospital and inpatient unit)

The program includes inpatient, outpatient, and day treatment services. Its narrative treatment philosophy separates the disease from the person, focusing on the person, as opposed disease. This treatment asks questions with the assumption that the patient possesses the necessary answers and will become empowered through answering.

## Residential Treatment Centers

Montecatini
2516 La Costa Ave.
Rancho La Costa, CA 92009
Tel.: 760-436-8930

Montecatini is a female-only treatment center for eating disorders and chemical dependency. Two houses accommodate six patients each. One serves as the main treatment center; the other provides step-down care. The program lasts a minimum of three months. It has a twelve step orientation and is group therapy based. Patients are not allowed to be left alone for the first two months. Families come to the facility for intensive family treatment and lodge elsewhere.

Monte Nido Residential Treatment Facility
27162 Sea Vista Drive
Malibu, CA 90265
Tel.: 818-222-9534

Monte Nido is a private six-bed facility created by recovered professionals to heal women who have eating or exercise disorders. It offers a highly structured program on a secluded gated estate with hiking trails leading to the beach. With individual therapy at least three times a week, participants progress through a levels system, gaining increasing freedom as they heal. The average length of stay is two months.

Remuda Ranch
Box 2481 Jack Burden Road
Wickenburg, AZ 85358
Tel.: 800-445-1900 or 520-684-3913

Remuda Ranch is a Christian-oriented, women-only facility, with an emphasis on the twelve step approach and a mandatory family week that is used to confront family-based issues.

Renfrew Center
475 Spring Lane
Philadelphia, PA 19128
Tel.: 800-736-3739 or 215-482-5353

and

Renfrew Center
7700 Renfrew Lane
Coconut Creek, FL 33073
Tel.: 800-332-8415 or 954-698-9222

Renfrew provides comprehensive women's mental health services in a highly structured program, with family therapy and family telephone contact encouraged. The focus of treatment is psychological; group subjects include such issues as self-esteem, assertiveness, nutrition, body image, interpersonal relations, anger, psychodrama, women's issues, life skills, sexuality, risk-taking, family issues, and so forth.

### Hospital Programs

The community where you live will have fine hospitals, some of which may have eating disorder units and programs. You can scout around to discover the best local programs, assessing how they vary from one another and deciding which would best accommodate your child's needs.

## EATING DISORDER ORGANIZATIONS

The following organizations are sources for referrals, free groups, education, and/or newsletters.

National Association of Anorexia Nervosa and Associated Disorders (ANAD)
P.O. Box 7
Highland Park, IL 60035
Tel.: 847-831-3438
E-mail: anad20@aol.com

ANAD was the first association in the United States developed for the education and support of individuals and families dealing with eating disorders. Nationwide it offers public speakers, a newsletter, and free support groups that maintain phone chain lists (group members exchange telephone numbers so they can give each other additional support between meetings). ANAD provides referrals to therapists and other eating disorder specialists all over this country and abroad and also a crisis hot line for eating disorder care. It conducts legislative advocacy work at state and national levels, fighting for parity in insurance coverage of mental illness and against harmful advertising.

For eating disordered individuals encountering insurance discrimination, ANAD provides advice and assistance about appealing insurers' rulings in court and to state commissioners. It makes pro bono lawyers available to the public to read any insurance policy in an effort to help people understand their rights. The group is currently looking for patients willing to join a possible class action suit against discriminatory insurance companies.

Academy for Eating Disorders
6728 Old McLean Village Dr.
McLean, VA 22101
Tel.: 703-556-9222; fax: 703-556-8729

The academy is primarily a professional organization of providers, researchers, and prevention specialists.

American Anorexia Bulimia Association, Inc. (AABA)
165 W. 46th St.
New York, NY 10036
Tel.: 212-575-6200

AABA provides treatment referrals and educational outreach.

Anorexia/Bulimia Treatment and Education Center (ABTEC)
621 South New Ballas Rd., Suite 7019B
St. Louis, MO 63141
Tel.: 314-569-6898 or 314-569-6565

Free support groups are available at ABTEC, as is evaluation for admission to a hospital psychiatric unit.

The Body Positive
2417 Prospect St., Suite A
Berkeley, CA 94704

This organization has created a model for eating disorder prevention in the schools and for starting support groups. It sells an educational video called *Body Talk,* in which teens talk about their bodies, eating disorders, and activism. It makes professional referrals in its immediate area.

Eating Disorder Awareness and Prevention (EDAP)
603 Stewart Street, Suite 803
Seattle, WA 98101
Tel.: 800-931-2237 or 206-382-3587

This nationally based organization distributes awareness and prevention materials and offers curriculum materials for the schools. It sponsors the annual Eating Disorder Awareness Week each February, and Go Girls, a program designed to empower girls of high school age. It will provide referrals to eating disorder specialists.

The Feldenkrais Method
Anat Baniel
Feldenkrais International
Tel.: 800-386-1441 or 415-464-0777
E-mail: anatbaniel@feldenkrais-intl.com

Overeaters Anonymous (OA)
World Services Offices
P.O. Box 44020
Rio Rancho, NM 87124
Tel.: 505-891-2664

Look for your local OA group in the Yellow Pages; also, the central office will make referrals to groups worldwide. OA is a twelve step program patterned after Alcoholics Anonymous but dealing specifically with food and overeating. Free, peer-run support groups help people stop abusing food.

## ON-LINE SUPPORT GROUPS

Research studies are being conducted on the use of the World Wide Web to deliver support to eating disordered individuals. Though studies of the effectiveness of Internet-based intervention are so far inconclusive, researchers at Stanford and California State Universities are excited by responses that show study participants are being supportive to each other and are learning significantly from the experience.[1] Keep an eye out for groups on the Web that might be of help to you.

## WEB SITES FOR SUPPORT AND INFORMATION

Most of the following Web sites offer links to additional sites with information and other resources for eating disorders.

| | |
|---|---|
| National Association for Anorexia Nervosa and Associated Disorders | members.aol.com/anad2o/index.html |
| American Anorexia Bulimia Association | www.aaba.inc.org |
| Anorexia Bulimia Nervosa Association | www.span.com.au/anorexia |
| Center for Eating Disorders | www.eating-disorder.com |
| Deaconess Medical Center medical information | www.geocities.com/ HotSprings/2846/eatdis.html |
| Grant Me the Serenity Self-Help and Recovery | www.open-mind.org |
| Healthy Weight Network | www.healthyweight.net |
| Laureate mental health clinic and hospital | www.laureate.com |
| Something Fishy Web Site on Eating Disorders | www.somethingfishy.org |

# Notes

## CHAPTER ONE

1. In order to represent both genders equally and avoid continual use of such constructions as "he or she" in referring to the eating disordered child, I will alternate the third-person pronoun gender from chapter to chapter.

2. American Psychiatric Association, *Diagnostic and Statistical Manual of Mental Disorders* (4th ed.) (Washington, D.C.: American Psychiatric Association, 1994), p. 547.

3. "Chemical Dependency and Eating Disorders: A Hidden Connection?" The Willough in the News. *Addiction and Recovery,* Mar.–Apr. 1993.

4. American Psychiatric Association, *Diagnostic and Statistical Manual of Mental Disorders,* p. 541.

5. C. Costin, *The Eating Disorder Sourcebook* (Chicago: Contemporary Books, 1996), p. 17.

6. Costin, *The Eating Disorder Sourcebook,* p. 13.

7. Costin, *The Eating Disorder Sourcebook,* p. 15.

8. A. E. Becker, S. K. Grinspoon, A. Klibanski, and D. B. Herzog, "Eating Disorders: Current Concepts," *New England Journal of Medicine,* Apr. 8, 1999, *340*(14), p. 1092.

9. Costin, *The Eating Disorder Sourcebook,* p. 49.

10. T. Moore, *Care of the Soul* (New York: HarperCollins, 1992).

11. The names and circumstances in all case studies and examples have been changed to protect the privacy of the involved parties.

12. J. C. Piscatella, *Fat-Proof Your Child* (New York: Workman, 1997), p. v.

13. Piscatella, *Fat-Proof Your Child,* p. 35.

14. Piscatella, *Fat-Proof Your Child,* p. 34.

15. W. H. Kaye and M. Strober, "Neurobiology of Eating Disorders," in D. E. Charney, E. J. Nestler, and B. S. Bunney (eds.), *Neurobiological Foundations of Mental Illness* (New York: Oxford University Press, forthcoming).

16. "Research Links Single Gene to Addictive Behaviors," *Chicago Tribune,* Mar. 15, 1994.

17. Ernest P. Nobel, quoted in "Research Links Single Gene to Addictive Behaviors."

18. L. R. Lilenfeld and W. H. Kaye, "Genetic Studies of Anorexia and Bulimia Nervosa," in H. W. Hoek, J. L. Treasure, and M. A. Katzman (eds.), *Neurobiology in the Treatment of Eating Disorders* (New York: Wiley, 1998), p. 186.

19. Lilenfeld and Kaye, "Genetic Studies of Anorexia and Bulimia Nervosa," p. 186.

20. C. Johnson, *Psychodynamic Treatment of Anorexia Nervosa and Bulimia* (New York: Guilford Press, 1991), p. 278.

21. C. Dare, D. le Grange, I. Eisler, and J. Rutherford, "Redefining the Psychosomatic Family: Family Process of Twenty-Six Eating Disorder Families," *International Journal of Eating Disorders,* 1994, *6*(3), pp. 211–226.

## CHAPTER TWO

1. D. M. Garner and P. E. Garfinkel, "Eating Attitudes Test" (EAT), in D. M. Garner and P. E. Garfinkel (eds.), *Handbook of Psychotherapy for Anorexia Nervosa and Bulimia* (New York: Guilford Press, 1985).

2. C. Johnson, "Diagnostic Survey for Eating Disorders" (DSED) (initial consultation for patients with bulimia and anorexia), in D. M. Garner and P. E. Garfinkel (eds.), *Handbook of Psychotherapy for Anorexia Nervosa and Bulimia* (New York: Guilford Press, 1984).

3. A. E. Becker, S. K. Grinspoon, A. Klibanski, and D. B. Herzog, "Eating Disorders: Current Concepts," *New England Journal of Medicine,* Apr. 8, 1999, *340*(14), p. 1092.

4. C. Costin, *The Eating Disorder Sourcebook* (Chicago: Contemporary Books, 1996), p. 30.

5. Costin, *The Eating Disorder Sourcebook,* p. 30.

6. C. Johnson, remarks at Eating Disorder Conference, sponsored by ANAD, Chicago, 1989.

7. K. Springer, "Making Calories Count," *Newsweek,* Summer–Spring 1999 (Health for Life Special Edition), p. 88.

## CHAPTER THREE

1. Epigraph: Elie Wiesel won the 1986 Nobel Prize and is the Andrew W. Mellon Professor at Boston University, Boston, Massachusetts. A world ambassador for peace and a champion of the disadvantaged, Wiesel has written more than thirty books.

2. Piscatella, *Fat-Proof Your Child,* p. 5.

3. H. C. Ginott, *Between Parent and Teenager* (New York, Avon Books, 1971), p. 97.

4. T. Apter, *Altered Loves* (New York: St. Martin's Press, 1990).


# CHAPTER FOUR

1. M. Feldenkrais, *The Potent Self: A Guide to Spontaneity* (2nd ed.) (San Francisco: HarperCollins, 1992), p. 4.

2. Feldenkrais, *The Potent Self,* p. xii.

3. Feldenkrais, *The Potent Self,* p. 4.

4. Feldenkrais, *The Potent Self,* p. 4.

5. M. Feldenkrais, San Francisco training, 1976.

6. C. Johnson and R. A. Sansone, "Integrating the Twelve Step Approach with Traditional Psychotherapy for the Treatment of Eating Disorders," *International Journal of Eating Disorders,* 1993, *14*(2), pp. 121–134. To obtain reprints, write to Laureate, 6655 S. Yale, Tulsa, OK 74136.

7. I. Eisler, C. Dare, G. F. M. Russell, G. I. Szmukler, L. Dodge, and D. le Grange, "Family and Individual Therapy for Anorexia Nervosa: A Five-Year Follow-Up," Archives of General Psychiatry, 1997, 54, pp. 1025–1030.

8. Quoted in S. S. Swartz, *Bar Mitzvah* (New York: Doubleday, 1985), p. 45.

9. The National Association for Anorexia Nervosa and Associated Disorders (ANAD) provides such groups nationwide. Contact ANAD (see Appendix C).

10. A. Schauss and C. Costin, *Zinc and Eating Disorders* (New Canaan, Conn.: Keats, 1989).


# CHAPTER FIVE

1. D. le Grange, I. Eisler, C. Dare, and G. Russell, "Evaluation of Family Treatments in Adolescent Anorexia Nervosa: A Pilot Study," *International Journal of Eating Disorders,* 1992, *12*(4), pp. 347–357.

2. American Medical Association, http://www.AMAassn.org; American Academy of Pediatrics, http://www.aap.org.

3. C. Fox, "Starved Out," *Life,* Dec., 1997, p. 80.

4. Legal assistance is provided by ANAD. See Appendix C.

5. National Association for Anorexia Nervosa and Associated Disorders, *ANAD Ten-Year Study* (Data was compiled by the National Association for Anorexia Nervosa and Associated Disorders, 1994–1995, Highland Park, Illinois. Results of this survey can be obtained by contacting ANAD, Box 7, Highland Park, IL 60035).

# CHAPTER SIX

1. K. M. Pike, "Long-Term Course of Anorexia Nervosa; Response, Relapse, Remission, and Recovery," *Clinical Psychology Review,* June 1998, *18*(4), 447–475.

2. National Association for Anorexia Nervosa and Associated Disorders, *ANAD Ten-Year Study* (Data was compiled by the National Association for Anorexia Nervosa and Associated Disorders, 1994–1995, Highland Park, Illinois. Results of this survey can be obtained by contacting ANAD, Box 7, Highland Park, IL 60035).

3. A. Andersen, remarks at Eating Disorder Conference, sponsored by Highland Park Hospital, Highland Park, Illinois, 1989.

4. A. E. Becker, S. K. Grinspoon, A. Klibanski, and D. B. Herzog, "Eating Disorders: Current Concepts," *New England Journal of Medicine,* Apr. 8, 1999, *340*(14) p. 1094.

5. P. S. Hurst, J. H. Lacey, and A. H. Crisp, "Teeth, Vomiting and Diet: A Study of the Dental Characteristics of Seventeen Anorexia Nervosa Patients," *Postgraduate Medical Journal,* June 1977, *53,* pp. 298–305.

6. W. H. Kaye, M. Strober, "Neurobiology of Eating Disorders," in D. E. Charney, E. J. Nestler, and B. S. Bunney (eds.), *Neurobiological Foundations of Mental Illness* (New York: Oxford University Press, forthcoming), p. 892.

7. Becker, Grinspoon, Klibanski, and Herzog, "Eating Disorders," p. 1092.

8. M. Chase, "Health Journal: Anorexics Face Hurdles with Insurance Plans Over Costly Treatment," *Wall Street Journal,* Mar. 15, 1999, p. B1.

9. M. Albom, *Tuesdays with Morrie: An Old Man, a Young Man, and Life's Greatest Lesson* (New York: Bantam, Doubleday, Dell), 1997, p. 105.

# CHAPTER SEVEN

1. R. Grossinger, *Planet Medicine: Modalities* (Berkeley, Calif.: North American Books, 1995) p. 260.

2. See the information for Feldenkrais International in Appendix C.

3. M. Chase, "Health Journal: New, No-Fault Therapy for Anorexics Takes Blame off the Parents," *Wall Street Journal,* Mar. 22, 1999; p. B1.

4. M. Chase, "New, No-Fault Therapy for Anorexics Takes Blame Off the Parents," p. B1. Quote by James Lock, Stanford psychiatrist who is leading a U. S. study using the therapy approach.

5. D. le Grange, "Family Therapy for Adolescent Anorexia Nervosa: JCLP/In Session," *Psychotherapy in Practice,* 1999, *55*(6), pp. 1–13. Copyright © 1999 John Wiley &

Sons, Inc. Corrspondence and requests for reprints should be sent to Daniel le Grange, Ph.D., The University of Chicago, Dept. of Psychiatry, 5841 S. Maryland Ave., MC 3077, Chicago, IL 60637.

6. M. Chase, "New, No-Fault Therapy for Anorexics Takes Blame Off the Parents," p. B1.

## APPENDIX C

1. American Psychological Association, *APA Monitor,* Mar. 1997.

# About the Author

Abigail H. Natenshon, M.A., L.C.S.W., B.C.D., is a recognized psychotherapist, author, and speaker with thirty years of experience and expertise in the treatment of eating disorders with individuals, families, and groups. A graduate of the University of Chicago School of Social Service Administration and a faculty member of the Institute for Educational and Professional Development, she provides consultation for educators and health professionals nationwide, conducts training workshops for professionals and parents, and lectures widely on the topic of eating disorders. Her work has been published in magazines, professional journals, and newspapers, and she has made numerous appearances on national television, radio, and the Internet.

Ms. Natenshon is the co-founder and director of Eating Disorder Specialists of Illinois: A Clinic Without Walls. Her informative and interactive Web site, www.empoweredparents.com, counsels parents about how to prevent eating disorders in children, how to intervene to find the most effective professional care, and how to participate with the child and health professionals to facilitate the child's timely and lasting recovery. Ms. Natenshon's body-image friendly site, www.empoweredkidz.com, is specifically designed for children (seven and older) and teenagers who wish to learn to eat and manage their weight healthfully.

# Index

ment of nuclear family, 54–56; of origin, 53–54; and shared responsibility, 120–121

Family therapists, 141–142

Family therapy: and conjoint family therapy, 142; and family counseling, 142; and mutual responsibility, 120–121

Fasting, 9

Fat phobia, 4

Fear, dealing with, 9, 63–65, 193–195

Feedback, child's, listening to, 228–229

Feeling content, 79–81

Feeling gauges, 18

Feelings, disorders of, 18–19

Feldenkrais, M., 96–97

Feldenkrais Method, 96–97, 238, 262

Food: analysis of personal attitudes toward, 24, 49–51, 52–53; fear of, 9, 193–195; and how food works, 12–13; looking beyond, 13, 19–21; as metaphor, 23–24; restrictions of, in history, 12; sample journal format for, 14

Food fears, 193–195

Food restriction: history of, 12; and task for food restricters, 9

Free choice, capacity for, in behavior, 48–49

Friend, versus parent obstacle, 65

G

Genetic factors, for eating disorders, 27–28

Goal redefinition, 143

Goal setting, 97–101

Good judgement, teaching, 231–232

Grazing, 11

Greek system syndrome, 35

H

Health Insurance Company, 163–165

Healthy parenting, 51–52

Hidden agendas, 75–76

Higher power, 116

*Holy Anorexia* (Bell), 12

Hospital personnel, 146

Hospitalization, 130–131

I

Identity, disorders of, 16–17

Institute of Psychiatry (Medical University of South Carolina), 241, 257–258

Internists, 145–146

Intervention: creating of, 233–234; sample script for, 83–85; and use of consultant, 234–236

Ipecac syrup, 9–10

J

Johnson, C., 116

Journal keeping, 7, 13, 14

K

Klonopin, 127

L

Laureate program, 256

Laxative use, 6

LCPCs. *See* Licensed clinical professional counselors

Licensed clinical professional counselors (LCPCs), 141

Lifestyle, disorders of, 17

Linden Oaks Hospital (Naperville, Illinois), 256

Lodahl, M. B., 9

Loren, S., 11

Luvox, 126

M

Maudsley Hospital (London), 241

Maudsley model for treating anorexics, 241–242

Meadows program, 256

Media, 17

Medical University of South Carolina, 257–258

Medication alternative, 123–127

Menninger Clinic, 256

Menses, absence of, 9

Mental illness, 25–26

Messages, feeling content in, 79–81

Milieu. *See* Treatment milieu

Monoamine oxidase inhibitors (MAOIs), 126

Monroe, M., 11

Monte Nido Residential Treatment Facility, 259

Montecatini treatment center, 259

Mood: disorders of, 7; regulation of, through bulimia, 10

Myths, common: about eating disorders, 4–7, 24; about parents, 6; about treatment, 92–95

## N

Nardil, 126
National Association for Anorexia
Nervosa and Associated Disorders (ANAD), 133, 205, 238, 255, 260–261
Nefazodone, 126
Neuro Psychiatric Institute and Hospital, 258
Neurochemical factors, for eating disorders, 28
Noncommunicative family obstacle, 66
Norpramine, 126
Nuclear family, assessing, 54–56
Nutritional supplements, 127
Nutritionists, 143–144

## O

Obesity, 11
Obstacles: and adolescent moods, 64; and burden of proof, 65; and friend versus parent dilemma, 65; and noncommunicative family, 66; and overweight fear, 64–65; to parental advocacy, 62; and personal attitude toward constraints, 66; personal recognition of, 67–70; and professional advice, 64; and support, 65
Organic factors, for eating disorders. *See* Genetic factors, for eating disorders
Overeaters Anonymous (OA), 115, 116, 262
Overweight fear, 64–65

## P

Pamelor, 126
Parent, friend versus, 65
Parent trap, 62–63
Parental advocacy, obstacles to, 62
Parental confrontation: and adolescent mood, 64; and burden of proof obstacle, 65; and fear, 63–64; and friend versus parent obstacle, 65; and making contact, 61–62; and noncommunicative family, 66; and obstacles to parental advocacy, 62; and overweight fear, 64–65; and parent traps, 62–63; and personal attitude toward con-

straints, 66; and professional advice, 64; and recognition of child's idea of support, 67–70; and recognizing own obstacles, 67–70; and support, 65
Parenting: and confrontation of children, 59–71; and empowered parenting, 230–233; and healthy parenting, 51–52; and resistant parents, 51–52
Parents: as advocates to team, 229–230; assessment of therapist response to intervention by, 226–227; common myth about, 6; contributions of, to disease, 20–31; and dealing with insurance company, 232–233; and empowered parenting, 230–232; and entering treatment, 223–224; influence of, on disease and recovery process, 214–216; and joining with therapist, 225–226; openness of, to alternative treatments, 238; role of, in confrontation of children, 59–71; treatment of, 223–225; and treatment team, 162–163
Parity, 164
Parnate, 126
Pathology, normalcy versus, 48–49
Paxil, 126
Pediatricians, 145–146
Personality, 8
Physicians, 6
Power struggles, rethinking, 89
Professional advice obstacle, 64
Professional help: and disease recognition, 41–42; and initial telephone contact, 136–139; and notification of insurance company, 139–140; problems with, 151–161; and referral sources chart, 133–134; search for, 133–140; what to expect from, 147–151
Prozac, 124, 126. *See also* Antidepressants; Medication alternative; Selective serotonin reuptake inhibitors
Psychiatrists, definition of, 140
Psychodevelopmental factors, for eating disorders, 29
Psychodynamic therapy, 111
Psychologists, definition of, 140
Psychopharmacologists, 140
Psychotherapists, options in, 140–147
Purging, 6, 9. *See also* Binge-eating disorders